MW01674234

CRIMINAL JUSTICE IN AUSTERITY

This book offers a timely and detailed examination of the reality of criminal legal practice today. Drawing upon extensive anonymous interviews with criminal lawyers in England and Wales, it illuminates how financial pressures arise within the criminal justice system and how lawyers seek to navigate them.

The work of criminal lawyers is frequently depicted in the news and media as exciting, well-paid and worthwhile, with prosecutors aiming to convict the guilty and defence lawyers fighting against miscarriages of justice. In contrast, the picture reported by many is of an already creaking and under-resourced system, now exacerbated by fallout from the COVID-19 pandemic. Against this backdrop, the book considers whether the criminal legal aid system really can continue to provide those unable to afford a lawyer with access to justice and whether the Crown Prosecution Service can provide justice to victims of crime.

The book presents detailed findings about the work and experiences of both prosecutors and defence lawyers, how financial pressures influence this and to what extent this has changed with the new ways of working brought about by the COVID-19 pandemic.

Criminal Justice in Austerity

Legal Aid, Prosecution and the Future of Criminal Legal Practice

James Thornton

•HART•

OXFORD • LONDON • NEW YORK • NEW DELHI • SYDNEY

HART PUBLISHING

Bloomsbury Publishing Plc

Kemp House, Chawley Park, Cumnor Hill, Oxford, OX2 9PH, UK

1385 Broadway, New York, NY 10018, USA

29 Earlsfort Terrace, Dublin 2, Ireland

HART PUBLISHING, the Hart/Stag logo, BLOOMSBURY and the Diana logo are trademarks of Bloomsbury Publishing Plc

First published in Great Britain 2023

Copyright © James Thornton, 2023

James Thornton has asserted his right under the Copyright, Designs and Patents Act 1988 to be identified as Author of this work.

All rights reserved. No part of this publication may be reproduced or transmitted in any form or by any means, electronic or mechanical, including photocopying, recording, or any information storage or retrieval system, without prior permission in writing from the publishers.

While every care has been taken to ensure the accuracy of this work, no responsibility for loss or damage occasioned to any person acting or refraining from action as a result of any statement in it can be accepted by the authors, editors or publishers.

All UK Government legislation and other public sector information used in the work is Crown Copyright ©. All House of Lords and House of Commons information used in the work is Parliamentary Copyright ©. This information is reused under the terms of the Open Government Licence v3.0 (http://www.nationalarchives.gov.uk/doc/open-government-licence/version/3) except where otherwise stated.

All Eur-lex material used in the work is © European Union, http://eur-lex.europa.eu/, 1998–2023.

A catalogue record for this book is available from the British Library.

A catalogue record for this book is available from the Library of Congress.

Library of Congress Control Number: 2023941336

ISBN: HB: 978-1-50995-531-2
ePDF: 978-1-50995-533-6
ePub: 978-1-50995-532-9

Typeset by Compuscript Ltd, Shannon

To find out more about our authors and books visit www.hartpublishing.co.uk. Here you will find extracts, author information, details of forthcoming events and the option to sign up for our newsletters.

ACKNOWLEDGEMENTS

I cannot thank my family, friends, colleagues and mentors enough for supporting and encouraging me. I could not have written this book without you.

Special thanks to Jonathan Doak, David Gurnham, Harry Annison, Daniel Newman and Amanda Parker, for commenting on draft chapters, and to my interviewees for sharing their stories with me.

James Thornton
24 March 2023
NG1, Nottingham

TABLE OF CONTENTS

Acknowledgements ... *v*
Abbreviations ... *xi*

1. Investigating Austerity in Criminal Law ... 1
I. Introduction ... 1
II. Context ... 1
III. Studying Criminal Law/Practice and Austerity ... 4
IV. Remaining Structure of Book ... 7

2. Studying the Work of Legal Practitioners ... 8
I. Introduction ... 8
II. Fundamental Challenges of Understanding Practice ... 8
A. The Relevance of Both Individual Agency and Environmental Pressures ... 8
B. Objectivist and Subjectivist Approaches to Understanding Practice ... 9
III. Studies on the Work of Legal Practitioners ... 11
A. Some Examples of More Subjectivist and Objectivist Studies on Criminal Legal Practitioners ... 11
B. Heroes and Villains ... 14
C. Avoiding Dichotomy ... 16
IV. Understanding Practice with Bourdieusian Concepts ... 18
A. How Bourdieu Moves Beyond Objectivism versus Subjectivism ... 18
B. Some Further Bourdieusian Concepts and their Value ... 22
V. Understanding the Work of Legal Practitioners ... 28

3. Legally Aided Criminal Defence at Police Stations in Austerity ... 31
I. Introduction and Context ... 31
A. Challenges of the Police Station Setting ... 32
B. The Legal Aid System in Police Stations ... 33
II. Financial Challenges of Criminal Legal Aid Work at Police Stations ... 35
A. Fundamental Profitability Issues ... 35
B. Time ... 37
C. Burnout/Demoralisation ... 46

D. Using Less Experienced Lawyers/Reps 47
E. Attendance In-person versus Remote 49
III. The Logic of Legally Aided Criminal Defence Practice in Police Stations 52

4. Magistrates' Court Defence and Prosecution Practice in Austerity 54
I. Introduction and Context 54
A. The Legal Aid System in Magistrates' Courts 55
B. Crown Prosecution in Magistrates' Courts 56
II. Financial Challenges of Magistrates' Court Practice 56
A. Money and its Connection with Time 57
B. Lack of Time to Prepare before Court 59
C. Trial and Plea-hearing Preparation 61
D. Time for Prosecution Disclosure 63
E. Time at Court 65
F. Time for TLC 68
G. Plea Advice 75
H. Less Experienced Lawyers 79
I. Burnout/Demoralisation 82
III. The Logic of Criminal Prosecution and Defence Practice in Magistrates' Courts 84

5. Crown Court Defence and Prosecution Practice in Austerity 87
I. Introduction and Context 87
A. Legal Aid in the Crown Court 89
B. Crown Prosecution in the Crown Court 90
II. Financial Challenges of Crown Court Practice 90
A. Money and its Connection with Time 90
B. Lack of Time to Prepare before Court 91
C. Time at Court and Appeals 97
D. Time for Prosecution Disclosure 98
E. Time for TLC 102
F. Prosecution Targets/Box-ticking 104
G. Gold Dust and Loss-making Defence Cases 108
H. Less Experienced and Reduced Staff 110
I. Plea Advice 112
J. Burnout/Demoralisation 120
III. The Logic of Criminal Prosecution and Defence Practice in the Crown Court 124

6. The Future of Criminal Court Practice in Austerity 127
I. Introduction 127
II. Measures from COVID-19 127

A. Summary of Criminal Courts' COVID-19 Mitigations 127
B. Basic Technology Enhancements 129
C. Online Hearings (CVP) 132
D. Blessing in Disguise or Trojan Horse? 138
III. Sustainability 142
A. Criminal Legal Aid Solicitors 142
B. Publicly Funded Criminal Bar 148
C. Sustainability of Crown Prosecution 153
IV. New Technology, Old Problems and Sustainability 155

7. Understanding the Work of Legal Practitioners in Austerity 157
I. Understanding Practice 158
II. Understanding Criminal Lawyers in Austerity 161

Bibliography 164
Index 171

ABBREVIATIONS

AGFS	Advocates' Graduated Fee Scheme
ASBO	Antisocial Behaviour Order
BSB	Bar Standards Board
CILEX	Chartered Institute of Legal Executives
CLAR	Independent Criminal Legal Aid Review
CLSA	Criminal Law Solicitors' Association
CPS	Crown Prosecution Service
CTL	Custody Time Limit
CVP	Cloud Video Platform
DPP	Director of Public Prosecutions
DSCC	Defence Solicitor Call Centre
EHRC	Equality and Human Rights Commission
GBH	Grievous Bodily Harm
HMCPSI	Crown Prosecution Service Inspectorate
HMCTS	HM Courts and Tribunals Service
HMICFRS	Inspectorate of Constabulary and Fire & Rescue Services
HMSO	HM Stationery Office
KC	King's Counsel
LAA	Legal Aid Agency
LCCS	London Criminal Courts Solicitors' Association
LGFS	Litigators' Graduated Fee Scheme
MA	Magistrates' Association
MoJ	Ministry of Justice
NPM	New Public Management

NPCC	National Police Chiefs' Council
PACE	Police and Criminal Evidence Act 1984 and its associated Codes of Practice
PPE	Pages of Prosecution Evidence
PTPH	Plea and Trial Preparation Hearing
RASSO	Rape and Serious Sexual Offences
SRA	Solicitors Regulation Authority
VHCC	Very High Cost Cases

1

Investigating Austerity in Criminal Law

I. Introduction

This book examines how external pressures, particularly austerity, influence criminal lawyers' work. The research is based upon 50 in-depth qualitative interviews with criminal lawyers, spanning both sides of the criminal process (defence and prosecution), professions (litigator and advocate), geography and experience (from the senior to the trainee). The book takes the England and Wales jurisdiction as its empirical case study, but many of the issues raised by austerity will be pervasive across multiple jurisdictions.

It is also concerned with a much more fundamental question though: the relationship between external/environmental structure and individual freedom. To explore this, we need to understand the working practices of practitioners who are both subject to external pressures (such as austerity) and also have some level of individual freedom/autonomy in how they work. This tension between individual agency and environmental structures has proven to be fundamental to my understanding of how austerity influences criminal lawyer work and, I contend, for understanding the work of practitioners more broadly. In examining the influence of external pressures on practice, knowing where that external influence ends and individual agency begins is critical. If the beginning of individual agency is the end of an external pressure, we can then better understand the effects of that external pressure, as distinct from the results of individuals' choices.

Ultimately, however, my argument throughout this book is that this is a false promise. Professional practice cannot be understood properly until these two seemingly distinct concepts (of environmental influence and individual freedom) are reconciled, and their interdependence appreciated. Having done so, the book suggests that our understanding of the way that external pressures influence individual practice, exemplified by how austerity influences practice in criminal law, may need to be completely re-conceptualised.

II. Context

In terms of 'austerity', to begin with it is worth considering what is meant by that term in this context. For the criminal justice process, Porter has defined austerity as 'spending within one's means'.[1] Similarly, British politicians (of both left and right) have spoken of the imperative of cutting the country's/treasury's 'deficit', particularly following the Global Financial Crisis from 2008 onwards.[2] However, the idea that (for a country, as opposed to a household), 'the books must be balanced' is itself by no means settled within the discipline of Economics and has even been argued to be 'economically illiterate'.[3] Thus, as Bramall et al argue (and Porter acknowledges), austerity is a political concept, not an economic one – unlike, say, a 'recession', which does have economic definition/s of sorts.[4] For example, 'austerity' can simply refer to this basic idea that 'the books must be balanced', or it can go further and also refer to a belief that the books must be balanced *by* 'quite severe spending cuts',[5] as opposed to, for example, increasing taxation.[6] The former definition would even include the Labour party under Jeremy Corbyn, which accepted the basic premise that the books needed to be balanced, but thought the way to do that was by cracking down on tax avoidance, rather than reducing public spending.[7] This book is concerned with the impact that external funding pressures have on the work of lawyers. In other words, we are concerned with the *effect* of austerity in the sense of 'quite severe spending cuts' to criminal defence and prosecution services, rather than examining the political arguments over what 'counts' as austerity. In doing so, the book takes as a starting point UK Governments' criminal law funding practices following the Global Financial Crisis, which began under the outgoing Labour Government and accelerated under the 2010 UK Coalition Government and those which have followed. In 2010, the Coalition Government took the view that 'deficit reduction, and continuing to ensure economic recovery, is the most urgent issue facing Britain'.[8] They therefore promised to 'significantly accelerate the reduction of the structural deficit … with the main burden of deficit reduction borne by reduced spending rather than increased taxes'.[9]

In terms of criminal law, the first 'severe spending cut' in recent times was arguably the 13.5 per cent reduction in defence advocacy fees from 2010–2012.[10]

[1] A Porter, *Prosecuting Domestic Abuse in Neoliberal Times: Amplifying the Survivor's Voice* (Palgrave Macmillan, 2020) Ch 4.

[2] eg 'David Cameron Urges "Further and Caster" Deficit Cut' (*BBC News*, 27 February 2013) www.bbc.co.uk/news/uk-politics-21605818; J McDonnell, 'Jeremy Corbyn Would Clear the Deficit – But Not by Hitting the Poor' (*The Guardian*, 11 August 2015) www.theguardian.com/commentisfree/2015/aug/11/jeremy-corbyn-close-deficit-poor-labour-economy.

[3] R Bramall et al 'What is Austerity?' (2016) 87 *New Formations* 119, 121.

[4] ibid 119.

[5] ibid 120.

[6] See also M Blythe, *Austerity: The History of a Dangerous Idea* (Oxford University Press, 2013) and commentary by H Thompson, 'Austerity as Ideology: The Bait and Switch of the Banking Crisis' (2013) 11 *Comparative European Politics* 729.

[7] Bramell et al, 'What Is Austerity?' (n 3) 121; eg, Labour Party, *The Labour Party Manifesto* (2017) Ch 1 – 'Balancing the Books'.

[8] *The Coalition: Our Programme for Government* (2010) 15.

[9] ibid.

[10] C Bellamy, *Independent Review of Criminal Legal Aid* (*CLAR*) (November 2021) 22; Criminal Defence Service (Funding) (Amendment) (No 2) Order 2010, SI 2010/1181.

Further radical proposals followed with the publication of *Transforming Legal Aid*, which proposed saving around £220m from the criminal legal aid budget (the Ministry of Justice's entire budget was to be cut by a third).[11] Not all the suggested means of doing this were enacted,[12] but there was an 8.75 per cent cut to general criminal law solicitors' fees and a 30 per cent reduction in solicitor fees for the most complex and lengthy cases (Very High Cost Cases – VHCCs). Advocates' fees (outside of the exceptional VHCCs, for which a 9 per cent cut was introduced and later replaced with a system of negotiation) were also in the firing line, but these cuts were, following industrial action, suspended[13] and eventually dropped following a change in Justice Secretary.[14] After much argument and 'cost neutral' fee system reforms, there was an increase of around 1 per cent in advocate fees in 2019, however, at best, this is a reduction in real terms.[15] The recent *Independent Criminal Legal Aid Review* (*CLAR*) estimated that defence had received real term cuts of one-third when compared to 2008 for police station and Crown Court work and a half compared to 1996 for magistrates' court work.[16] Surface-level consequences appear alarming. The following headlines, summarised in *CLAR*, are instructive:

- 'In 2014/15 133,370 solicitors held practising certificates, of which 14,790 worked for a Criminal Legal Aid (CLA) firm. In 2018/19 145,530 solicitors held practising certificates, of which 11,760 worked for a CLA firm.'[17]
- The average age of a duty solicitor (those on-call to assist at police stations and magistrates' courts) was 47–49 from 2017–2019. Many schemes are threadbare (32 schemes have seven solicitors or fewer for a 24/7 rota).[18]
- Between 2015–2020 'a significant fall in criminal barristers concentrated in the 8–22 years of practice group. The latter part of this group includes a significant reduction in the number of [K]Cs' (the most senior advocates).[19]

In response to these findings, *CLAR* made a number of recommendations in relation to fee schemes and structures, many of which will be noted in their context in later chapters. However, in terms of raw numbers, it also recommended a 15 per cent increase to much of solicitors' and barristers' fees for criminal legal

[11] Ministry of Justice, *Transforming Legal Aid: Delivering a More Credible and Efficient System* (2013) and Ministry of Justice, *Transforming Legal Aid: Government Response* (2014).

[12] In the Criminal Legal Aid (Remuneration) Regulations 2013, as amended.

[13] 'Agreement between Ministry of Justice, Bar Council and Criminal Bar Association' (Ministry of Justice, 27 March 2014) https://consult.justice.gov.uk/digital-communications/transforming-legal-aid-next-steps/user_uploads/advocacy-note.pdf.

[14] A MacDonald, 'Bar Council Responds to Ministry of Justice Announcement on Legal Aid' (Bar Council, 10 June 2015).

[15] The argument over which benchmark is used to suggest increases or cuts is summarised by Bellamy, *CLAR* (n 10) at 27.

[16] ibid [6.28]–[6.35].

[17] ibid [6.20].

[18] ibid.

[19] ibid 109.

aid work.[20] The Government enacted many, but not all, of these uplifts.[21] Most notably, it did not apply this increase to substantial parts of Crown Court litigators' fees, on the basis that the system was to be reformed in due course anyway.[22] It is also worth noting that *CLAR* reported in November 2021, when the percentage change of inflation over the preceding 12 months was 7.1 per cent (RPI) and 4.2 per cent (CPI).[23] By the time the Government had enacted these fee uplifts, in September 2022, this had risen to 12.6 per cent (RPI) and 10.2 per cent (CPI).[24] In real terms, therefore, the increases that *CLAR* had recommended to address the effects of many of the previous 'severe spending cuts' discussed above were instead largely used up in offsetting sudden inflation, unforeseen at the time *CLAR* made those recommendations.[25] Thus, whilst this did reduce the impact of runaway inflation on an already greatly diminished area of public spending, the earlier financial deficits, which *CLAR*'s recommendations set out to correct, were not addressed in real terms.

On the other side, the Crown Prosecution Service (CPS)'s budget was cut by 26 per cent (£185m) between 2009–10 and 2015–16. Although this was reduced by a later increase of around £85m, this is of course still a deficit of £100m and was done in anticipation of a corresponding increase in workload from police officer recruitment.[26] As with criminal legal aid, this also ignores inflation since 2009–10: in real terms the reduction is greater. Likewise, surface-level consequences are disquieting: the independent HMCPS Inspectorate has found that 'Many CPS Areas were lacking grip on casework: the core function of the CPS' and that 'budget and staff reductions have had an impact on delivery', with many issues relating to 'the challenges of resourcing – with many Areas under-resourced in terms of the number of lawyers they had in place'.[27]

III. Studying Criminal Law/Practice and Austerity

Against that backdrop, this book takes that austere environment of criminal defence and prosecution as its case study, in order to understand how austerity impacts lawyer work and, more broadly, to understand the operation, conflict and relationship between external pressures and professionals' individual agency in

[20] Bellamy, *CLAR* (n 10) Ch 16.

[21] Criminal Legal Aid (Remuneration) (Amendment) Regulations 2022, SI 2022/848.

[22] Ministry of Justice, 'Government's Response to the Criminal Legal Aid Independent Review and Consultation on Policy Proposals' (HM Government, 2022).

[23] ONS, 'Inflation and Price Indices' (2023) www.ons.gov.uk/economy/inflationandpriceindices.

[24] ibid.

[25] The increasing inflation coincided with then Prime Minister Liz Truss and Chancellor Kwasi Kwarteng's 'mini budget' in September 2022: Kwasi Kwarteng, *The Growth Plan* (CP743, 2022).

[26] CPS, *Annual Report and Accounts 2019–20* (House of Commons, 2020).

[27] HMCPSI, *Annual Report 2019–20* (House of Commons 2020) 17.

such settings. The following chapter addresses these issues in some detail, although at the outset it is trite that the basic methodology of the study is explained.

This is a semi-structured interview study and the limitations of these are well-known.[28] Whilst good for a qualitative study,[29] 50 interviewees are still obviously not representative of all criminal lawyers in England and Wales. Rather, they show what is *capable* of happening, and has happened, amongst a set of lawyers on both sides, in various locations, firms and chambers, and at many different levels of experience. Such findings are still valid, dependable,[30] and generalisable in terms of, as Peräkylä put it when interviewing counselling professionals, what those who were not included in the study *could* do – given that they have similar options available to them.[31] However, they do not establish what happens everywhere. Put crudely, as a qualitative study, this book seeks to answers questions about *how* austerity can impact criminal lawyer work, not *how many* criminal lawyers are influenced in that way. That said, responses were remarkably consistent across locations, roles and seniority, and often concur (at least to some extent) with a voluminous quantity of previous empirical literature.

To be specific, of those 50 participants, 22 were barristers, 25 were solicitors and 3 were caseworkers. The first phase of (29) interviews took place between 2015 and 2017 (with a greater focus on legal aid/defence), with a second tranche taking place from 2021–2022 (with a greater, but not exclusive, focus on prosecution and lessons learnt from COVID-19 measures, such as online hearings). The vast majority of barrister interviewees did some work for the CPS, as well as defence. In addition, seven interviewees were either CPS employees or had recently been. Although anonymised, participants can be distinguished by the side/s they represented and their work ('Pros' = CPS employed; 'Pros+Def-Bar' = barrister doing prosecution and defence work; 'Def-Bar' = barrister doing defence work; 'Def-Sol' = solicitors firm etc). For the most part, all levels of seniority were represented (from pupil to head of chambers and paralegal to partner). Whilst CPS *managerial* staff were not involved,[32] the focus of the study was on the impact of austerity on criminal *legal* work rather than the work of management and the struggles on that front are readily apparent from the reports of HMCPS Inspectorate.

I adopted a variety of recruitment methods. Solicitor participants were recruited via an invitation letter sent to criminal legal aid firms listed by the Legal

[28] See, for example, D Silverman (ed), *Qualitative Research*, 5th edn (SAGE, 2020); HR Bernard, *Social Research Methods: Qualitative and Quantitative Approaches* (SAGE, 2012).

[29] See S Baker and R Edwards (eds), 'How Many Qualitative Interviews is Enough? Expert Voices and Early Career Reflections on Sampling and Cases in Qualitative Research' (National Centre for Research Methods, 2012) http://eprints.ncrm.ac.uk/2273/4/how_many_interviews.pdf.

[30] L Webley, 'Qualitative Approaches to Empirical Legal Research' in P Cane and H Kiritzer (eds), *The Oxford Handbook of Empirical Legal Studies* (Oxford University Press, 2010) 934–35.

[31] A Peräkylä, 'Reliability and Validity in Research Based on Naturally Occurring Social Interaction' in D Silverman (ed), *Qualitative Research: Theory, Method and Practice*, 2nd edn (SAGE, 2004) 297.

[32] In other words, whilst senior lawyers themselves participated, those making strategic human resource decisions did not.

Aid Agency (LAA) as undertaking criminal legal aid work in England. The Law Society and Young Legal Aid Lawyers also advertised the study to their members. Based on the comparatively much smaller pool of practising criminal barristers,[33] a slightly different approach was taken. Letters were sent to the treasurers of each of the four Inns of Court (every barrister must join an Inn to qualify as a barrister) explaining the research and the need for participants. Three of the Inns responded and advertised the research to their members. A similar approach was taken with the Criminal Bar Association, who agreed to advertise the research in their weekly newsletter for several months. Social networks and snowball sampling via professional contacts were also utilised.

Interviews were conducted either in-person or via telephone/online (the vast majority by telephone/online). Participants were asked open-ended questions about the challenges of criminal practice/impact of finance reduction on their work (in the context of recent and proposed cuts), general questions about the cases they had recently done, as well as more specific questions about finance reduction – often based upon things other interviewees had mentioned in order to triangulate claims. As Chan points out, 'different accounts of the same phenomenon' are a useful cross-referencing tool.[34] More recent interviewees were also asked about how COVID-19 mitigations fitted within that and whether there were any they especially thought worth keeping or removing (including as a way of improving any issues they had already discussed). At all points, in accordance with the discussions in the next chapter, I sought to 'disrupt practitioners' absorbed coping, [throwing] them into a mode of deliberation' in order that they 'step back from their practice to reflect on how they practice'.[35]

In terms of transcripts, some changes were made for easier reading: for example, repeated words, filler discussion and interviewer replies of 'yes' etc are omitted. Text within square brackets is either a paraphrase of something an interviewee said (to save space), or to clarify how or what was said. Some particularly unique expressions were modified to ensure anonymity. Interviewee transcripts were then imported into qualitative research analysis software (NVIVO) and thematically coded. To an extent, this adopted a 'grounded' approach,[36] in that early data was sorted into codes, which were (over time) developed into 'tentative analytical categories'. Taken to its 'grounded theory' conclusion, these categories become more developed until they can eventually be formed into a theory: an 'abstract theoretical understanding of the studied experience'.[37] The theory is 'grounded' because it starts from and is created by the data, rather than being imposed on the data.

[33] The Bar Standards Board estimated around 5000 barristers specialise in criminal law (compared with 2,262 solicitors firms): Ministry of Justice, *Litigators Graduated Fees Scheme and Court Appointees Equality Statement* (2017) 3.

[34] J Chan, *Doing Less Time: Penal Reform in Crisis* (Institute of Criminology, 1992) 19.

[35] J Sandberg and H Tsoukas, 'Grasping the Logic of Practice: Theorizing Through Practical Rationality' (2011) 36 *Academy of Management Review* 338, 350.

[36] K Charmaz, *Constructing Grounded Theory* (SAGE, 2006) 2.

[37] ibid 3–4.

However, my approach was not fully 'grounded'. I knew what I was looking for (in terms of subject matter: the study examined impacts of austerity and external pressures) and, as will be seen in the next chapter, at a meta-level I had already developed an overarching theory to assist in making sense of the data.[38]

IV. Remaining Structure of Book

The remainder of the book analyses the effects of the above austere context on lawyers' work across different areas of criminal practice. Before examining the empirical data, Chapter 2 sets out my argument as to how to understand the work of practitioners in this area in terms of conflict between environmental structures and individual agency. This culminates in an overarching meta-analytical approach/theory for understanding the empirical data that follows. As will become clear there, whilst at times complex, it is very difficult to understand the nuances of the moral dilemmas and ethical challenges in this context without such a theoretically heavy analytical approach. The following three chapters (3–5) then apply this analytical lens to three key arenas of criminal practice: the police station; the magistrates' courts; and the Crown Court, respectively. Finally, having analysed the present, Chapter 6 considers the future of criminal practice in austerity, both in terms of technology (of which the COVID-19 pandemic provided a unique and fast-paced testing ground) and financial sustainability.

[38] See M Grenfell (ed), *Pierre Bourdieu: Key Concepts*, 2nd edn (Routledge, 2012) Ch 13, for a general introduction to this approach.

2

Studying the Work of Legal Practitioners

I. Introduction

This chapter sets out my argument for how to analyse the work of lawyers in this context, providing the conceptual framework underpinning the rest of the analysis in this book. In particular, how concepts from French sociologist Pierre Bourdieu's work can enable an understanding of the complex interaction between individual agency and the external environment, in order to explain practice. Initially, I will set out the significance of each of these aspects of individuals' practices (environmental and individual), to illustrate the need for conceptual frameworks that account for both. Relatedly, I first discuss conflicting social science perspectives and approaches to understanding individuals' practices. Second, I examine how those issues of principle have filtered through to previous studies on the work of legal practitioners. This serves both to illustrate the point regarding the necessity of appreciating both aspects of practice and to situate the Bourdieusian framework relied upon here within wider literature on legal practitioners. Third, the majority of the chapter then explains the Bourdieusian framework and, I argue, its merits for understanding the work of legal practitioners in this book and elsewhere.

II. Fundamental Challenges of Understanding Practice

A. The Relevance of Both Individual Agency and Environmental Pressures

To begin, it is important to appreciate both the power and influence that individual practitioners can have, as well as the formal and informal limits on that power. In 1980, American sociologist Michael Lipsky's seminal work, *Street-Level Bureaucracy*, established the critical role of individual *discretion* in understanding the work of public service workers (teachers, social workers, police, prosecutors, public defenders, etc).[1] For Lipsky, the exercise of this discretion *becomes* policy

[1] M Lipsky, *Street-Level Bureaucracy*, 30th anniversary edn (Russell Sage, 2010).

in a way that is just as important (perhaps more so) as top-down policy from lawmakers and high-ranking administrators. A remarkable British example of this (coincidentally from around the same time) illustrates the point in the criminal justice context. Despite apparent government policy to be tough on youth crime, there was a very substantial (over 81 per cent) fall in youth imprisonment during the 1980s, in which youth justice practitioners played a significant part.[2] Clearly, front-line public practitioners can have more substantial power and influence, in spite of contrary government policy, than might appear intuitively to be the case. That said, there are limits to this. Most obviously, formal rules limit the theoretical scope of practitioner discretion – for example, in the legal context: rules of law, evidence, procedure etc. However, less obviously, the exercise of such discretion is also limited (or even driven) by more practical constraints on time, information and other resources.[3] Such constraints produce more informal, but no less influential, limits on discretion: 'large classes, huge caseloads, and other challenging workload pressures … defeat their aspirations as service workers'.[4] Indeed, in practice, such limits may be more influential than abstract/official rules. Hence, the challenge in studying the work of legal practitioners is to understand how both those external pressures and the individual interact to shape the work that practitioners do.

B. Objectivist and Subjectivist Approaches to Understanding Practice

That challenge cuts across one of the most fundamental divisions in social science, specifically the division between analyses that take a more 'objectivist' approach and those which take a more 'subjectivist' approach. Fundamentally, I would regard taking an objectivist approach here as that which treats practice as if there is a single overarching *objective* reality that can be uncovered.[5] This suggests that research on practitioners ought to aim at uncovering this reality. In contrast, I would regard a subjectivist approach as that which focuses on practitioners' perspectives: only the individual can decide and know for sure who they are[6] and we can only be absolutely certain of that which we are self-aware of and which is self-evident (eg a reflection).[7] From a subjectivist perspective, objective

[2] M Telford and S Santatzoglou, '"It Was About Trust" – Practitioners as Policy Makers and the Improvement of Inter-professional Communication within the 1980s Youth Justice Process' (2012) 32 *Legal Studies* 58, 61.

[3] Lipsky, *Street-Level Bureaucracy* (n 1).

[4] ibid xiv.

[5] AJ Ayer, *Language, Truth and Logic* (first published 1936, Courier Corporation, 2001) exemplifies the extreme of this: if assertions are not verifiable by empirically observable reality, they are nonsense.

[6] J Sartre, *Being and Nothingness* (Routledge, 1958).

[7] ibid. See also J Sartre, *The Psychology of the Imagination* (Routledge, 1971).

knowledge is therefore, at best, probable rather than certain.[8] In contrast therefore, this suggests that research on practitioners ought to consider those practitioners' *subjective* realities (including accepting that there is more than one 'reality').

Unsurprisingly, both of these rather absolutist ways of understanding the world have their problems. Bourdieu highlights two key issues with 'objectivist' approaches. First, the desirability of becoming a truly neutral or objective spectator is highly questionable. Being absolutely objective can simply result in such an incomplete understanding as to be misleading. As Weber argues, it takes us away from 'the richness of reality'.[9] Bourdieu likens such an approach to trying to understand a speech purely from the perspective of a grammarian.[10] No doubt verb placement and punctuation have their roles but clearly there is more to a speech and its effect than that. The result is that objectivist analyses tend to (wrongly) see reality as a pre-set puzzle to be decoded or as 'rules' which 'govern[s], direct[s] or orient[s] behaviour' rather than rules 'which fit[s] the observed regularity in a purely descriptive way.[11] For example, the saying 'as a rule, the train is always late' could be suggesting either that this is a deliberate policy, or that it is what usually tends to happen.[12] Bourdieu's criticism is that objectivist analyses (in their search for that single, logical overarching, reality) tend to assume such a *deliberate policy* understanding of conduct/phenomena. These can often be wrong: trains are deliberately made late only rarely.

Second, it is greatly debateable whether the absolutely objective perspective on social phenomena described above can ever be reached by human beings in any case. In other words, so-called 'objective' approaches can in practice just end up presenting the researcher's own perspectives and taken-for-granted assumptions about what is going on and why as 'the reality'.[13] In doing so, we might claim to be or think we are being more 'objective', but in fact we have just replaced one *subjective* view (the practitioner's) with another (our own): biased 'accounts of [others'] accounts'.[14] The above tendency to assume *deliberate policy* understandings of phenomena might therefore be explained by this often being what the researcher expected to find or (a critic might say) went looking for.

The subjectivist approach is problematic too. In short, subjectivist approaches 'cannot go beyond a description of what specifically characterises "lived" experience of the social world'.[15] In doing so, such approaches accept the same taken-for-granted assumptions about the world as the practitioners' being studied.[16] In other

[8] ibid.

[9] M Weber, '"Objectivity" in Social Science and Social Policy' in E Shils and H Finch (eds and trans), *The Methodology of the Social Sciences* (Free Press, 1949) 80.

[10] P Bourdieu, *The Logic of Practice* (R Nice tr, Polity Press, 1990) 31.

[11] ibid 39.

[12] ibid 40; P Ziff, *Semantic Analysis* (Cornell University Press, 1960).

[13] Bourdieu, *The Logic of Practice* (n 10) 28–29.

[14] ibid 26.

[15] ibid 25.

[16] ibid.

words, whilst we might critique some objectivist approaches for adopting and presenting the *researcher's* taken-for-granted assumptions about the world as 'the reality', it is little better to adopt (to a greater or lesser extent) the observed *practitioners'* taken-for-granted assumptions instead. Doing so wrongly presents each practitioner action as 'a kind of antecedent-less confrontation between the subject and the world'.[17] In fact, individuals are influenced by their own taken-for-granted assumptions about the world as much as they are by conscious analysis. We shall return later to Bourdieu's suggested solution to these issues, which entails very close engagement with those taken-for-granted assumptions. First, though, I will illustrate how the above rather abstract conflict in views can influence research on the work of legal practitioners.

III. Studies on the Work of Legal Practitioners

A. Some Examples of More Subjectivist and Objectivist Studies on Criminal Legal Practitioners

A classic example[18] is the disparity between, on the one hand, both McConville, Sanders and Leng's *The Case for the Prosecution*[19] and McConville et al's *Standing Accused*[20] and, on the other hand, Travers' *The Reality of Law*.[21] Given the glaring disparity in findings and subsequent critique, it is necessary to first set out each study in some detail.

The Case for the Prosecution examined both police and prosecutor practice from arrest to conviction (including the, then relatively new, CPS – the study viewed 'the prosecution' as equalling the police plus the CPS).[22] It also made incidental findings on defence lawyer practice. Findings were negative for all involved, although (given this book's emphasis) I focus here on those in relation to prosecution lawyers, rather than police. These were so explosive that the then Director of Public Prosecutions (DPP) refused to approve a number of prosecutor interviewee quotes for publication (which was a precondition of access).[23] The role of the CPS reviewing lawyer was found to be largely relegated to rubber-stamping previous police decisions to prosecute, regardless of the Code for Crown

[17] ibid 42.

[18] Highlighted by D Newman, *Legal Aid Lawyers and the Quest for Justice* (Hart Publishing, 2013).

[19] M McConville et al, *The Case for the Prosecution: Police Suspects and the Construction of Criminality* (first published 1991, Routledge, 2017).

[20] M McConville et al, *Standing Accused: The Organisation and Practices of Criminal Defence Lawyers in Britain* (Oxford University Press, 1994).

[21] M Travers, *The Reality of Law: Work and Talk in a Firm of Criminal Lawyers* (Ashgate, 1997).

[22] McConville et al, *The Case for the Prosecution* (n 19) 12.

[23] ibid 9.

Prosecutors' evidential strength and public interest requirements.[24] Similarly, at court, behaviour was unethical: prosecutors do not seek 'a plea to what they can *prove*, but to what they can bluff or "arm-twist" defendants into … Bluff and tactics – rather than Truth, Justice, Guilt or Innocence – are what "good" prosecution is all about.'[25] Even defence lawyers 'more or less contribute' to this situation, unnecessarily accepting charge/plea bargains in 'case after case' and pressurising clients to plead guilty accordingly.[26]

Standing Accused then studied criminal defence work in-depth.[27] Conclusions were similarly damning. At the Crown Court, defence 'barristers evince little interest in scrutinising the evidence' and '"the evidence" is reified, set up as a totality, and invested with a force which irresistibly points to guilt'.[28] Magistrates' court work was no better: 'For the most part, solicitors do not see magistrates' courts as trial venues but as places where defendants can be processed through guilty pleas.'[29] Equally, before court, their view was: 'conviction is achieved in the office of their [the defendant's] adviser through a process whose methodologies most nearly resemble those of the police themselves'.[30]

However, *The Reality of Law* also studied criminal defence work and made very different findings. Travers focused on two episodes. First, a lawyer advising a guilty plea and consequently securing the best outcome (a substantial sentence reduction to reflect the plea) for a defendant who would likely have been convicted at trial regardless.[31] Second, the opposite situation in the Crown Court, where the outcome was difficult to predict.[32] Again, the account is of a dedicated lawyer acting in their client's interests and ultimately securing a not guilty verdict.[33]

The scathing account of criminal lawyers in the first two studies has been critiqued on the basis of those same abstract problems with objectivism discussed first. Whilst example after example is given in these studies of allegedly poor practice, there is little discussion as to why the individual decided to work in that way (and therefore their perspective/'reality' is missed). Poor practice is just presented as *the* objective reality. Travers provides a more subjectivist critique of the limits of such an approach.[34] Taking the example of the guilty plea from his book, Travers notes the multiple realities at play here, which more objectivist approaches risk missing. One view is that this was poor practice: 'a lawyer using her position of power to persuade a vulnerable client to plead guilty'.[35] However, from

[24] ibid 138–39.
[25] ibid 156.
[26] ibid 156–70.
[27] McConville et al, *Standing Accused* (n 20) 15.
[28] ibid 268.
[29] ibid 210.
[30] ibid 160.
[31] Travers, *The Reality of Law* (n 21) 157.
[32] ibid 147–48.
[33] ibid 125.
[34] ibid 157.
[35] ibid.

that practitioner's perspective this is the best outcome if the defendant would have been convicted at trial regardless (and given a consequently greater sentence).[36] That more positive interpretation may of course be argued to be wrong too: the key point is that good or poor practice is debateable, rather than a single objective reality.[37] The subjectivist view is that there is no single objective truth on the matter. Some would say that getting the best available outcome like that for the client is good practice (that good legal advice includes providing a realistic, and if necessary robust, appraisal). Others would take the view that the lawyer's job is to do what the client says, more or less unquestioningly. There are of course further approaches between those extremes too. However, the analytical approach of the above two studies tends to discourage consideration of that. The defence lawyer forcing their client into pleading guilty is just presented as the objective reality.[38]

Equally, though, some of the abstract problems highlighted earlier in relation to subjectivism limit Travers' study, *The Reality of Law*. This has been described as 'a glowing account'.[39] I agree. Unfortunately, as Bridges et al point out in response to Travers' criticism of their own work on *Standing Accused*, there is little room in *The Reality of Law* for criticism of the lawyers involved.[40] No matter what is said or seen, we must simply accept 'at face value practitioners' own rationalisations for their (mal)practices'.[41] We cannot understand the context, because there are multiple realities and their *subjective* reality is not our reality, and therefore we cannot judge. Reform for those involved (apart from perhaps asking the police or lawyers nicely to reflect on their practices)[42] is out of the question.[43] It is therefore just as open to critique of being one-dimensional as the more objectivist approaches are. For example, Newman notes it is always putting 'a positive shine' on examples given and 'refusing to countenance alternative, negative, readings'.[44] In terms of

[36] ibid.

[37] See T Smith, 'The "Quiet Revolution" in Criminal Defence: How the Zealous Advocate Slipped into the Shadow' (2013) 20 *International Journal of the Legal Profession* 111; and E Johnston, *The Role of the Defence Lawyer: Conceptions and Perceptions within a Changing System* (Lexington Books, 2021).

[38] M Travers, 'Preaching to the Converted? Improving the Persuasiveness of Criminal Justice Research' (1997) 37 *British Journal of Criminology* 359, 366. NB, beyond the issues of principle, Travers also argued that findings based on the former are, practically, 'remarkably easy' to criticise (ie *you just don't understand the reality of our work*) and therefore unlikely to change or improve the behaviour complained of. D Smith similarly critiqued these studies on this practical basis: 'Reform or Moral Outrage – the Choice is Yours' (1998) 38 *British Journal of Criminology* 616. Several articles from these academics made their way into the 1998 *British Journal of Criminology*. They make for interesting, if lively, reading; however, the focus here is on the methodological disagreements rather than those about the best way to influence policy.

[39] Newman, *Legal Aid Lawyers and the Quest for Justice* (n 18) 24.

[40] L Bridges et al, 'Can Critical Research Influence Policy? A Response to Max Travers' (1997) 37 *British Journal of Criminology* 378.

[41] ibid 379.

[42] Travers, 'Preaching to the Converted?' (n 38) 372.

[43] Bridges et al, '"Can Critical Research Influence Policy?"' (n 40) 380–81, rightly pointing out the many concrete reforms *Standing Accused* instigated on custodial legal advice and Law Society training materials and even *The Case for the Prosecution* on police interviewing methods.

[44] Newman, *Legal Aid Lawyers and the Quest for Justice* (n 18) 28.

Bourdieu's general critique of subjectivism discussed earlier: it 'cannot go beyond a description of what specifically characterises "lived" experience of the social world',[45] simply adopting the same 'taken for granted' assumptions about the world as the practitioners.[46]

B. Heroes and Villains

Clearly, both approaches can result in an incomplete understanding of practice. However, I also contend that there are patterns in the severity of critique between more subjectivist studies and more objectivist ones, which are partly driven by these differing analytical perspectives.[47] Although not an absolute rule (more a *tendency*), more objectivist studies appear to demonstrate greater capacity to be critical, whereas more subjectivist approaches appear to demonstrate greater capacity to be sympathetic towards practitioners being studied.

In terms of this critical tendency of more objectivist studies, we have already seen how scathing *The Case for the Prosecution* and *Standing Accused* were and Travers' critique of that, but other, more recent, work demonstrates this too. For example, in relation to defence lawyers, *Legal Aid Lawyers and the Quest for Justice* presents one defence practitioner calling their client a 'toe rag' behind their back:

> [Harold] skimmed through the papers and remarked:
>
> > 'It hasn't got a chance; the magistrates will never believe one toe rag over three police officers.' (Harold, partner, *Radford Hope*, IC)

The commentary which follows suggests: 'Harold, then, had neither the ability nor the inclination to thoroughly prepare the case for the trial.'[48] However, this is not the only way to understand what occurred here. For example, on one view, this perhaps says more about [Harold]'s views/assumptions about magistrates' potential prejudices (towards his client) than his own prejudices. I am not blind to the practicalities of empirical research. It may not have been practical to question [Harold] further about his own views of this incident (this was a throwaway comment as he read the case papers, not a formal interview), or, on balance, not necessarily right to accept that rationalisation even if he did volunteer it. It *is* a useful example of where viewing one interpretation as the (only) objective reality might limit our understanding of why [Harold] behaved in the way that he did though. [Harold]'s own interpretation/rationalisation for this comment would have been illuminating. More objectivist approaches having a tendency towards severer critique also accords with Bourdieu's point in relation to their tendency in

[45] Bourdieu, *The Logic of Practice* (n 10) 25.

[46] ibid.

[47] In agreement with Newman, *Legal Aid Lawyers and the Quest for Justice* (n 18) and Travers, *The Reality of Law* (n 21).

[48] Newman, *Legal Aid Lawyers and the Quest for Justice* (n 18) 134.

principle to see deliberate policy rather than propensity (as in his example of the phrase 'as a rule, the train is late'). Applied in this context, more objectivist studies on legal practitioners appear likelier to view a practitioner as making a deliberate and free choice (for which said practitioner can therefore be criticised), rather than responding to an imperfect and prejudiced justice system.

In terms of more subjectivist studies tending towards sympathy, we likewise saw how glowing an account *The Reality of Law* was and associated critique by Bridges et al, but more contemporary (albeit not quite as glowing) examples can also be seen. For example, Welsh's qualitative study of fixed fees and means testing on the work of criminal defence solicitors found that the introduction of fixed fees disincentivised work on cases.[49] However, Welsh was keen to stress (and here expressly disagreed with *Legal Aid Lawyers and the Quest for Justice*) that the lawyers involved felt 'torn' between client and business needs.[50] Whilst acknowledging that interviewees understood all too well that there was 'a temptation to "cut corners" or perform as little work as possible in order to maximize profit',[51] these are blamed on legal aid cuts,[52] conflicting duties between courts, clients, firms and government[53] and challenges to their professional self-image/status.[54] Whilst Welsh is certainly more realistic about the challenges and the implications for clients than Travers, this approach still does not readily lend itself to critique: is criminal legal aid the only profession in the world with no bad apples? No lawyers out there inclined to take advantage of the opportunities of a fixed fee scheme to make big profits through cutting corners? Again, this accords with the earlier issues discussed in relation to subjectivism in the abstract. If the starting point or underlying assumption is that individuals' own accounts are their own realities and objective knowledge is, at best, probable,[55] one is also quite naturally going to be more inclined to accept those practitioners' own rationalisations for behaviour (the same 'taken for granted' assumptions about the world)[56] than a more objectivist approach is.

Nothing I say here should be taken as criticism of the rigour or value of the particular studies I happen to have used as examples. All of them were most illuminating and worthwhile. They uncovered things worth uncovering and the discipline is better-informed for it. My criticism is not about what *was* found, but rather the lost opportunity to uncover even more: an analytical blind spot. Those with a more objectivist slant, focusing on a single objective reality that the researcher 'finds', lead us away from other ways of viewing or understanding

[49] L Welsh, 'The Effect of Changes to Legal Aid on Lawyers' Professional Identity and Behaviour in Summary Criminal Cases: A Case Study' (2017) 44 *Journal of Law and Society* 559.
[50] ibid 576.
[51] ibid 576.
[52] ibid 585.
[53] ibid 584.
[54] ibid 585.
[55] Sartre, *Being and Nothingness* (n 6) and Sartre, *The Psychology of the Imagination* (n 7).
[56] Bourdieu, *The Logic of Practice* (n 10) 25.

the incidents in question. These may or may not be legitimate or open to criticism, but exploring them would give us a 'richer' view of reality[57] than assuming (to a greater or lesser extent) that there is only one 'objective' view: the researcher's. Equally, those taking a more subjectivist slant, focusing on multiple (subjective) realities (and giving primacy to the research participants' realties) have their own blind spots, carrying with them a danger of accepting individuals' rationalisations for malpractice.

C. Avoiding Dichotomy

The result, however, is that we appear to have some quite unattractive options. At one extreme, we can judge (potentially unfairly) what we see from an academic pedestal as the only objective reality. At the other, we can accept participants' attempts to self-justify poor practice. Alternatively, we might try somewhere on the scale between those two extremes. Much other work on lawyers (particularly more recently) does not go to quite the same extremes as (in one direction) *The Case for the Prosecution* and *Standing Accused* or (in the other) *The Reality of Law*. However, only rarely is this division acknowledged, let alone addressed. Even when it is,[58] it is all too easy to still end up somewhere on a binary scale between being more objectivist or more subjectivist, even if not at the polar positions.

One recent legal study that has moved away from this somewhat is Moorhead, Vaughan and Godinho's analysis of the work of in-house lawyers and their capacity for agency (eg in 'saying no' in the face of institutional pressure). Moorhead et al used the concept of 'institutional logics',[59] building upon more generalist work on this concept[60] (derived significantly from Bourdieu's work).[61] The institutional logics concept is teased out at the individual level as role and professional orientations (of commercial, ethical, independence, integrity, society etc).[62] This requires

[57] Weber, '"Objectivity" in Social Science' (n 9) 80.

[58] See eg Newman, *Legal Aid Lawyers and the Quest for Justice* (n 18) Ch 1. Newman expressly wished to move away from the above dichotomy but, as argued above in relation to the example of [Harold]'s comments, not always successfully. *cf* later papers suggesting a move towards a more subjectivist approach, eg R Dehaghani and D Newman, 'Criminal Legal Aid and Access to Justice: An Empirical Account of a Reduction in Resilience' (2022) 29 *International Journal of the Legal Profession* 33: 'to understand how lawyers' experience practice, we should approach their accounts in good faith and understand that deviation from an ideal standard … may be due to factors outside of their control'.

[59] R Moorhead et al, *In-house Lawyers' Ethics: Institutional Logics, Legal Risk and the Tournament of Influence* (Hart Publishing, 2018).

[60] See P Thornton and W Ocasio, 'Institutional Logics' in R Greenwood and C Oliver (eds), *Sage Handbook of Organizational Institutionalism* (SAGE, 2008); W Ocasio et al, 'Advances to the Institutional Logics Perspective' in R Greenwood et al (eds), *Sage Handbook of Organizational Institutionalism* (SAGE, 2017); P Thornton et al, *The Institutional Logics Perspective: A New Approach to Culture, Structure and Process* (Oxford University Press, 2012).

[61] Moorhead et al, *In-house Lawyers' Ethics* (n 59) 207 and Thornton and Ocasio, 'Institutional Logics' (n 60).

[62] Moorhead et al, *In-house Lawyers' Ethics* (n 59) 196, Table 8.5.

recognition that in-house lawyers exist in a 'sub-system nested within the broader systems of their profession and their host organisations, where they compete for job satisfaction, influence and status'.[63] For Moorhead et al, the crucial issue is how these lawyers' social world is 'made sense' of: 'sense-making constructs how a problem and its potential solutions are understood. It occurs with each interaction between the system, organisation, and individual.'[64] This 'sense-making' analytical lens (strikingly similar, as we shall see, to key elements of Bourdieu's concept of *habitus*) helped Moorhead et al move beyond the ability of in-house lawyers to 'say no' to management as a measure of independence and ethicality. Rather, they argued that:

> saying 'no' is part of a continuum of context specific responses, and one requiring significant effort as well as internal human capital. An in-house lawyer may need to be both well-placed in the tournament of influence, but also resourceful and willing to organise alliances within the organisation, before they can say 'no'. 'No' is both decided and negotiated. It is also often avoidable if the in-house lawyer wants to avoid it.[65]

Doing so allowed Moorhead et al to move beyond some previous academic work on in-house lawyers, which focused on (rather objectivist-sounding) analyses of 'agents failing in their choices'.[66] On the other hand, this is hardly subjectivist. They did not assume or adopt individuals' own taken-for-granted assumptions about the world. Indeed, as noted, they examined such taken-for-granted 'sense-making' and construction of problems/potential solutions closely. Ultimately, they maintained that 'some in-house lawyers plainly are unwilling to ever say "no" to their employers, and that this is a problem'.[67]

The specifics of the *institutional logics* approach is potentially less useful outside of the specific context of in-house lawyers (it is hard to see where the Legal Aid Agency or austerity politics would fit within this lens, which places the *institution* of the organisation, (sub)profession, etc front and centre as an influence on practitioner behaviour). However, I build upon this work in principle, using Bourdieu's framework (a significant influence on the development of the institutional logics approach).[68] I contend (and illustrate with this book) that returning to Bourdieu's concepts can provide a helpful and more generally applicable approach for both this and future studies on the work of practitioners. In doing so, this framework unlocks analyses that take account of both subjectivism and objectivism (and, crucially, their interaction) in the context of examining environmental pressures and individual agency.

[63] ibid 7–8.
[64] ibid 207.
[65] ibid 24.
[66] ibid 46.
[67] ibid 10.
[68] ibid 207; J Sandberg and H Tsoukas, 'Grasping the Logic of Practice: Theorizing through Practical Rationality' (2011) 36 *Academy of Management Review* 338.

IV. Understanding Practice with Bourdieusian Concepts

Bourdieu's work has covered a great variety of topics, such as Algerian kinship,[69] the social structure of academia,[70] social class[71] and contemporary social strife.[72] However, what I am concerned with here are his broader ideas about how to understand practice. These are of great assistance when it comes to the dilemma between objectivism and subjectivism discussed in the previous section.

A. How Bourdieu Moves Beyond Objectivism versus Subjectivism

Bourdieu challenged this division as 'the most fundamental and most ruinous' in social science.[73] To do so, he developed the concepts of *habitus*, *field* and *capital*. These concepts incorporate both subjective and objective elements. They also all interact. Hence, Bourdieu argued that neither subjectivism nor objectivism alone is sufficient: rather it is both together *and* their interaction which explains practice. Combined, therefore, the objective and subjective can be more than the sum of their parts. Consequently, the above division is 'set up' and 'artificial', rather than inevitable.[74]

Habitus consists of 'systems of durable, transposable dispositions'. These are 'structured structures predisposed to function as structuring structures, that is, as principles which generate and organise practices'.[75] Breaking that down, *habitus* is a *disposition* in the sense that it refers to something inherent about an individual. This *generates* and *organises* their practices, ie it influences what an individual is inclined/tends to do and how they make sense of the world around them. These dispositions are a *system*: it is not a basic emotional 'disposition' like being tired or upset, but much more entrenched and complex. In fact, *habitus* is 'the basis of the perception and appreciation of all subsequent experiences'.[76] It is also both *structured* by that individual's past experiences and *structuring*, because it will influence how that person understands the world and behaves in it now and in future. That future behaviour and its consequences will itself result in further experiences, which further contribute to that individual's *habitus*. Of course, if

[69] Bourdieu, *The Logic of Practice* (n 10).

[70] P Bourdieu, *Homo Academicus* (P Collier tr, Stanford University Press, 1988).

[71] P Bourdieu, *Distinction: A Social Critique of the Judgement of Taste* (R Nice tr, first published 1987, Routledge, 2010); P Bourdieu, *The State Nobility: Elite Schools in the Field of Power* (L Clough tr, Polity Press, 1996).

[72] P Bourdieu (ed), *The Weight of the World: Social Suffering in Contemporary Society* (P Parkhurst Ferguson tr, Polity Press, 1999).

[73] Bourdieu, *The Logic of Practice* (n 10) 23.

[74] ibid 23.

[75] ibid 53.

[76] ibid 54.

someone's understanding and decisions today are indeed closely influenced by their previous ones (a 'present past'),[77] and their decisions and understandings today also influence their future decisions and understandings, then this will tend to reinforce itself over time. Hence, these systems of dispositions are also said to be *durable*.

Bourdieu argues that this understanding transcends the conflict between (objective) determinism and (subjective) freedom. Instead, it allows an understanding of a 'conditioned and conditional freedom':[78] 'the *habitus* makes possible the free production of all the thoughts, perceptions and actions inherent in the particular conditions of its production – [but] only those'.[79] This is largely imperceptible to the individual involved, who will feel like they are making unique and individual choices (because in some ways they are, even if, at the same time, those choices are restricted and influenced by their *habitus*).[80] Accordingly, just like two highly accurate synchronised clocks, two people with a similar *habitus* can behave in a logical and similar way because of their similar mechanical structures. Nobody would sensibly claim the clocks are consciously trying to copy the other, or are aware that they are synchronised though.[81]

Bourdieu would go on to make use of this concept in a variety of contexts, but his initial focus was on understanding foreign (to him) cultures, particularly social standing, kinship and ritual in Algeria.[82] To take a crude example from closer to home, some individual middle class people will insist (and, more importantly, often believe themselves) that they genuinely like classical music and golf more than drill music and boxing and that this has nothing to do at all with their upbringing.[83] This ignores the fact staring us in the face that:

> [t]hough it is impossible for all (or even two) members of the same class to have had the same experiences … it is certain that each member of the same class is more likely than any member of another class to have been confronted with the situations most frequent for members of that class.[84]

Beyond analysing Algerian kinship rituals or the French class system, *habitus* illustrates a more general point about practice here. How one can simultaneously be making (somewhat) autonomous decisions, and feel like one is, yet at the same time be heavily influenced by one's previous experiences, decisions and environment, without necessarily realising it (and indeed, its influence is all the more potent because of that). This provides room for an understanding of individual

[77] ibid.
[78] ibid 55.
[79] ibid.
[80] ibid 58–59.
[81] ibid 59.
[82] ibid, Preface. The empirical portion of *The Logic of Practice* was the culmination of ethnographic work with the Kabylian people in Northern Algeria.
[83] If one finds this example too crude, the same point could be made regarding tastes for clothing, furniture, leisure activities, or even dinner menus. See Bourdieu, *Distinction* (n 71).
[84] Bourdieu, *The Logic of Practice* (n 10) 60.

(subjective) agency, but one that also acknowledges objective (and somewhat predictable/standardised) structures.

It is difficult to talk about *habitus* in isolation. Where exactly does it come from? If it is made up of the past, how does it interact with someone's current environment? The concept of *field* provides the other side of the coin. If *habitus* addresses how an individual (by reference to their previous experiences) sub-consciously 'makes sense' of the (or rather *their*) world or social environment, then *field* examines what that world is and how it functions. Bourdieu likens it to a game. The *field* is the 'objective structures within which it is played out',[85] including the pitch/board and its territorial limits (each is a 'separate universe governed by its own laws').[86] It closely interacts with *habitus* though. A person with a *habitus* well adapted to a particular *field* (including a sub-conscious grasp of the unspoken and imperceptible rules of that *field:* its *doxa*) is said to have a 'feel for the game',[87] much like an Olympic athlete can perform on an almost subconscious level on the sports field.[88] Equally, one's *habitus* can be poorly adapted to a particular field, which can be greatly distressing or disorientating. Bourdieu's concept of *hysteresis* addressed the phenomenon of rapid social change, whereby previously well-adapted *habitus* become less so.[89] For example, workers dealing with the 'restructuring' of the western steel industry.[90] *Fields* need not be so narrow as sport or industry though. For example, Bourdieu studied contemporary French society as a whole in *The Weight of the World*.[91]

All *fields* are a site for struggle. Bourdieu's 'game' is a competitive one and, at a societal level, the stakes are very high indeed (compare the life expectancy, chances and experiences of oppressed groups in societies with those of dominant groups). The concept of *capital* provides a way to measure this positioning/power in a *field*.[92] Part of that is the traditional understanding of 'capital': wealth. However, for Bourdieu this is only one form of *capital* (economic *capital*).[93] The other (often more important) form is 'symbolic *capital*'.[94] This opens up broader ideas about what capital can be, such as 'social *capital*' (who an individual knows), or 'cultural *capital*' (someone's taste and lifestyle).[95] However, this itself is linked to *habitus*,

[85] ibid 66.

[86] P Bourdieu, *The Social Structures of the Economy* (C Turner tr, Polity Press, 2005) 7.

[87] Bourdieu, *The Logic of Practice* (n 10) 66.

[88] For some helpful practical illustrations from combat sports, see R Sánchez García and DC Spencer (eds), *Fighting Scholars: Habitus and Ethnographies of Martial Arts and Combat Sports* (Anthem Press, 2013).

[89] Bourdieu, *The Logic of Practice* (n 10) 62.

[90] P Bourdieu, 'Jonquil Street' in Bourdieu (ed), *The Weight of the World* (n 72) 6.

[91] Bourdieu (ed), *The Weight of the World* (n 72).

[92] P Bourdieu, 'The Forms of Capital' in P Bourdieu and JG Richardson (eds), *Handbook of Theory and Research for the Sociology of Education* (Greenwood Press, 1986) 243.

[93] ibid 242.

[94] Bourdieu, *The Logic of Practice* (n 10) 119.

[95] Bourdieu, 'The Forms of Capital' (n 92) 243.

because the ultimate form of symbolic *capital* is to have the tastes, values, lifestyle etc of the dominant group's *habitus* in that *field*: a perfect feel for the game.[96]

As can be seen, each of these concepts interlinks with the others. Some of them also incorporate objective and subjective elements in themselves. Symbolic *capital* is held by individuals, but its value is defined by dominant groups as part of a somewhat fluid back-and-forth process (consider eg the vicissitudes of fashion).[97] *Habitus* is subjectively held and structured by an individual's decisions, but those are also structured by previous experiences and upbringing. *Field* is perhaps the most objective concept, but nonetheless closely interacts with the others. Together, these concepts can bridge the above dichotomy between objectivism and subjectivism and provide a more realistic picture of practice: the *logic* of practice.[98]

Those concepts are not without problems of their own though. First, as Maton points out, whilst *habitus* as a concept highlights something significant and provides a way of thinking about that, it is abstract.[99] It is difficult to specify that *this* person's *habitus* is **X** and not **Y**. I have previously suggested that a model of extreme rational/economic self-interest might be helpful for understanding *habitus* in the context of legal aid cuts, as an ideal-type,[100] to compare against.[101] This is fine as far as it goes, but it does not fully solve the problem. Most people do not think like that (ideal-types represent extreme positions), so whilst such a model might help to understand, eg that an individual's *habitus* is *not* **Y** (or that it would be in one's interest for it to be **Y**), it still does not tell us what it *is*. Alone, that approach can seem a little unrealistic (as most people will not conform to an ideal-type). Relatedly, *habitus* as explained thus far also seemingly does not account for the well-meaning but unethical practitioner. Whilst it does permit some appreciation that one's behaviour can be similar to others' without consciously trying to be (like hypothetical synchronised clocks), it does not account for the phenomenon of somebody consciously trying to behave in a certain (ethical) way, but ultimately not succeeding. Can one end up behaving (unconsciously) in one way if they are consciously trying to do differently? Second, *habitus, field* and *capital* could together be critiqued as unduly determinist. Despite trying to move away from an objective versus subjective dichotomy, there is seemingly not a lot of room left for subjectivity in the sense of free choices or thoughts. The concepts thus far permit free will only in a very limited (both conditioned and conditional) sense. A particularly bleak reading may suggest we are all simply slaves to our *habitus* (and, by

[96] ibid 244–45.

[97] Bourdieu, *Distinction* (n 71). Even economic *capital* has this element to some extent though. Money, stocks and (especially) newer assets like cryptocurrencies are only worth what someone is willing to exchange for them. Their value derives from group attitudes and tastes external to the thing itself.

[98] Bourdieu, *The Logic of Practice* (n 10).

[99] K Maton, 'Habitus' in M Grenfell (ed), *Pierre Bourdieu: Key Concepts*, 2nd edn (Acumen, 2012) 48, 62–63.

[100] Weber, '"Objectivity" in Social Science' (n 9) 97–98.

[101] J Thornton, 'The Way in Which Fee Reductions Influence Legal Aid Criminal Defence Lawyer Work: Insights from a Qualitative Study' (2019) 46 *JLS* 559.

implication, our previous experiences and upbringing), though Bourdieu would dispute this.[102] I will therefore now introduce some of Bourdieu's more advanced concepts, which provide a more detailed understanding of the above concepts and address those issues: *interest/illusio, doxa, symbolic violence* and *conatus.*

B. Some Further Bourdieusian Concepts and their Value

First, the concepts of *interest/illusio, doxa*, and *symbolic violence* provide a helpful way of avoiding reliance on crude (ideal-type) understandings of human motivations. Undoubtedly, most people are (occasionally) selfish and some are even evil, but understanding how well-meaning practitioners can still behave unethically permits recognition of a much broader variety of human behaviour.

For Bourdieu, *interest/illusio* is a way of understanding the interaction between *habitus* and *field.* In short, those who adapt to a particular field (by spending time in it, who gain something of a 'feel for the game' and its *doxa* – see above) also gain an interest, investment or stake in its continued existence as it is.[103] Importantly for our purposes, Bourdieu was clear that this was different from more deliberate/conscious forms of self-interested action. *Illusio* is an unconscious phenomenon and all the more 'total and unconditional' for it.[104] It operates due to the fact that, as a result of the influence of an individual's well-adapted *habitus* on the way they see and make sense of their world, they will be inclined to see that *field* and its *doxa* as sensible, common-sense, the way things obviously should be etc, no matter how arbitrary it may actually be or appear to an outsider.[105] The use of the word '*illusio*' (as in 'illusion') highlights this element of self-deception well. *Illusio* is for an individual to 'acknowledge what is at stake' in the *field*, even if to others it seems meaningless or arbitrary.[106] To the person well-adapted to a particular game, however, it *has to* matter. Try telling a distraught Olympic athlete, who has just missed out on gold, to calm down because it's only a game.[107]

Sport is a good example because most people might eventually be brought round to agree that the score does not really matter in the grand scheme of things. However, with other *fields*, breaking away from *illusio* is much harder. Bourdieu was originally concerned with foreign cultures. Having known nothing else since birth, the idea that your own culture's eg family or marriage rituals etc might be arbitrary or pointless is difficult to even conceptualise, let alone agree with. It is not that people rationally calculate that the way things are is in their own self-interest (they may in fact be worse off) and consciously decide to follow that, but that the

[102] Bourdieu, *The Logic of Practice* (n 10) 55.
[103] ibid 66.
[104] ibid 67.
[105] ibid 66.
[106] ibid.
[107] ibid 67.

operation of *habitus* and *field* is to remove the impetus for that calculation at all. For the person with a well-adjusted *habitus* to that *field*, the benefits or rightness of the ways things are appear so obvious, such common sense, that it is unlikely to even occur to anyone to challenge it, or to be able to comprehend that challenge even if someone did. *Illusio* is (and helps explain) the phenomenon of why *fields* and their *doxa* remain, even if they are ultimately arbitrary, counterproductive, or harmful. It is the acquisition of *interest* and investment in the *field*. Signing up to this game is rarely voluntary/considered at all. It is not the same as signing a contract or joining a profession, but an acceptance, through experience/practice, of how the social world within it works and a reluctance and (in time) growing *inability* to question that or look at it critically anymore.[108]

The relevance of this to analysis of the work of practitioners is that it permits an understanding of those who act seemingly selfishly or in their own interests at the expense of others (eg clients or the interests of justice), but without necessarily realising it or even if consciously trying to do the opposite.[109] It permits an understanding that there is more to practitioner behaviour than *consciously* deciding either to prioritise one's own interests at others' expense or to sacrifice one's own interests for the greater good. A good example of this use of *illusio* to understand well-meaning, but ultimately harmful, practitioner behaviour (unconsciously influenced by *interests/illusio*) is Greenhalgh et al's analysis of infection control measures in the early stages of the COVID-19 pandemic.[110] As they point out, during the early stages of that pandemic, infection control measures focused on a 'droplet theory' of transmission (COVID-19 was said to spread primarily through coughed out droplets from sufferers, whether directly onto others or indirectly via ending up on surfaces which were then touched by others). The possibility of an 'airborne route' (that COVID-19 also spread via microscopic droplets breathed or coughed out, which, rather than just landing on surfaces or people, circulate in the air before being breathed in) was initially ignored and rejected.[111] Hence, an early emphasis on handwashing and plastic screens (to physically remove the droplets from hands or block them respectively), rather than masks and ventilation. It is easy to forget just how uncompromising this messaging was. For example, the World Health Organisation (WHO) tweeted in late March 2020 that 'COVID-19 is NOT airborne' and that contrary science was 'fake news'.[112] In the UK, a medical academic speaking to the media provided a useful example of the dismissive tone in relation to scientists who suggested otherwise: 'Most of them are chemists,

[108] ibid.

[109] The phenomenon of 'ethical fading' is an example of this in operation. See AE Tenbrunsel and DM Messick, 'Ethical Fading: The Role of Self-Deception in Unethical Behaviour' (2004) 17 *Social Justice Research* 223.

[110] T Greenhalgh et al, 'Orthodoxy, *Illusio*, and Playing the Scientific Game: A Bourdieusian Analysis of Infection Control Science in the COVID-19 Pandemic' (2021) 6 *Wellcome Open Research* 126.

[111] ibid 6.

[112] ibid.

engineers, owners of ventilation companies … They do not have a broad understanding of disease transmission mechanisms.'[113]

Belatedly, it was accepted that COVID-19 *was* an airborne virus and that ventilation was in fact extremely important. Greenhalgh et al raise a number of troubling political issues re the WHO, national governments and policymakers, however their primary interest (and ours) was what key scientists in good faith 'believed to be scientifically true … and why they considered [other] facts to be untrue'.[114] In brief, Greenhalgh et al argued (via case studies of advice and publications) that the Western scientific *field* is hierarchically skewed in favour of expertise, experience, qualifications etc of hospital doctors (schooled in the traditions and values of Medicine). These therefore carried greater *symbolic capital* than those of aerosol scientists (mostly lab-based scientists schooled in Engineering and Chemistry).[115] They contrasted this with the Japanese scientific *field*, where aerosol science received a warmer reception from the start.[116] The result was a collection of responses which in hindsight seem bizarre, but highlight the arbitrary nature of *doxa* well: eg *outdoor* playgrounds being quickly shut and taped-over for fear of children touching infected equipment, but mandatory mask wearing in crowded *indoor* settings not appearing in England until autumn 2020, despite the latter being more of an infection risk than the former.[117]

Importantly, Greenhalgh et al were not suggesting bad faith on the part of medical scientists who did not accept airborne spread earlier, but rather that their *habitus* and dominant positioning in their *field* blinded them to the twin possibilities that they might have been wrong and that the chemists and engineers may have had a point: 'the nature of *illusio* … over time prevents the players from developing a healthy view of the game once they are heavily vested and entrenched in it'.[118] The power of the concept of *illusio* and the lesson we can take from these medical scientists is that practitioners can be inclined to act in their own self-interests (and those of their group) at the expense of others, at the expense even of things which they consciously value (no one is suggesting doctors do not value public health) without consciously trying to or even realising that they are. Well-meaning medical practitioners with honestly held views nonetheless advocated infection control strategies which upheld their own privileged position in the scientific *field* and dismissed those which could have reduced the spread of COVID-19. Put simply, well-meaning practitioners, acting in good faith, can nonetheless end up doing

[113] ibid 12. See J Krisch, 'Is the coronavirus airborne? Evidence is scant, infectious disease experts say' (*Live Science*, 8 July 2020) www.livescience.com/coronavirus-airborne-transmission-debate.html.

[114] Greenhalgh et al, 'Orthodoxy, *Illusio*, and Playing the Scientific Game' (n 110) 5.

[115] ibid 10–11.

[116] ibid 12. The point here is not to castigate 'The West' and praise 'The East', it is simply that comparisons between countries allow us to recognise that hierarchies are arbitrary. Why prioritise medical science over natural science? The problem is that there was less impetus to even ask this question in The West. It was just accepted as the way things obviously are/should be.

[117] See the various iterations of Regulations made under the Public Health (Control of Disease) Act 1984, ss 45B, 45C, 45F and 45P.

[118] Greenhalgh et al, 'Orthodoxy, *Illusio*, and Playing the Scientific Game' (n 110).

harm for personal gain. *Illusio* – seeing the current *field* and its *doxa* and hierarchies as natural, objective and the way things ought to be – is a potent trap which permits harmful, arbitrary, and dysfunctional practices to become normalised and accepted even by the well-meaning.

Greenhalgh et al were largely concerned with the conduct of those in a dominant/privileged position in their *field* (the medical scientists) inadvertently acting in their own self-interests to uphold the current *field* and their powerful position/*capital* within it, however, such is the power of it, this operation of *habitus* and *field* can be equally potent even in those who personally stand to lose under such an arrangement. Bourdieu's concept of *symbolic violence/suffering* makes the point that even oppressed groups (or those with much less *capital* in a *field*) can nonetheless come to accept and act in accordance with their *field* (as this is preferable to the unpleasant effect of *hysteresis*: having a *habitus* out of sync with the *field*). It is 'misrecognised and internalised' by all members of society.[119] 'Without violence, art or argument', for example, a working class teenager may simply accept that certain universities, professions, etc are 'not for the likes of us'.[120] As Bourdieu points out, this is often more effective than physical violence at upholding orthodoxy, because physical violence is at least visible and can sometimes be resisted or protested. With *symbolic violence*, the individual complies without threat or compulsion: it 'is something you absorb like air, something you don't feel pressured by; it is everywhere and nowhere, and to escape from that is very difficult'.[121] This is worth mentioning because of the complex position that criminal lawyers are sometimes in. Whilst they are, in one sense, powerful and dominant in their field (compared to, for example, criminal clients), it has been argued that they are in another sense very much vulnerable.[122] The concepts of *interest/illusio* and *symbolic violence* provide the intellectual space to understand that, whichever perspective one takes on the position of lawyers, the possibility for well-intentioned, but harmful (including potentially to oneself) conduct is ever-present. Indeed, Bourdieu considered that there was no such thing as a purely disinterested act[123] (although he was hopeful that this mechanism could be manipulated, such that we could work towards social conditions whereby it was in one's interests to be virtuous or ethical).[124]

The second issue (that *habitus*, *field* and *capital* risk a purely determinist understanding of human behaviour) is guarded against by Bourdieu's understanding of the concept of *conatus*. Bourdieu did not invent the word 'conatus' any more than he invented the word 'interest' ('conatus' has a long and complex philosophical

[119] JD Schubert, 'Suffering/Symbolic Violence' in M Grenfell (ed), *Pierre Bourdieu: Key Concepts*, 2nd edn (Acumen, 2012).

[120] Bourdieu, *The Logic of Practice* (n 10) 56.

[121] P Bourdieu and T Eagleton, 'In Conversation: Doxa and Common Life' (1992) 191 *New Left Review* 111, 115.

[122] Dehaghani and Newman, 'Criminal Legal Aid and Access to Justice' (n 58).

[123] P Bourdieu and L Wacquant, *An Invitation to Reflexive Sociology* (Polity Press, 1992) 166.

[124] M Grenfell, 'Interest' in Grenfell (ed), *Pierre Bourdieu: Key Concepts* (n 119) 165.

history), however it is Bourdieu's own conception of the word that we are concerned with here. 'Conatus' is Latin for (roughly) 'having tried to do something', although Bourdieu was more concerned with it in terms of a 'trajectory' in one's life.[125] In terms of (and building upon) the previously discussed concepts of *habitus* and *interest*, *conatus* is:

> that combination of dispositions and interests associated with a particular class of social position which inclines agents to strive to reproduce … the properties constituting their social identity, without even needing to do this deliberately or consciously.[126]

Conatus then, is a further example of people's capacity to be unconsciously inclined to behave in a particular way in order to perpetuate a group's current position, but in the sense of staying on a trajectory, rather than just enhancing one's group's interests randomly. Like continuing to follow the direction of a satnav's outdated map even though the road layout has changed and without realising you are doing so. As Fuller puts it, 'habitus is to conatus … as position is to momentum'.[127]

Like many of the other concepts discussed thus far, *conatus* also draws attention to a particular form of self-deception. Fuller provides an interesting Anglophone example: Apted's *7Up* documentary series, where a diverse group of British children were interviewed in 1964, aged seven, and then every seven years thereafter. Apted's focus was on the British class system. From that perspective, it was a bleak program: there was little evidence of social mobility.[128] For Fuller, though, it is not just the outcome that is important:

> Moreover, the subjects tend to rationalise both personal failure and personal success so as to uphold the overall logic of the social order from which they emerged. This is what Bourdieu, now drawing on Nietzsche's Latin … called amor fati, literally love of fate. The mark of conatus is that people adjust their subjective expectations to match their objective chances … The word amor is appropriate in this context because Apted's subjects do not credit/blame either themselves or others for their fate. Rather, they come to accept their fate as how it was meant to be, such that they believe that everyone is best served by how they turned out.[129]

It is not, then, that *habitus*, *field*, etc are fully deterministic. People do have choices, rather the operation of *habitus* means they cannot always see them. This human tendency to rationalise what happens to us and what we do as 'just the way it is' can be just as effective as physical barriers. In terms of this study, many lawyers for example are not happy and satisfied with the social order or *field* of criminal law work as a whole. Indeed, many were speaking to me precisely *because* they were not. However, that does not mean that, for example, subjective expectations as

[125] S Fuller, 'Conatus' in Grenfell (ed), *Pierre Bourdieu: Key Concepts* (n 119) 169.
[126] Bourdieu, *Homo Academicus* (n 70) 176.
[127] Fuller, 'Conatus' (n 125) 176.
[128] M Apted, *7Up* (Heinemann, 1999).
[129] Fuller, 'Conatus' (n 125) 173.

to likelihood of conviction, profitability, etc are never adjusted to mark previous objective experience. Successes and failures (whether that individual's fault or not) are rationalised – the guilty pleader was always going to be convicted anyway –[130] and this rationalisation implicitly accepts and is influenced by the *field* conditions being worked within. Far from being determinist though, this can be hopeful. In drawing back the curtain and appreciating that what we so often take as self-evidently true might not be, we can realise opportunities for change. Some things really are as impossible as they seem, but others are not.[131] On the other hand, drawing back that curtain is extremely difficult, as one must fight against one's own *habitus*, *field* and (individual and group) *interests* to do so. We have already seen how people with the best of intentions can nonetheless fall into these traps.[132] *Conatus* provides a realistic balance between freedom and determinism when it comes to understanding individual behaviour through Bourdieu's concepts.

To summarise, through *interest/illusio, doxa* and *symbolic violence* we can avoid undue reliance on crude understandings about (purely deliberate) human motivations and appreciate how, much like some medical scientists in the early days of the COVID-19 pandemic, even well-meaning practitioners can nonetheless end up prioritising their own (and their group's) self-interests by operation of a structured set of taken-for-granted assumptions about the world or *how things are* (embodied in their *habitus*). Indeed, this can function in the opposite direction too: *symbolic violence* permits an understanding of how powerless or oppressed groups can work against their own interests, via the same mechanism, again without realising or even when consciously trying not to. Through *conatus*, we can end on a more hopeful note. One need not be a slave to the above mechanisms. Individuals and groups do have options: powerful people and groups need not follow the old script and use their power to enrich themselves and oppress others, nor are those who feel less powerful always as powerless as it might seem to them.[133] The problem (which *conatus* – that sense of trajectory and the self-deception that following it is inevitable and the best outcome anyway – reveals) is that the joint operation of *habitus* and *field* makes it very difficult for individuals to tell the difference between the genuinely impossible and genuine opportunities in their *fields*.

[130] Travers, *The Reality of Law* (n 21).

[131] eg Spinoza's arguments (a strong influence on Bourdieu), whilst apparently counselling acceptance of life, in fact 'demystified people's acceptance of their fate'. Whereas in the past they would have attributed this to an unquestionable God's will, 'Spinoza suggested that each person … is complicit in his or her acceptance of how things are …. There is no supreme entity called "God" holding them back': Fuller, 'Conatus' (n 125) 174.

[132] Greenhalgh et al, 'Orthodoxy, *Illusio*, and Playing the Scientific Game' (n 110).

[133] Many of the anti-child-custody practitioners in Telford and Santatzoglou's study (n 2) must have initially felt powerless to resist the incoming policies of the 1979 Government, with its manifesto commitment to 'short sharp shock' custodial sentences and subsequent enactment of the Criminal Justice Act 1982 along similar lines. How many at the time would have believed that by the end of the decade, and under the same Government, youth custody rates would have *reduced* by over 80% instead?

V. Understanding the Work of Legal Practitioners

Understanding the work of practitioners is challenging. We have seen how an apparent dichotomy between more objectivist and more subjectivist approaches to doing that falls short in many crucial respects, both at an abstract/theoretical level and in some seminal research work on criminal lawyers. With this book, I contend that a very helpful way to avoid such dichotomy in understanding the work of practitioners is to use Bourdieu's conceptual framework.

It is true that Bourdieu's work has had a variable reception within Anglophone legal discourse. On the one hand, given his reputation in France as a public intellectual, it has been queried why he is nowhere near as well-known (or cited) in legal research as other famous French intellectuals (in comparison to, say, Michel Foucault).[134] A dense writing-style and an apparent focus on topics at first blush of little relevance to legal academics (unless they happen to specialise in those areas themselves) – such as French colonialism in Algeria,[135] the social structure of academia[136] and social class –[137] perhaps does not assist either. Whilst he has not been ignored, it is fair to say that much Anglophone legal work focuses exclusively on one of those specific issues. For example, race, gender and social class (and using Bourdieu's concept of *habitus*) in understanding access to the legal professions and/or prestigious universities,[138] or analysing the role of lawyers as a profession, at an international level.[139] Comparatively fewer studies have utilised Bourdieu's work to understand legal practitioner behaviour/practices generally (the *logic* of their practice, as set out in the book of the same name), but those which have taken steps in this direction are encouraging. For example, Sommerlad's examination of quality initiatives in legal aid used two of Bourdieu's concepts (*habitus* and *doxa*) to make sense of a move towards New Public Management, beyond simple overt/calculated lawyer resistance or acceptance of it. Rather, 'a new [implicit] 'common sense' emerges to dominate understandings and actions'.[140] More recently, Pivaty has made similar use of *habitus* and *field* to assist understanding the occupational

[134] Y Dezalay and M Madsen, 'The Force of Law and Lawyers: Pierre Bourdieu and the Reflexive Sociology of Law' (2012) 8 *Annual Review of Law Social Science* 433, 434.

[135] Bourdieu, *The Logic of Practice* (n 10).

[136] Bourdieu, *Homo Academicus* (n 70).

[137] Bourdieu, *Distinction* (n 71); Bourdieu, *The State Nobility* (n 71).

[138] L Webley et al, 'Access to a Career in the Legal Profession in England and Wales: Race, Class, and the Role of Educational Background' in S Headworth et al (eds), *Diversity in Practice: Race, Gender, and Class in Legal and Professional Careers* (Cambridge University Press, 2016); C Epstein, 'Faulty Framework: Consequences of the Difference Model for Women in the Law' (1990) 35 *New York Law School Review* 309.

[139] Y Dezalay and B Garth, *Dealing in Virtue: International Commercial Arbitration and the Construction of a Transnational Legal Order* (University of Chicago Press, 1996). See also Dezalay and Madsen, 'The Force of Law and Lawyers' (n 134).

[140] H Sommerlad, 'The Implementation of Quality Initiatives and the New Public Management in the Legal Aid Sector in England and Wales: Bureaucratisation, Stratification and Surveillance' (1999) 6 *International Journal of the Legal Profession* 311.

cultures of police station advisers.[141] Outside work on lawyers, Robinson et al have also taken a similar approach to Sommerlad for understanding quality in probation officers' work[142] and Callaghan has used some Bourdieusian concepts to provide an extensive analysis of the effectiveness of anti-bullying initiatives within the police.[143] Likewise, Young (whilst by his own admission not providing particularly 'extensive mapping' of Bourdieusian theory himself) has sought to 'encourage' legal researchers to utilise Bourdieusian frameworks more extensively in understanding courtroom workers.[144] With that challenge in mind, what I hope to have demonstrated with this chapter (and the analysis that follows in this book) is that such 'extensive mapping' of Bourdieu's attempts to understand practice bears a great deal of fruit when it comes to studying the work of legal practitioners. In particular, engaging with Bourdieu's framework (including the more advanced concepts discussed in the latter parts of this chapter, beyond just *habitus*, *field* and *capital*) can avoid the subjectivist-objectivist binary that has limited social science and fed into studies on the work of lawyers, in order to provide a much more comprehensive understanding of the logic of practice in this context.

Bourdieu's approach is neither subjective nor objective. The concepts discussed above, first, incorporate elements of both and, second, go beyond the sum of their parts (objective plus subjective) by also permitting an understanding of how these *interact* with one another rather than being in conflict. In doing so, they allow this 'dichotomy' to instead be understood as two sides of the same coin, in order to explain the logic of practice. Practically, this permits a range of more nuanced judgements to be made. First, like many other approaches, it still permits analysis that lauds those who wilfully act ethically and critiques those who do not. Bourdieu does not claim that heroes and villains do not exist. The more complex underlying operations of *habitus* etc are in addition to those possibilities. They do not exclude them. Second, though, the interaction between *habitus*, *field* and *capital* (as illuminated by *interest*/*illusio*) also permits analysis of those who (unknowingly) act unethically/in their own and their group's self-interests (including even where they are consciously trying not to) and the impact of their environment on that. Indeed, this can even occur (in the case of *symbolic violence*) where it is ultimately counterproductive and harmful to individuals' own interests too. It also still permits analysis of those who are powerless to resist causing bad things to happen, even if they know it.[145] Although difficult to always know what genuinely is and is not possible in one's practice (as opposed to what one's *habitus* etc might lead one to

[141] A Pivaty, *Criminal Defence at Police Stations* (Routledge, 2019) 168, 177–81.

[142] G Robinson et al, 'Understanding "Quality" in Probation Practice: Frontline Perspectives in England & Wales' (2014) 14 *Criminology & Criminal Justice* 123.

[143] D Callaghan, 'Seeing through a Bourdieusian Lens: A Field-level Perspective of Anti-Bullying Interventions in a UK Police Force' (PhD Thesis, University of Liverpool, 2019).

[144] R Young, 'Exploring the Boundaries of the Criminal Courtroom Workgroup' (2013) 42 *Common Law World Review* 203, 226.

[145] See eg Thornton, 'The Way in Which Fee Reductions Influence' (n 101).

believe), reflexivity is possible (both for the powerless[146] and the relatively powerful).[147] One can be genuinely powerless in some scenarios, although appreciating that is sometimes conceptually difficult or impossible (illustrated by *conatus*). For the truly powerless, this is bleak, but it can also be empowering in itself by partially freeing people from a particularly vicious and insidious form of violence (*symbolic violence*, remember, is effective precisely because so much of it is self-imposed).[148]

Having established the analytical framework, we can now analyse this study's empirical data for details of the structure of the criminal law *field* itself, the positions of those within it (as demonstrated by *symbolic capital*, and what that is in this particular *field*) and their *habitus*. Ultimately, doing so provides an understanding of the logic of practice of criminal lawyers in austerity. The next chapter begins this, by considering the work of lawyers at the police station stage. As will be seen, understanding the *field* these practitioners operate in and how this impacts (and is impacted by) their *habitus* provides an illuminating understanding of the many dilemmas austerity and financial concerns throw up in that context.

[146] Bourdieu and Eagleton, 'Doxa and Common Life' (n 121) 126.

[147] See Bourdieu and Wacquant, *An Invitation to Reflexive Sociology* (n 123); S Armstrong et al (eds), *Reflexivity and Criminal Justice* (Palgrave Macmillan, 2017) and Greenhalgh et al, 'Orthodoxy, *Illusio*, and Playing the Scientific Game' (n 110) – the medical scientists came round to accepting airborne transmission eventually.

[148] Bourdieu and Eagleton, 'Doxa and Common Life' (n 121) 126, on how awareness of the operation of *habitus* and *field* smooths out internal contradictions/dissonance that participants have otherwise been struggling with for years: 'often, the individuals experience a sort of intellectual pleasure; they say "Yes, I understand what happens to me"'.

3

Legally Aided Criminal Defence at Police Stations in Austerity

I. Introduction and Context

At first sight, the police station is one of the better-covered areas for legally-aided criminal defence. Unlike later stages of the criminal justice process, anyone, regardless of means, offence type, etc is entitled to unconditional free legal advice and assistance in the police station.[1] Indeed, this plays a key role in legitimising the otherwise very wide-ranging police powers and obvious scope for abuse in this context.[2] However, as we shall see, this contrasts starkly with the reality for many defence lawyers. Work in the police station is regarded by some as a loss-leader and by many as the worst remunerated area of criminal defence work. For this reason, it sometimes falls on more junior (and inexperienced) staff. For those doing this work, it is tiring, stressful and frequently requires antisocial hours. Further, by the very nature of the setting, the suspects they help will at best be stressed and far outside their comfort zones. At worst, suspects may have spent significant time in the cells, be sleep-deprived, mentally ill, angry, violent, or under the influence of drugs and/or alcohol. This chapter first outlines some of these inevitable challenges, as important context, before considering the criminal legal aid system and its implications for the logic of criminal defence practice in police stations across five key themes:

(1) profitability;
(2) time;
(3) burnout;
(4) inexperience; and
(5) in-person versus remote attendance.

[1] See Legal Aid Agency, *Standard Crime Contract 2022* and the Criminal Legal Aid Regulations made under the Legal Aid Sentencing and Punishment of Offenders Act 2012. Albeit that, for less serious offences, eg non-imprisonable offences, this is over the telephone via 'Criminal Defence Direct'.

[2] Eg (in the context of Art 6, ECHR compliance) *S v Switzerland* (1991) 14 EHRR 670; *Brennan v UK* (2001) 34 EHRR 507. Domestically, see Police and Criminal Evidence Act 1984, s 58. PACE Code C (HMSO, 2019) para 6 also refers to free legal advice.

A. Challenges of the Police Station Setting

Challenges of legal advice work in the police station are numerous and well-covered in both established and more recent literature. To give just one example, evidence disclosure has been shown to be a key challenge. The point at which police disclose evidence (and how much of it) to defence lawyers in the police station affects defence advice and strategy in relation to suspects' interviews. Sukumar et al have found somewhat inconsistent levels (and timings) of such disclosure and that this impacted on the advice lawyers gave. Earlier and/or more extensive disclosure tended to result in greater cooperation from lawyers and their being less likely to advise no-comment interviews than if given no disclosure before interview.[3] They found that lawyers sometimes play an active role in interviews and can secure further evidence/disclosure if they do.[4] Other studies suggest police openness with defence lawyers re evidence/disclosure has been variable or poor,[5] although, in contrast, Sukumar et al suggest police are 'generally quite open', albeit not always.[6] This divergence may reflect differing cultures between forces and/or the approaches of individual officers. Given their other findings, Sukumar et al also suggest that greater disclosure can be tactical: to encourage lawyers to be more cooperative in suspects' interviews.[7] In turn, lawyers say good disclosure is required to advise clients properly and allows cases to be completed more quickly.[8] Other challenges are more basic, but nonetheless make the job needlessly difficult. For example, interviewees in Kemp's study of Anglo-Welsh police station legal advice reported officers ignoring phone calls from the lawyer assigned to a case as the on-call duty solicitor:

> It can be very frustrating if you're woken up by the DSCC [Defence Solicitor Call Centre – which notifies on-call lawyers when/where they are needed] at two in the morning and when you call the station it rings and rings and ends up cutting you off.[9]

Police disclosure and 2.00am starts are just two such examples and there are many more in the literature.[10] These broader challenges are significant, but the focus of

[3] D Sukumar et al, 'How the Timing of Police Evidence Disclosure Impacts Custodial Legal Advice' (2016) *International Journal of Evidence and Proof* 200.

[4] D Sukumar et al, 'Behind Closed Doors: Live Observations of Current Police Station Disclosure Practices and Lawyer-Client Consultations' [2016] Crim LR 900, 912, Case 5.

[5] M McConville and J Hodgson, *Custodial Legal Advice and the Right to Silence* (HMSO, 1993); V Kemp, *Bridewell Legal Advice Study – BLAST: An Innovation in Police Station Legal Advice* (Legal Services Research Centre, 2012) (BLAST I); and V Kemp, *Bridewell Legal Advice Study: Adopting a 'Whole Systems' Approach to Police Station Legal Advice* (Legal Services Research Centre, 2013) (BLAST II).

[6] Sukumar et al, 'Behind Closed Doors' (n 4) 913.

[7] ibid.

[8] V Kemp, *Effective Police Station Advice: Country Report 2: England and Wales* (University of Nottingham, 2018) 13.

[9] ibid 4.

[10] See eg M McConville et al, *The Case for the Prosecution: Police Suspects and the Construction of Criminality* (first published 1991, Routledge, 2017); A Pivaty, *Criminal Defence at Police Stations*

this book and chapter is the role that austerity for lawyers plays here. Hence, whilst I say little more about them, the fact that the finance issues discussed below operate in an already very challenging context is important to bear in mind throughout.

B. The Legal Aid System in Police Stations

In terms of the system for police station legal aid,[11] defence firms apply for contracts with the Legal Aid Agency (LAA) directly. There is no limit on the number available, but minimum quality requirements apply (as might be expected from a public sector contracting exercise). Coverage is split between 'own client' and 'duty'. Own client work simply involves advising and assisting those who, when arrested, ask for that particular firm/solicitor, eg because of previous positive experiences. Duty work involves being 'on-call' and ready to attend the police station to advise and assist clients who do not already have their own solicitor (or whose own solicitor is unavailable to attend). It is usual to do both. Indeed, duty work is a way of bringing in own client work for those arrested and/or charged in future, as a (literally) captive audience of potential clients. Duty work is organised across geographic areas through a system of rotas and slots, depending on where the firm's office/s are, etc. To ensure these slots are fairly allocated, those with a 'slot' must complete a specific volume of duty work in each period to retain it.

Those sent to advise at the police station can be, but are not always, qualified lawyers. 'Accredited police station representatives' (who need not be solicitors/ CILEX)[12] can also attend on a firm's behalf, notionally under supervision from one of the firm's duty solicitors (although said solicitor need not be present at the station with them). Regardless of the qualifications of the person doing it, this work is paid for via a fixed fee for each client.[13] These differ depending on the particular police station and reflect historic waiting/travel times and the type of work/offences that tended to be dealt with at that station when the scheme was first drawn up (circa 2008). It has been acknowledged that these measures are crude and the MoJ has committed to introducing a new scheme (based on time-spent, but still fixed fee based), currently in development.[14] However, at present, subject

(Routledge, 2019); R Pattenden and L Skinns, 'Choice, Privacy and Publicly Funded Legal Advice at Police Stations' (2010) 73 *MLR* 349; E Cape, 'No Defence: The Erosion of PACE Rights' in J Robins (ed), *No Defence: Miscarriages of Justice, Lawyers and Poor Representation, London* (The Justice Gap, 2013).

[11] For details, see eg V Ling and S James, *Legal Aid Handbook 2022/23* (Legal Action Group, 2022) and Legal Aid Agency, *Standard Crime Contract* (n 1).

[12] Representatives are required to complete an accreditation process, including assessments, in their first 12 months of work. See SRA, 'Police Stations Representatives Accreditation Scheme' https://www.sra.org.uk/solicitors/resources/continuing-competence/cpd/accreditation/police-station-representative-accreditation-scheme/.

[13] Criminal Legal Aid (Remuneration) Regulations 2013, Schedule 4. NB: given the clear link between individual police stations and fees due, references to specific fees in interview quotes have been made deliberately vague to support anonymity.

[14] C Bellamy, *Independent Review of Criminal Legal Aid* (2021); Ministry of Justice, *Government's Response to the Criminal Legal Aid Independent Review and Consultation on Policy Proposals* (2022).

to very limited exceptions, the fixed fee applies regardless of how much work, how many attendances etc are required in the case and it is important to appreciate that this covers all further associated work, such as follow-up advice, unless/until any court work begins. The exception is where so much time is necessarily spent on a case that a very high 'escape fee' threshold is crossed. In such cases, the lawyer can apply to the LAA for further payments at hourly rates for any further work they do beyond (but not up to) that escape threshold.[15]

From the client perspective, suspects are entitled to unconditional free advice and assistance in the police station from either the on-call duty solicitor or their choice of available legal aid lawyer (unless, as mentioned above at footnote 1, the offence is covered by Criminal Defence Direct). This can be in-person or by telephone, if preferred. This needs to be explained to them by the custody officer upon arrival at the police station and reasons recorded if they refuse such advice and assistance.[16] In reality, the adequacy of this explanation by custody officers has always been questionable.[17] Myths also persist that (illogically) either only guilty people or only innocent people need solicitors,[18] or that it will mean spending longer in detention etc,[19] and these myths are sometimes perpetuated by the police.[20] Similarly, some lawyers and suspects also 'internalise' a belief that the police station does not matter very much and that the court is the most important forum (another reason, it has been suggested, for the poor take-up of legal advice).[21] Such beliefs can be dangerously misconceived, as McConville et al illustrate: a suspect in their study without a lawyer told them the police interview 'did not matter as "nothing happened"'. In fact, the suspect had just confessed in interview and been charged.[22] Hence, even before considering any consequences of austerity, the initially rosy picture is already highly questionable. Remarkably, research suggests less than half of detainees request legal advice and less than a third eventually receive it.[23]

The remainder of this chapter will discuss austerity issues with police station legal aid work and what this means for the logic of defence lawyer practice here.

[15] Criminal Legal Aid (Remuneration) Regulations 2013, Schedule 4.

[16] Police and Criminal Evidence Act 1984, s 58; PACE Code C (n 2) para 6.

[17] A Sanders et al, *Advice and Assistance at Police Stations and the 24 Hour Duty Solicitor Scheme* (Lord Chancellor's Department, 1989); Kemp, *BLAST I & II* (n 5).

[18] V Kemp, 'Digital Legal Rights: Exploring Detainees' Understanding of the Right to a Lawyer and Potential Barriers to Accessing Legal Advice' [2020] Crim LR 129. When asked why they declined legal advice, some suspects said it was because they were guilty, whereas others said it was because they had done nothing wrong.

[19] ibid.

[20] Kemp, *England and Wales Country Report* (n 8) 6–7.

[21] McConville et al, *The Case for the Prosecution* (n 10) Ch 8.

[22] ibid.

[23] P Pleasence et al, 'The Justice Lottery? Police Station Advice 25 Years on from PACE' [2011] Crim LR 3. Kemp's (n 18) more recent, but geographically limited, work suggests around half requested a lawyer in 2017, although this was as low as 35% and as high as 67% in some forces. This may reflect differing police forces' approaches/cultures to explaining rights.

It is structured thematically, in accordance with themes which emerged from the empirical data and, where relevant, existing literature. However, it should always be borne in mind that these operate in addition to the systemic challenges of the legal aid scheme in the police station setting from the broader literature, including those examples above (and in addition to the fundamental challenges of the police station setting discussed first).

II. Financial Challenges of Criminal Legal Aid Work at Police Stations

A. Fundamental Profitability Issues

The first key theme seen from both the literature and interview data is the simplest and, in many ways, the bedrock upon which other issues stand. The police station fixed fee scheme, combined with the low level of the fees themselves, has long been regarded as simply unprofitable. Hence, this chapter is largely concerned with the consequences of that for the logic of defence lawyer practice here. The tenor of my data on this point reflects that of Kemp's interviewees' views: 'probably 70–80% of our police work is uneconomical',[24] and likewise Dehaghani and Newman's respondents more recently: 'you lose money hand over fist on your general police station work'.[25] Most of my solicitor interviewees viewed police station work as a loss-leader:[26]

> Def-Sol-11: I think every firm works on the basis that police stations are in effect loss-leaders. The idea is that you're servicing your own client base and also you're then following a reasonable percentage of cases through the court process.
>
> Def- Sol-04: Last night, I was on duty, three cases, three rapes. Now two of them have been 'no further action', but one is probably going to run and when that runs to court, it's probably worth [£thousands]. I wouldn't have picked that up if I wasn't on duty.

Hence, this work is only justified by the hope of bringing in court work from the same client in future (either in the same case or, if a repeat 'customer', future cases), or out of some feeling of altruistic obligation,[27] rather than being financially worthwhile in itself. Even the aforementioned 'escape fee' scheme[28] did not change

[24] Kemp, *England and Wales Country Report* (n 8) 20.

[25] R Dehaghani and D Newman, 'The Crisis in Legally Aided Criminal Defence in Wales: Bringing Wales into Discussions of England and Wales' (2021) 41 *Legal Studies* 234, 244.

[26] Exceptionally, Def-Sol-09 did not regard it as lossmaking, but still considered it the worst compared with both magistrates' court and Crown Court work.

[27] See eg an interviewee from Kemp, *England and Wales Country Report* (n 8) 24: 'The job isn't about the fee, it's about the ethos of the firm in doing a good job. Giving good advice and representing people well'.

[28] See section I.B above.

this assessment, partly because the level was just very high, so numerous time-consuming cases would nonetheless fail to trigger it:

> Def-Sol-09: if you've got somebody who's got 4–5000 [indecent] images [of children] on his computer, and the police want to interview them, you could be there seven or eight hours, and you wouldn't get into the next threshold.

As that example shows, such cases need not be trivial. Indeed it illustrates that, counter-productively (up until the escape fee threshold is breached), the more serious and complex (and therefore, time consuming) the work, the less money it is worth.[29] In contrast, simple and trivial matters (which can therefore be dealt with quickly) are more financially worthwhile under such a system (Def-Sol-09 gave the example of driving whilst disqualified).

The administrative burdens of applying for (and arguing about) the escape fee also play their part:

> Def-Sol-02: you'll complete the application and it'll come back from the Legal Aid Agency – and they'll say, 'well no, we're not going to give it to you because of this, or because of this' – and you don't get paid to keep going back and forth.

This reflects previous literature on escape fees, with one solicitor telling Kemp that only a 'tiny proportion' of cases were covered by escape fees and lamenting their arguments with the Legal Aid Agency in order to get them.[30] Interestingly, many of my interviewees, whilst acknowledging that the police station payment scheme was arbitrary (with its differing fees for each police station and inadequate escape fee thresholds), did not see the basic principle of fixed fees here as the problem:

> Def-Sol-06: they are too low. I think that some of them are utterly insulting. I don't have a problem with the idea of it, the premise of it.

The Criminal Legal Aid Review,[31] whilst recommending fee increases, also devoted much time to reforming the fee system (as did the Government response).[32] The primacy of concern for fee *levels* as an issue here, rather than the fixed fee *system*, ought therefore to be borne in mind.

In terms of effects on practice, at the very least, this leads to frustration, as Def-Sol-01 demonstrated:

> A rape case could take a good six hours. So six hours … [calculations by reference to particular police stations in one city] … the market rate of pay is about [£50–£70], that's all I'm getting. To God damn represent someone for rape. Absolutely fucking scandalous, that's what it is. What will I get for going to [other city police station]? [calculations]. Works out to be [circa £10] an hour … no concept of inflation, no anti-social times factored into it, no bank holidays, no increased fee for Christmas.

[29] See also Kemp, *England and Wales Country Report* (n 8) 32–33.
[30] ibid 21.
[31] Bellamy, *Criminal Legal Aid Review* (n 14).
[32] Ministry of Justice, *Criminal Legal Aid Review: Government Response* (n 14).

Alternatively, Def-Sol-04, who was more experienced (and, I dare say, jaded) had a different approach:

> I spend half my time working out how I can make the most money, rather than advising on law.
>
> Interviewer: right, OK. And how do you do that then, what's the strategy?
>
> Def-Sol-04: the old Tesco: pile it high, sell it cheap.

As Cape has noted, fixed fees reward lawyers for doing minimal work[33] and most legal advisers in Kemp's study admitted that fixed fees made them more 'commercially aware' and reduced time spent on cases.[34] I argue in this chapter that Def-Sol-04's approach (as someone who had been working in the *field* for quite a while) illustrates the *habitus* that this *field* rewards and makes dominant: the *habitus* of highest *symbolic capital.* The frustration and anguish demonstrated by Def-Sol-01 (who was at an earlier career stage) shows the consequences of having a different *habitus* in this *field.* Def-Sol-01 must either adapt/reconcile their *habitus* (values, disposition, world-view, etc) to this reality, like Def-Sol-04 or be forever frustrated and disempowered within it as someone with little *symbolic capital* (or leave the *field* entirely). We shall now consider more specific examples of the implications of this for police station work.

B. Time

The first strategic consequence for defence lawyer practice is the use and perception of time. As Morison and Leith pointed out many years earlier in relation to barristers: time 'dictates much in the life of the barrister'. Managed properly, a barrister can 'cover enough cases to be busy and successful'.[35] However, in 'the hostile barristerial world … time is short and pressures are constant'.[36] The data here highlight the equal importance of time for solicitors in police stations. Financial concerns permeate this:

> Def-Sol-12: you try to spend as little time as possible in the police station … you have a competition in your own mind between doing the job properly and doing it quickly. So, are you going to spend two hours discussing with somebody the ins and outs of a small shoplifting case in a police station, or are you going to try and do that in 30 minutes … because you're gonna get paid the same.[37]

[33] Cape, 'No Defence' (n 10) 17.

[34] Kemp, *BLAST I* (n 5) 50–51.

[35] J Morison and P Leith, *The Barristers World and the Nature of Law* (Open University Press, 1992) 19.

[36] ibid 91.

[37] Dehaghani and Newman's interviewees similarly reported this dilemma, stating that it was 'only natural' to want to minimise time spent in the station on this basis: R Dehaghani and D Newman, 'Criminal Legal Aid and Access to Justice: An Empirical Account of a Reduction in Resilience' (2022) 29 *International Journal of the Legal Profession* 33, 39–40.

Pivaty found this to be equally true of the independent agents various law firms send out (indeed, Pivaty also argued that reduced fees incentivised firms to make greater use of agents), both for their own income and to meet business commitments to their law firm customers.[38] Hence, observed consultations of two 'first-timer' clients 'felt rushed'. In his research interview, the agent in question stated he could 'squeeze in' up to 100 visits to police stations per month, with an average of around 20 cases per week.[39]

Equally though, immediate, more operational, concerns also come down to a lack of time on the part of lawyers in the police station:

> Def-Sol-03: There are fewer lawyers practising in criminal defence than there ever have been, but people still get arrested at the same rate. So what we now have are situations where we've got four people in custody down at a police station, and two people to cover them: one done, onto the next, wrap up the next one.

Kemp has also noted issues of firms 'juggling' small numbers of solicitors for out of hours police work due to employee cutbacks and resultant attempts to 'stack' cases[40] and likewise one suspect told Skinns that: 'there's just one duty solicitor … they're trying to split between ten people. Initially, they just come and see you, sit down with you for two minutes, tell you exactly what's happening and then they cut out'.[41]

These examples are an illuminating illustration of how financial concerns impact both directly and indirectly here. In terms of the indirect impacts, whilst the issues mentioned by Def-Sol-03 are indeed *operational* in nature, the fact that law firm partners do not pay/employ more people to go out to police stations was itself acknowledged by interviewees to be a consequence of the fundamental unprofitability of police station work. Whether they like it or not (or realise it or not), the *field* condition has influenced how those making staffing decisions make sense of the world in this context: their *habitus*. The prospect of hiring more is either not considered or dismissed as fanciful. Those with a different *habitus*, inclined to employ more, are financially punished for doing so. Their *habitus* is of less *symbolic capital* in this *field*. That does not mean nobody is altruistic. The interview data shows some lawyers *would* like to employ more here. For them though, they experience an unpleasant dissonance (*hysteresis*) between their *habitus* and the *field*, which can be seen in the low morale reported in this and other studies.[42] I now consider some more specific examples of how this financial

[38] Pivaty, *Criminal Defence at Police Stations* (n 10) 144.

[39] ibid.

[40] Kemp, *England and Wales Country Report* (n 8) 4.

[41] L Skinns, 'The Right to Legal Advice in the Police Station: Past, Present and Future' [2011] Crim LR 19.

[42] See section II.C below and eg D Newman, 'Are Lawyers Alienated Workers?' (2016) 22 *European Journal of Current Legal Issues* 3; J Thornton, 'Is Publicly Funded Criminal Defence Sustainable? Legal Aid Cuts, Morale, Retention and Recruitment in the English Criminal Law Professions' (2020) 40 *Legal Studies* 230.

imperative to spend as little time as possible on police station work influences the logic of defence lawyer practice here.

i. *Work before Attending the Station and Pre-interview*

Previous work has identified a phenomenon of lawyers focusing closely on the police interview, at the expense of other police station work. In some cases, not even speaking to clients before arriving just in time for interview.[43] As Kemp points out, this can be hours after being referred for legal advice, contrary to PACE ('as soon as practicable') and their LAA contract (within 45 minutes of referral).[44] A sense that operating otherwise was simply impossible permeated many of my interviewees' comments. Whilst Def-Sol-05 considered substantial work pre-attendance to be an integral part of 'proper' service, they did not regard this as possible for legal aid clients:

> If you're going to do it properly, you might want to see them beforehand, prepare it properly, like I do for my private clients. Come up with a proper strategy, go to the police station with them, give them follow up advice. In a private case, I would charge someone [£thousands] for that. On a legal aid case … what the law firm will say is, 'oh we'll just spend 10 minutes on the phone with you now, and we'll see you at the police station', because they just want you to be in and out as quick as possible, because the firm will only get [£fee].

Similarly, Def-Sol-13, whilst unhappy, had come to accept only attending immediately before the interview as just 'the way it is':

> The way we used to be paid, you would go up there and see your client as soon as you could when they got arrested. Quite often people have never been in that situation before, so simply seeing you, talking to you, you are able to manage the situation. Get a grip on things. Now you can't do that because if they're gonna take an hour to sort themselves out before they can interview you, that's an hour's time gone. When effectively you're achieving nothing and bearing in mind you're on a fixed fee, you want to spend that time doing the coalface work when the interview's actually going to take place, when decisions are going to be made. So it's, [pause] sad, but it's the way it is I'm afraid.

On the other hand, as we saw, Def-Sol-01 could spend hours in the police station for some cases, although the result of doing so is to put their hourly rate down to around £10. Like Def-Sol-04, Def-Sol-13 had been in the job significantly longer than Def-Sol-01. For them, this was just 'the way it is'. Again, we see the consequence of staying in the *field*. Their well-adapted *habitus* means that what might previously have been considered 'absolutely fucking scandalous' (as Def-Sol-01

[43] V Kemp, '"No Time for a Solicitor": Implications for Delays on the Take-up of Legal Advice' [2013] Crim LR 184; D Newman, *Legal Aid Lawyers and the Quest for Justice* (Hart Publishing, 2013); Kemp, 'Digital Legal Rights' (n 18); Kemp, *England and Wales Country Report* (n 8) 19–20.

[44] Kemp, 'Digital Legal Rights' (n 18) 6.

put it) is now an unquestionable fact of life, albeit one that is 'sad' (it might also explain Def-Sol-13's fairly abrupt reappraisal, having just set out the benefits of early attendance, that such work 'achieve[s] nothing'). They certainly will no longer be spending hours in the police station before interview for less than minimum wage, like Def-Sol-01 does, though, no matter how sad it is.

ii. Investigations/Work at the Station

Once (potentially belatedly) at the station, finance remains a heavy influence, although, as before, not always overtly. Rather, a practical logic can be seen which has its roots in financial issues, even if these are not always clear to the lawyers involved, who may 'conceal, even from themselves, the true nature of their practical mastery as learned ignorance'.[45]

Def-Sol-02 noted the tendency on the part of some solicitors to advise no comment interviews, as a time-saving measure:

> many solicitors think, 'well if you're only going to get a fixed fee for it, let's just quickly do a no comment interview and get out of there', but that's not always the best for clients.

Beyond maximising returns on the fixed fee by saving time, a 'no comment' interview may in some cases carry further financial advantages (compared to an early admission) as it can lead to (more lucrative) court work later on. Certainly, the best outcome from a client's perspective (released with no further action) is going to pay least of all. We shall consider this issue in more detail in later chapters on the courts, but even at the police station stage, some of Kemp's BLAST project interviewees complained of others who advise no comment in order to take lucrative cases to Crown Court trial, or even, when working for another firm, being directly instructed to '[t]ell them to make no comment and we can get a trial out of it'.[46] There are other ways of saving time though, for example, where there is no prospect of a lucrative Crown Court trial (because it is a less serious offence) an admission might be even quicker and more preferable than a no comment interview. As one of Kemp's interviewees explained 'If the police provided us early on with comprehensive disclosure then this can help us to get things dealt with a lot quicker. It's in our financial interest to encourage a client to make an admission'.[47] Another put this even more strongly: 'There's nothing stronger than showing a suspect CCTV evidence and asking if it's them. There are targets in the criminal justice system to achieve early guilty pleas and we need the police to understand that disclosure is key here'.[48] Previous literature has also found slightly less extreme forms of keeping interviews short in response to the fixed fee scheme. Eg one of Kemp's interviewees, although not going as far as advising going completely 'no

[45] P Bourdieu, *The Logic of Practice* (Richard Nice tr, Polity Press, 1990) 102.
[46] Kemp, *BLAST I* (n 5) 54–55.
[47] Kemp *England & Wales Country Report* (n 8) 13.
[48] ibid 12.

comment' or encouraging admissions to save time, noted 'anything like an interjection or stopping the tapes is going to cause a delay and for some solicitors all they see is that their hourly rate starts to drop'.[49] Similarly, once the interview has concluded, there is pressure to move on to the next client as soon as possible:

> Def-Sol-03: You don't then have an hour to spend chatting away with a client in a consultation booth after you've done your interview, who might say to you, 'well there's something on my mobile phone that I'd like the police to look at' … It puts an enormous onus upon us as the defence lawyer to still be diligent enough to capture those things, so that you can satisfy your obligations, but try to run a business as well. Trying to be a profitable business and not lose the next case that's waiting down the corridor for you, because he's suddenly going to say, 'I'm fed up of waiting, I'm going to go in on my own'.

As with previous examples, this is potentially not even perceived as a choice, suggesting it is a more ingrained feature of the necessary *habitus* to survive in this *field* for long. Def-Sol-03 regards the time to discuss things with the client post-interview as a commodity they just do not possess, rather than a choice they make about case management. The potential consequences of this approach for clients are clear from the literature:

> You're generally limited to ringing up but by that time you might be told that your client has been remanded. You can try and overturn the decision but it's a bit late in the day. You don't tend to get the heads up from the police about what happens next unless you're hanging around.[50]

Equally though, 'hanging around' is untenable when solicitors have many other cases to work on. Again, it is not only a case of some lawyers behaving unethically. As operational and financial concerns blur, there are also altruistic justifications for concluding your time with one client quickly, like the fact that – as Def-Sol-03 perceived it – the next one needs you. Clearly, financial concerns can colour advice and approach to interviews in indirect ways, which may not always be appreciated by the lawyers involved. Such influence may explain the otherwise puzzling finding of Blackstock et al: that some lawyers advised on interrogation strategy 'in quite strong terms' before they had even had sight of the evidence and that, instead, the adviser accepted 'at face value' what the police had told them.[51] For some, no doubt this is an extremely cynical and unethical way of maximising profits, but others remain driven to spend hours (like Def-Sol-01) acting heavily against their own interests. The *field*, however, rewards those with the *habitus* who are inclined to take the former view (indeed, to an extent, it creates or structures such a *habitus* in people over time). As Blackstock et al acknowledged, whilst 'professional cultures' are important factors driving conduct here, these 'do not develop in a vacuum and there is an important interrelationship between the attitudes of lawyers and

[49] ibid 16.
[50] ibid 17.
[51] J Blackstock et al, *Inside Police Custody: An Empirical Account of Suspects' Rights in Four Jurisdictions* (Intersentia, 2014) 291.

external factors'.[52] The data thus far suggest that financial factors, including austerity, impact significantly on the time lawyers invest in police station advice, both directly and indirectly. Indeed, through *habitus*, they can impact the extent to which defence lawyers can even perceive of having the choice to do so.

iii. *Further Investigations/Work after First Attendance*

Work related to further investigations/appearances after the first visit to the police station was also influenced significantly by financial pressures. Whilst notionally included in the fixed fee, even Def-Sol-06, who did do this sort of work, regarded it as pro bono:

> In two weeks' time, you are called back to be further interviewed. Now that's the same matter, which means you won't get any more money. So that's free work, isn't it?

The results where the lawyer is not so dedicated can be seen from the BLAST project (which found non-attendance at subsequent interviews/police station visits was 'common practice'): without their lawyer in later interviews, observed 'suspects were likely to respond to police questions and to accept an out-of-court disposal'.[53] Similarly, Pivaty has noted a 'tendency towards being selective in exercising activities which were not part of the "standard package" of police station legal assistance', such as charging decisions, bail appointments and ID parades.[54] As one of Dehaghani and Newman's interviewees reported bluntly: '[c]ontractually we don't need to, and in the quality standards we don't need to, so we don't'.[55] Robust challenging of police and prosecution pre-charge (after interview) is another thing lost to this lack of (paid) time. However, this can be extremely effective when done well. As Pros-02 explained in relation to what (before moving to the CPS) private funding allowed them to do (which was not done with legal aid):

> 'frontloading' a case: taking all the client's instructions, reviewing all the evidence before they're charged, putting in letters of representations to the police and the Crown Prosecution Service. And cases were being dropped. Whereas if I hadn't done that work beforehand, then they're getting prosecuted.[56]

[52] ibid 416–17.

[53] Kemp, *BLAST II* (n 5) 29.

[54] Pivaty (n 10) 143–44.

[55] Dehaghani and Newman (n 37) 40.

[56] Under legal aid, where the case comes within the scope of the police station scheme, no further fee is payable. All work pre-charge is covered by the initial police station fixed fee unless and until the escape fee threshold is crossed. A similarly penurious scheme (Advice and Assistance) is available for those cases where the police or other agencies with powers of arrest are not involved, such as an interview with a benefit fraud investigator (as they do not have powers of arrest). Unlike the police station scheme, this is also subject to means and merits tests. More recently, parts of this approach have been formalised via a 'Pre-charge Engagement' scheme. As Johnstone and respondents to his study on this note, money available for this work on legal aid makes it most unattractive where the client is not private paying: E Johnstone, 'Pre-charge (Lack of) Engagement: An Empty Gesture?' [2022] Crim LR 737, 747–48.

Similarly, one of Def-Sol-07's clients paying privately permitted much earlier engagement of a drug driving expert and their evidence, which was then used to influence the charging decision. The consequences would otherwise have been severe:

> That all had to be done privately: cost him about £1500 for us to do it and for the expert. It came back that he wasn't driving with drugs in his system, but we could not have done that on legal aid at that stage. Just wouldn't have been possible. And it meant that he didn't get recalled to prison.

Although not mentioned here, there is also the fact that (as considered above in relation to those advising no comment in the hope of things progressing further) it is not just that further work to get charges dropped early does not bring in any more money (a *negative* incentive). There is also a (*positive*) financial reward from the fees of progressing such cases to trial instead. This also develops a more general point from the BLAST project that (at least where, unlike in the previous two examples, the client is legally aided rather than privately funded): 'The effect of solicitors pulling back on the amount of work undertaken in cases, as well as spending less time in police stations, seems to have helped marginalise them from the pre-charge process.'[57]

All these examples demonstrate clear financial pressure to minimise investigations after the first interview. This encourages practices which are not to clients' benefit (and indeed, against wider public interests too: getting hopeless cases dropped before court, as some of the examples related to, saves public resources and time). Conversely, 'good practice' leads to financial punishment. In practice, this can result in a challenging dilemma to navigate. Def-Sol-12 comes across as somewhat torn:

> Going to a police station four times, spending several hours, getting paid the same as if you were in and out in 30 minutes. You have to think, effectively, strategically about this. You have to think to yourself, what's most cost effective? To make sure that I'm doing what I'm required to do in providing the appropriate level of service to the client, but not bankrupting the firm while I'm doing it. So you're gonna make a judgment call. It does mean that there are certain things which in the old days you would do without thinking, nowadays you do think about quite hard.

As we saw in relation to the need to save time at earlier stages (before attending the police station and whilst at the police station), this is not spoken of in terms of something that is optional/a decision. Rather (for Def-Sol-12), thinking strategically is perceived as something you simply 'have to' do. Likewise (for Def-Sol-07 above) substantial post-interview (pre-charge) work 'just wouldn't have been possible' on legal aid, even where this is vital in preventing recall to prison. Individuals' *habitus* structured by an austerity *field* means that what might previously have been considered a choice is now just an unfortunate fact of life.

[57] *BLAST I* (n 5) 53.

This is enforced frequently: those doing otherwise are financially punished[58] and those doing so to the greatest extent are rewarded the most.

iv. Time for TLC

The final theme where lack of time influences the logic of defence lawyer practice is what might, in healthcare professions, be termed 'tender loving care'. This is difficult to quantify or explain in the abstract, but it is important, just as it is for a doctor's patients. Def-Sol-02 provided examples from their own practice:

> They need someone to speak to, [they say eg]
>
> 'well I'm trying, I'm trying, but I can't get anywhere … I'm struggling with my drug habit and I've asked the support worker and I'm not getting anywhere.'
>
> 'Yes I did steal that, but I stole it because I'm withdrawing, and I need to have my next fix.'
>
> 'I'm a victim of domestic violence; she's always going to be listened to, because she is the female.'
>
> And for me to sit there and say to my clients, 'do you know what, I'm fully aware that men are victims of domestic violence', give them some examples of when I have seen it and make them feel comfortable that they can actually speak to me about it. And then try to focus their energy on what they should be doing to help themselves rather than just go back into that situation again. I don't have to provide that level of service, I don't have to say to them, 'if you're feeling quite angry and vulnerable, you should be going out for a run', or 'you should be looking after your own mental health'.

Others did provide some level of 'TLC' but, due to finances, either viewed it as 'pro bono', or something for private clients only:

> Def-Sol-06: The client calls, their family call, you've got to send a letter. It's all just free; it's all pro bono work.
>
> Def-Sol-07: If someone's paying us privately, outside of the police station they can come in for conferences. It makes them feel a bit more at ease most of the time.

This accords with Pivaty's prediction that cuts and payment structures could result in undue focus on 'legal' issues, at the expense of 'broader clients' concerns'.[59] Pivaty's observed consultations focused on substantive criminal law issues and the upcoming interview, rather than other important things that could influence interview performance, eg entitlements to food (even after six hours), police obstruction of a phone call to a relative/friend,[60] or mental health.[61] Likewise, Skinns has noted that resources and payment structures mean lawyers are 'unlikely to have the time or the money to hold a suspect's hand whilst they waited at the

[58] And arguably personally punished too, see section II.C below.
[59] Pivaty (n 10) 163.
[60] Contrary to PACE Code C (n 2) para 5.
[61] Pivaty (n 10) 76–77.

police stations'.[62] Def-Sol-06 provided a specific example of this in being unable to be with the suspect when a charging decision is made:

> Your client felt as though they had somebody there with them, and they felt looked after, and they felt protected … and charge is a point where, if you say something, it is recorded down, and it can be used against you. If you've got somebody vulnerable, especially if they feel intimidated by the police, then it could be quite key. And that's just never done anymore.

Nowadays, Def-Sol-06's approach was: 'You just finish your interview, and you talk to them and then you go.' This was done reluctantly, but with that same sense of inevitability we have seen in earlier sections:

> It's not so much of an immediate decision that a firm might make … I think really, most firms are like this, they really do want to do a good job … But I think over the last 15 years firms have just gradually, in some areas, just had to lower their expectations.

Hence, the level of support mentioned at the beginning of this sub-section by Def-Sol-02, whilst admirable, is also exceptional and certainly not compatible with the imperative of being in and out of the police station as quickly as possible. This is driven out of the defence lawyer *habitus* by the financial conditions of the *field* (or the defence lawyer themself is driven out of the *field*: Def-Sol-02 had moved towards spending much of their time in a different practice area). The ultimate structure for the dominant *habitus* in this *field* in terms of TLC is therefore exemplified by some that Pivaty 'regularly observed commenting that their clients were "obviously lying" or telling a "load of bollocks"'.[63] Regrettably, there is little room for any wasted time on TLC in the police station in such a case.

v. *Final Thoughts on Time*

We have seen that, when it comes to the issue of time, the distinction between financial concerns (maximising meagre fee income) and operational concerns (just getting through your list of clients) can easily become blurred. It is not (always) the case that one is consciously aiming to be in and out of police stations as quickly as possible to maximise fees. Even the more altruistic can feel the systemic pressure to finish with one client in order that you might help the next one, who is currently alone on police turf and at risk of being bullied into saying something unwise, or deciding that they have waited long enough for a lawyer and going into the interview room alone.[64] Alternatively, it may be as simple as just wanting to get through the night and go home. This pressure of time, and the sense of immediacy and

[62] Skinns, 'The Right to Legal Advice in the Police Station' (n 41) 31.

[63] Pivaty (n 10) 155.

[64] Although such pressure is itself a consequence of the way businesses must be run in order to make a profit in the financial conditions of the *field*.

uncertainty it imposes, is crucial for understanding the logic of practice.[65] Much like a boxer in the heat of a match,[66] defence lawyers are not mechanically deploying a series of moves, but nor are they all making purely detached and calculated decisions. As we can see, they do not have the luxury of time, or indeed complete freedom of choice of what to do. They can only play as best they can in that instant: demonstrating a 'practical' logic (as opposed to theoretical or 'logical logic'), which they may be unaware of, but is influenced by the austere financial *field* conditions: 'a kind of stylistic unity which, though immediately perceptible, has none of the strict, regular coherence of the concerted products of a plan'.[67]

C. Burnout/Demoralisation

A common theme thus far is of some (often more experienced) lawyers giving in to financial pressures, whereas others (often more junior) appeared to work all the harder, no matter the cost and terrible hourly rates this equated to. The issue can therefore appear simple: the cynical need to stop being so selfish and be more dedicated, like Def-Sol-01 spending hours in the police station getting it right, or Def-Sol-02 with their exemplary TLC. Unfortunately, such idealism can be exhausting. I set out the next passages at some length. It makes for uncomfortable reading, but illustrates well the toll such dedication can ultimately take:

> Def-Sol-07: I was Court Duty in [City]. I'd set off at 8am to get there, was there all day, and then I drove back, went straight to [other City] police station, I got in bed at 4am, then I had a court day again, and I had to wake up at 7am, so I had two hours sleep. I came back from court the next day at about 4pm-ish, So I did nearly a 30-hour shift. You shouldn't be doing that. It's just not healthy. But if you've got clients that are in court, that you've seen, and they're expecting you, you can't just say, 'I'm tired' … and you know that your colleagues – they're suffering just as much as you with everything going on – that if you don't turn up the next day, or if you lumber them with something, that's just one more thing for them to do. And it's just a vicious circle.
>
> Def-Sol-01: My mental wellbeing, my sanity, my physical and mental health's taken a battering. Burnout galore: two bouts of burnout in the last 18 months really made me unwell … the job has almost taken a piece from me. And it's the sacrifices you have to make. To get here is hard. And is it worth it? Sometimes yes, sometimes no. And if there's more negative than positive, then you have to really ask yourself, why am I doing this Law? Because if it's damaging you, then what's the point?

Such dedication, whilst admirable, is unsustainable. Hence, people quit or cut down on police station work:

> Def-Sol-06: I know people just stop doing it, because they don't want to do it anymore. Because they realise that it's just draining.

[65] See generally, Bourdieu (n 45) Ch 6, 'The Work of Time'.
[66] ibid 102.
[67] ibid.

The sense here is of being physically and mentally worn down because the work is tiring, but there is also a different sense of being tired too: in the sense of being fed-up or disillusioned:

> Def-Sol-10: I was working 16–14 hours a day, doing police stations and Crown Court cases. I was barely making a minimum wage … And you're not enjoying what you do, because it was effectively a white-collar factory … especially when you're a very junior lawyer, you have ideas of what being a lawyer is – you're going out and defending people's human rights, defending people against injustice – which to some extent you are, but the majority of us were just processing people through the system. It was very discouraging.

As Def-Sol-10 illustrates, not only is there the exhaustion that comes from working 16-hour days for minimum wage (because the margins are so tight), but also the sense of futility, that, for all that, it is not even worthwhile because of the business practices which those same tight margins require. You do not feel like you are really defending people against injustice.

Hence, it is not all that surprising that, oftentimes, those more experienced had (in some cases reluctantly) come to accept certain working practices which would shock their less cynical junior colleagues, or had simply got fed up and left (or least cut down on criminal law work). The result is that the *habitus* required to adapt (or survive) in the *field* contributes to a practical logic that sees certain kinds of conduct or practice as simply the way it is. The mental consequences for the individual of going against this are, as we have seen here, severe, beyond simple financial disadvantage and illustrate Bourdieu's concept of *hysteresis* well: where one's *habitus* is poorly adapted to a particular field, resulting in distress and disorientation.

D. Using Less Experienced Lawyers/Reps

As we have seen, much police station work is unprofitable, unpleasant, demoralising and draining. This all contributes to this work being of little appeal. Hence, it is unsurprising that another impact of those low fees is that some more experienced lawyers avoid police stations if possible, in favour of sending less experienced staff.

As interviewees noted, this is a financial decision for the firm:

> Def-Sol-02: if I was to go to the police station and do an interview where you only pick up [£fee], I could actually do a [other area of law] case initial consultation and pick up [£higherfee] for an hour.
>
> Def-Sol-06: [clients are] not going to get me anymore. They're going to get somebody who either is almost retired (who may have run out of steam a little bit, which does unfortunately happen to the best of us), or somebody very junior who doesn't quite know what they're up to yet.

Unfortunately, this is not simple work. Just training someone up properly, according to one of Kemp's interviewees, requires 'a massive input', including mentoring, in-house seminars/lectures, etc.[68] Doing so was unusual though: another stated that some firms were 'not bothered' about the police station and advisers would just sit back whilst clients spoke 'nonsense' in interviews, which the defendant was then extensively questioned about at court.[69] Def-Sol-10 provides an insight as to what this felt like, from their time working as an accredited police station representative:

> [management] were obviously trying to keep their business afloat, in any way they could, while trying to pay as little as they could. And the whole culture … A lot of people, including myself were not even considered employees at the firms we were working at. We were being told that we're workers without an entitlement to annual leave or sick leave, or any of that … So when you enter a career and you're effectively being used, it doesn't really leave any motivation for you to continue.

Another of Kemp's interviewees perhaps provides the management perspective: 'get rid of the case to a rep who's as cheap as possible. If the client gets charged, then all the better as they get another fee.'[70] Perversely, as noted above (in section II.A), such financial imperatives are worse for the more serious cases, as – unless they are so complex as to trigger the escape fee – they are likely to take longer and therefore be worth less in terms of the fixed fee when taking into account the time spent.[71] There are exceptions of course. Some (as we have already seen) are just very dedicated. Equally, whilst Blackstock et al noted that the 'bulk of the police station advice work' was done by accredited representatives,[72] more experienced solicitors still attended for 'prestige' clients and the (minimum) number of attendances required to keep their duty slot.[73]

Nonetheless, it is clear from the data here that, as a result of a funding scheme which both takes no account of lawyer experience and is so penurious as to be considered 'loss-leading' by most, some will respond (and indeed have responded) by sending the least experienced staff that can be got away with. Again though, illustrating impact on *habitus*, this is largely perceived as an ingrained fact of life; there is a 'culture' (Def-Sol-10) that many senior/experienced lawyers are just not going to attend the police station anymore (Def-Sol-06). Alternatively, those experienced lawyers who do decide to do police station work nonetheless (or who make management decisions to send them) will lose even more money (from something which is already considered a 'loss-leader', even when done by less experienced staff) and the lawyers themselves will feel undervalued. Such feelings may also then further contribute to the sense of frustration and burnout discussed above (see section II.C).

[68] Kemp, *England and Wales Country Report* (n 8) 24.
[69] ibid 24–25.
[70] ibid 25.
[71] See also ibid 32–33.
[72] Blackstock et al, *Inside Police Custody* (n 51) 282.
[73] ibid.

E. Attendance In-person versus Remote

Under normal circumstances (outside the COVID-19 pandemic and associated mitigation measures for police station work), telephone or (rarely) videoconferencing is available to suspects instead of in-person advice. For non-imprisonable offences, this is the only option available under legal aid (via Criminal Defence Direct). Telephone advice must also be offered where a suspect has initially refused the offer of free in-person legal advice (to guard against fear of delay being the reason).[74] Previous literature noted the importance of finance for lawyer practices in this context too. Some even went as far as arguing that remuneration is 'perhaps the most important' issue for determining attendance at interrogations.[75] Literature was also generally quite negative. One of Kemp's interviewees, when asked if he would provide telephone advice instead of in-person, replied: 'Absolutely not. That's no substitute for attendance. It's just a lazy solicitor who doesn't want to get out of bed'.[76] Others claimed there was a benefit simply from the lawyer's physical presence, which would be lost from telephone advice, both in giving suspects confidence/making them less easy to manipulate and in constraining police misconduct. Eg Blackstock et al critiqued telephone advice generally (pre-COVID-19), concluding that 'it was clear' suspects exercising their rights to silence benefited from lawyers being physically present with them.[77] Both police and lawyer interviewees stated that officers were 'more careful' when lawyers were in interviews and 'freer' when they were not.[78] Skinns further noted the more abstract, but no less important, emotional benefits of physically seeing 'a friendly face' in what is otherwise a depressing, isolating and frightening place and the opportunities it provided to resolve practical problems with the police (such as the 'suspect's need for a glass of water or a breath of fresh air').[79]

Although there has now been a return to the status quo, the COVID-19 infection control measures and protocols imposed from 2020–21 provide an interesting illustration of the operation of financial issues (and how the *habitus* derived from them can influence responses to new scenarios) here and what their influence might be as technology continues to change the criminal justice system in future. In brief, to enhance infection control, a protocol was agreed between the National Police Chiefs' Council, Crown Prosecution Service and defence representative bodies.[80] This permitted virtual police station attendance and advice, including in interviews.

[74] PACE Code C (n 2) para 6.5.

[75] Blackstock et al, *Inside Police Custody* (n 51) 388.

[76] Kemp, *England and Wales Country Report* (n 8) 19.

[77] Blackstock et al, *Inside Police Custody* (n 51) 284.

[78] ibid 409.

[79] Skinns, 'The Right to Legal Advice in the Police Station' (n 41) 36.

[80] See CPS, NPCC, Law Society, CLSA and LCCS, 'Coronavirus: Interview Protocol between National Police Chiefs' Council, Crown Prosecution Service, The Law Society, Criminal Law Solicitors' Association and London Criminal Courts Solicitors' Association' (CPS, 2 April 2020, as revised) www.cps.gov.uk/legal-guidance/coronavirus-interview-protocol-between-national-police-chiefs-council-crown.

Reflecting on their experiences of these extraordinary measures, some interviewees took a similarly negative view to the previous literature. For example, Def-Sol-06 was generally in favour of physical attendance:

> if they've got a complaint to raise about the police, if they've been mistreated, if they need to be assessed by the crisis team, if they're just in a massive state, then you need to be there to support them.

Others were very positive, for financial and convenience reasons, for example Def-Sol-05:

> the police love it – they don't have to deal with us face-to-face – and we love it – we don't have to [travel long distances] in the middle of the night.

Indeed, Def-Sol-04 (among others) considered that the convenience and efficiency permitted by online attendance, particularly regarding travel and waiting times, was so positive that it had (inadvertently) transformed the loss-leading police station fee scheme into something sustainable:

> [It] has become a sustainable model. If I could do that from home, and my total time commitment takes an hour and a half, well then that's a sustainable model. If I can do four of those in a night, it's really sustainable. If I can only do one, and I have to drive an hour to [City] and an hour back from there, and maybe spend an hour and a half at the police station, for the same money, I'm doing four and a half hours work and I'm only doing one case.

There was also agreement that some, simple, cases, or those with experienced suspects, did not require physical attendance:

> Def-Sol-07: When you've got somebody who goes into interview more [often] than I do, for a petty shop theft, where they're caught on CCTV doing it, and they're going no comment or they're accepting it, I don't need to be down at the police station.

Def-Sol-03 pointed out benefits for clients too, such as reducing delays and ensuring all cases were covered/continuity of representation:

> Truth be told, we could not have covered a lot of cases if we hadn't been able to do them by remote. We would have had to return some of them to the DSCC, or there would have been an unreasonable delay in getting somebody to the police station.

Surprisingly, some also noted there were practical advantages to having a virtual rather than physical presence in interview:

> Def-Sol-03: It's probably worked better sometimes, because when you are on a video screen in the interview room and you go, 'excuse me, something to say here', everybody shuts up … Whereas occasionally I've been in face-to-face interviews and an officer will just talk over you.
>
> Def-Sol-04: it works better because the client can see you, the officer can't. It [tablet/laptop] faces the client, so you can go to the client [mimes/gestures 'SHUT UP!'] which you would never do in an [in-person] interview.

This goes against (or perhaps adds nuance to) the (pre-COVID) literature suggesting that the defence lawyer's physical presence is needed to improve police behaviour.[81] There may be scope for a virtual 'presence' to accomplish the same thing or better. On the other hand, a more cynical view is that Def-Sol-04 and Def-Sol-03's opinions about the increased convenience and financial sustainability offered by virtual attendances play their part in their positive views stated here. Certainly, *habitus* structured in an austerity *field* may affect how clients' best interests are perceived. Indeed, most interviewees acknowledged hazards in relation to certain types of cases or suspects. Def-Sol-02 and Def-Sol-07 provided some examples of the benefits of being in-person for some clients especially:

> Def-Sol-02: with vulnerable clients, those who need appropriate adults, or those who've got mental health difficulties, or even youths who suffer with ADHD, it's always better to be there in-person because they can engage with you if you're there in person. They feel more comfortable … I would say, 'okay I can see that you're really anxious, here's a pen and paper, just so you can do some squiggles on it, so you can just focus your mind.' If you're doing video, you can't do that.
>
> Def-Sol-07: I had one [youth] who was getting interviewed, had denied the offence in interview [with me advising remotely]. Then the interview stopped, the police officer said to him, '[details removed to ensure anonymity].' Then I spoke to him [by phone] in the consultation room – so, between the interview room and the consultation room, a 20-second walk. And he said, 'I want to go in there and accept that I've done it' and it was just because [of what the officer told him]! That unnerves me, because you have complete control over it if you're there.

Hence, whilst virtual attendance is arguably appropriate for some suspects and, as Def-Sol-04 notes, can operate to make the police station legal aid scheme profitable again, this can often set up an all too familiar conflict we have seen in this context between defence lawyer financial pressures and client/suspect needs. Again, we can see evidence of some very dedicated (albeit self-reported) practice here, but not everyone is going to do that. The *habitus* that would not is rewarded with a newly sustainable fee scheme. Indeed, even for child suspects, preliminary survey research of appropriate adults by Transform Justice found breaches of the agreed COVID-19 Protocol's safeguards.[82] Given the dominance of a particular *habitus* which emphasises spending as little time as possible in the police station, to maximise the fee/time spent (as illustrated in the earlier themes/sections) such an outcome is not particularly surprising, albeit disheartening.

[81] See above, Blackstock et al, *Inside Police Custody* (n 51) 490.

[82] Transform Justice, Fair Trials and National Appropriate Adult Network, 'Not Remotely Fair? Access to a Lawyer in the Police Station during the Covid-19 Pandemic' (Transform Justice, 2021) 24–27.

III. The Logic of Legally Aided Criminal Defence Practice in Police Stations

At one level, the police station legal aid scheme looks reassuring: unconditional free legal advice and assistance for everyone arrested and/or interviewed. As we have seen though, in practice, this is one of the worst (arguably *the* worst) remunerated areas for legally aided criminal defence. This has consequences for the lawyers involved in the form of financial losses and/or even burnout, but also for the logic of their practice (and therefore on clients and the administration of justice). We have seen evidence of some very dedicated practice here (or at least claims of it), going well beyond the call of duty, such that effectively the fee is minimum wage or worse. Doing so involves working far against one's own interests in the *field* though and in that sense their *habitus* is out of sync with it. Put another way, their *habitus* is not worth much; it disempowers them: low symbolic *capital*. Bourdieu noted that, where *habitus* and *field* are not in sync, individuals are negatively sanctioned (in our context, both financially and through burnout).[83] For some, this will be self-correcting. Over a period of time, their *habitus* (and through that, their dispositions and subconscious understanding of how the world works and what is common sense within it) will slowly and imperceptibly adapt and change to match the conditions. For others, the difference will simply be too much. The consequences of this for individuals are troubling and can be seen above in section II.C on burnout/exhaustion.

Alternatively, in this context (unlike many of the subjects in Bourdieu's studies), lawyers do have the choice of simply leaving the *field* of legally aided police station criminal defence, and many do.[84] It is notable that most of those who reported going beyond the call of duty were either early in their career, or reflecting on how they used to practise before moving on to other things (to a greater or lesser extent). Some of the older hands were not so altruistic. Some even admitted more (charitably put) cynical practice. However, for the most part (albeit allowing for the biases of self-reporting), this was not the case. Instead, more common amongst those who had been in the *field* for a while (across all themes discussed here) was the attitude of acceptance/resignation (some more reluctantly than others) that this is just the way things are, of it not really being a matter of choice at all. As I mentioned in Chapter 2, when discussing the concepts of *conatus*, *interest* and *symbolic violence*, there is a very human need to rationalise and come to terms with 'the way things are', even to the extent of self-deception: 'people adjust their subjective expectations to match their objective chances'.[85]

[83] Bourdieu (n 45) 62.

[84] Illustrated well by the Law Society's duty solicitor average age and numbers awareness campaign: Law Society, 'Criminal Duty Solicitors: A Looming Crisis' www.lawsociety.org.uk/campaigns/criminal-justice/criminal-duty-solicitors.

[85] S Fuller, 'Conatus' in M Grenfell (ed), *Pierre Bourdieu: Key Concepts*, 2nd edn (Acumen, 2012) 173.

People are then inclined to perpetuate their positions, 'without even needing to do this deliberately or consciously'.[86] Eventually, people even gain a stake or *interest* in the way things are. They may then act seemingly selfishly or in their own interests (or even, in the case of *symbolic violence*, at their own expense) to keep things the way they are, but without necessarily realising it or even if consciously trying to do the opposite. Ultimately, the logic of the legally aided criminal defence lawyer in the police station is to make peace with the fact that they can provide only a very limited service: the best they can whilst trying not to bankrupt their firms or make themselves ill with burnout.

[86] P Bourdieu, *Homo Academicus* (Peter Collier tr, Polity Press, 1988) 176.

4

Magistrates' Court Defence and Prosecution Practice in Austerity

I. Introduction and Context

Contrary to the (often idealised) view of the jury trial in popular culture, the vast majority of criminal cases in England and Wales are dealt with by magistrates' courts. Government statistics show magistrates' courts' case numbers in the hundreds of thousands as opposed to tens of thousands in the Crown Court.[1] All cases begin in the magistrates' courts and around 95 per cent will end there.[2] What goes on in magistrates' courts therefore has a very significant impact (numerically speaking, the greatest impact of all) on people and their communities. Regrettably, as we shall see, this suffers from a similar funding problem to police station work. Some defence lawyers can regard it as a loss-leader for more remunerative Crown Court work and prosecutors report being snowed under with cases. After a brief introduction to the system of defence and prosecution in these courts, we shall then examine the implications of austerity for the logic of criminal legal practice here across four key themes emerging from the interview data and relevant literature:

(1) time (generally and in a number of key areas/moments);
(2) plea advice;
(3) inexperience; and
(4) burnout.

As with the police station, whilst the focus here is on financing, it should always be borne in mind that these themes operate in addition to the systemic challenges of this setting, already established by broader literature.[3]

[1] Ministry of Justice, 'Criminal Court Statistics' (Gov.UK) www.gov.uk/government/collections/criminal-court-statistics.

[2] 'About Magistrates' Courts' (Courts and Tribunals Judiciary) www.judiciary.uk/courts-and-tribunals/magistrates-courts/magistrates-court/.

[3] For recent appraisals, see eg J Ward, *Transforming Summary Justice: Modernisation in the Lower Criminal Courts* (Routledge, 2017) and L Welsh, *Access to Justice in Magistrates' Courts: A Study of Defendant Marginalisation*, Kindle edn (Hart Publishing, 2021).

A. The Legal Aid System in Magistrates' Courts

Like police station work, there is a magistrates' courts duty solicitor scheme.[4] Unlike police station work, one must be a qualified lawyer and pass a further specialist duty qualification to register with the Legal Aid Agency (LAA) as a duty solicitor here. Magistrates' court duty solicitor work involves helping defendants with advice and limited advocacy services if they do not have their own solicitor. Generally, this is limited to advocacy in relation to bail, guilty pleas and imprisonable offences. It is also generally limited to one hearing in the proceedings. After that, the defendant is expected to select their own lawyer (although this could be the same lawyer that was initially their duty solicitor if the defendant wishes). Work not within the limited scope of the duty solicitor scheme (eg trials) requires a Representation Order for a legal aid lawyer of the defendant's choice. This is much more restrictive than the police station scheme. There is both a financial (means) test and an interests of justice (merits) test, which is assessed by the LAA.[5]

From the lawyer's perspective, work is almost exclusively paid via fixed fees.[6] One first categorises the work into category 1B, 1A or 2. This is roughly in order of seriousness/complexity and, therefore, category 2 work attracts the highest fees. Category 2 includes, for example, contested trials. At the other end of the scale, category 1B includes summary offence guilty pleas and attracts the lowest fee. One can claim a lower standard fee, a higher standard fee, or a non-standard fee. One can claim a higher standard fee (still a fixed fee though) if, after calculating the overall costs of running the case,[7] a specified numerical threshold is crossed. One can then claim an even higher fee – the exact costs incurred – if the total crosses another, even higher threshold. So, in total, there are seven possibilities:

1. Lower 1B;
2. Higher 1B;
3. Lower 1A;
4. Higher 1A;
5. Lower 2;
6. Higher 2;
7. Full Case Costs Incurred.

Hence, whilst there is more scope for nuance here than under the police station scheme (which provides a fixed fee for work at each police station, regardless of the type of case or how complex it is until the escape fee threshold is crossed),

[4] For details, see V Ling and S James, *Legal Aid Handbook 2022/23* (LAG, 2022) and LAA, 'Guidance: Standard Crime Contract 2022' (Gov.UK) www.gov.uk/government/publications/standard-crime-contract-2022.

[5] Against criteria in the Legal Aid, Sentencing and Punishment of Offenders Act 2014, s 17.

[6] Criminal Legal Aid (Remuneration) Regulations 2013, SI 2013/435, Sch 4, para 5.

[7] These costs are set out on an itemised basis: ibid, Sch 4.

this is still a fixed-fee system. The best way of organising the scheme will always be debateable, but some have argued (and Government has accepted) that this method strikes the right balance between nuance and simplicity of administration, to the extent that a reformed police station scheme ought to adopt a similar approach.[8]

B. Crown Prosecution in Magistrates' Courts

Those prosecuting in the magistrates' courts are either qualified lawyers working in-house for the CPS (Crown Prosecutors),[9] qualified Associate Prosecutors working in-house for the CPS[10] (and notionally under supervision of a Crown Prosecutor),[11] or (qualified lawyer) agents instructed by the CPS for particular cases.[12] The last of these, whilst fully qualified, must take instructions from the CPS and are therefore not permitted to (for example) unilaterally decide to drop or reduce charges.[13] For efficiency reasons, there is likely to be more continuity for the CPS than the defence in a given courtroom on a given day (ie whilst there may be several different defence lawyers doing different cases on a given day, the same prosecutor could run all prosecution cases in that courtroom).

II. Financial Challenges of Magistrates' Court Practice

The fundamental financial challenge in this setting from the legal aid (defence) perspective, much like the police station, is that fee *levels* can make this work somewhere between a cashflow source and (at worst) a loss-leader, rather than profitable. Hence, as a starting point, it is important to appreciate that this work can be difficult to justify on a pure accounting/business basis. That is not to say there are *no* potential business benefits from such work though. Whilst there is certainly a sense of altruism/mission on the part of some, there is also the possibility of, for example, bringing in (much more remunerative) Crown Court work from the same client (later in the process or in future cases), and/or profiting from some magistrates' court cases on a high-volume basis. However, the point I seek to make here is that much of what follows (including practices which may be regarded

[8] C Bellamy, *Independent Review of Criminal Legal Aid (CLAR)* (2021) 85; Ministry of Justice, *Government's Response to the Criminal Legal Aid Independent Review and Consultation on Policy Proposals* (2022).

[9] Prosecution of Offences Act 1985, s 1(3).

[10] ibid, s 7A; DPP, 'Director's Instructions to CPS Associate Prosecutors' (CPS, 2014) www.cps.gov.uk/publication/directors-instructions-cps-associate-prosecutors.

[11] In practice, whether this is complied with (in some places at least) is highly questionable. See L Soubise, 'Prosecuting in the Magistrates' Courts in a Time of Austerity' [2017] Crim LR 847.

[12] Prosecution of Offences Act 1985, s 5.

[13] ibid s 5(2).

as problematic) results from the various approaches or 'strategies' that are considered necessary to get around this fundamental problem. Indeed, when it comes to considering the logic of practice here, I contend that a keen sense of this 'necessity' permeates many individuals' understanding of the world (via their adapted *habitus* from this *field*) and is somewhat required to thrive (or survive) in it.

Def-Sol-04 reflected the views of a number of interviewees on this point:

> We worked out, without two paper heavy[14] [Crown Court] cases a year, we couldn't pay the bills and keep the lights on, and I believe that to be the case across the profession … it's a loss-leader. I don't believe anyone is making profit from magistrates' court work.

In contrast to fee *levels*, the fee *system* in itself (see above) was largely considered acceptable in principle:

> Def-Sol-01: There's nothing wrong with the way the magistrates' court fee scheme works … but it's too low.

These support Welsh's view that a distinction ought to be drawn 'between payment by way of standard fee in principle and standard fee in practice'.[15] Respondents to the Westminster Commission on Legal Aid made the same point, with Vice-Chair James Daly noting that, in his own Bury firm, no money was made on magistrates' court work and it was hoped Crown Court work was sufficient to cover costs and to provide some profit.[16]

For those who did see any potential profit in magistrates' court work, this was contingent on a strategy of high case volumes. Unfortunately, as Def-Sol-12 notes, in a *field* where, realistically, time is always limited, increasing volume means reducing time spent on each individual case:

> the key is more cases, because since the payment for each case is fixed it doesn't matter whether you spend two hours, three hours or five hours, you're not gonna get paid any different for it.

Hence, just like with the police station, a fundamental issue arising from austerity practice here is the use and perception (and lack) of time; which we will therefore examine in some depth.

A. Money and its Connection with Time

Just as with police stations, Morison and Leith's comments in relation to barristers apply equally well to impacts of austerity for both defence and prosecution lawyers in magistrates' courts: time 'dictates much'. Managed properly, a barrister can

[14] This refers to the number of pages of prosecution evidence (PPE). Under the Crown Court fee scheme for litigators, higher PPE results in the fee 'graduating' upwards.

[15] Welsh, *Access to Justice in Magistrates' Courts* (n 3) 135–36.

[16] Westminster Commission on Legal Aid, 'Inquiry into the Sustainability and Recovery of the Legal Aid Sector' (All-Party Parliamentary Group on Legal Aid, 2021) [193].

'cover enough cases to be busy and successful'.[17] However, in 'the hostile barristerial world … time is short and pressures are constant'.[18] More recently, Newman and Dehaghani have argued that '"time" and "money" – are inextricably linked.' Their research participants had very limited financial resources or (consequently) time and felt 'pressure' to compensate for this by working faster.[19] The data in this chapter provide further evidence for that inextricable link and (whilst Newman and Dehaghani were concerned solely with legally aided defence) suggest this is equally the case for prosecution lawyers doing magistrates' court work. Lack of time was raised frequently by my defence and prosecution interviewees in several specific contexts (which I examine next), but was also expressed as a pervasive issue:

> Def-Sol-09: Fixed fees are great, but you've got to pile it high, sell it cheap haven't you? The more you do and the least amount of time you spend on it, the most money you'll make.
>
> Pros-01: there's so much to do and just not enough time in the day to do it. … fundamentally we just don't have the capability to do things as we want to … either time-wise or resource-wise.

Other recent data from Porter on prosecutors reflects Pros-01's view: interviewees were acutely aware of lack of time due to austerity.[20] As one reflected, if they 'really sat and thought about every case' they would be concerned about the victim being 'subject to a further serious or even fatal assault. But, we are dealing with so many of these cases, you know, on a daily basis that you have to kind of just get on with it'.[21]

Even just looking at these general comments, we can see a very clear practical logic or *habitus*: we 'just get on with it', we 'just don't have the capability to do things as we want to', 'you've *got to* pile it high, sell it cheap'. There is a sense of weary inevitability. These are the realities that defence and prosecution lawyers in magistrates' courts must come to accept, as just the way things are, 'something you absorb like air',[22] in order to have any chance of lasting in this *field*. We will now consider more detailed and specific consequences of this lack of time for magistrates' court work in their chronological context, starting with preparation for court.

[17] J Morison and P Leith, *The Barristers World and the Nature of Law* (Open University Press, 1992) 19.

[18] ibid 91.

[19] D Newman and R Dehaghani, *Experiences of Criminal Justice: Perspectives From Wales on a System in Crisis*, Kindle edn (Bristol University Press, 2022) 111. See also L Welsh, 'The Effects of Changes to Legal Aid on Lawyers' Professional Identity and Behaviour in Summary Criminal Cases: A Case Study' (2017) *JLS* 559, 574 and R Helm et al, 'Guilty Plea Decisions: Moving Beyond the Autonomy Myth' (2021) *MLR* 1, 28.

[20] A Porter, 'Prosecuting Domestic Abuse in England and Wales: Crown Prosecution Service 'Working Practice' and New Public Managerialism' (2019) 28 *Social & Legal Studies* 493, 505.

[21] ibid 509.

[22] P Bourdieu and T Eagleton, 'In Conversation: Doxa and Common Life' (1992) 191 *New Left Review* 111, 115.

B. Lack of Time to Prepare before Court

Austerity-driven lack of time for magistrates' court work often manifests well before any court hearing, in the form of inability to prepare adequately. However, this has effects further down the line. Campbell, during observation of 13 magistrates' courts in London during 2016–17, found legal aid lawyers 'did not appear to have adequately prepared their cases', 'failed to challenge police evidence and overall, they provided a poor defence'.[23] Welsh found this imperative for speed had its roots in austerity, with one respondent feeling 'torn' between doing things 'properly', as they wanted, and 'working for minimum wage', with a 'jaded approach' subtly developing.[24] For others though, this was more official: another of Welsh's interviewees noted a firm managing time spent by drawing up case plans (according to that case's fixed fees) and not going beyond them.[25] This sense of austerity-driven lack of preparation time was reflected by my defence lawyer interviewees:

> Def-Sol-03: You have to prioritise ruthlessly in terms of what needs to be done, and what we would like to be doing. I don't think I would speak out of turn in saying that in terms of case preparation, we do what we *have* to do. [emphasis added]

This point applies as much to support staff/paralegals as it does to their supervising solicitors, as can be seen from Def-Sol-10's reflections on that former career stage:

> I would have 4–5 police stations within the 24-hour period and after doing those, if people were being held on remand, and being sent to the magistrates' [court] straight away, I'd have to prepare instructions for the solicitor going to the court the next morning. So I'd finish work at 4am, and I'd have three or four cases that I'd need to write instructions of to the solicitor. And you end up with 40–50 cases at the same time. And interviewing witnesses when you're being paid £50 an hour is very difficult to do. Because it all takes time, and you simply don't have that time.

Alternatively, other firms simply cut such support staff entirely, placing greater burden (and therefore even less time) on solicitors already busy most of the day in court:

> Def-Sol-03: We used to have teams of caseworkers to do preparation on case files. We don't anymore. The solicitors who have conduct of those files are preparing them themselves, in whatever time they've got when they finally get back to the office [from court].

Unfortunately, as I illustrate in more specific detail over the next few sections, what (in Def-Sol-03's words, above) 'needs' to be done (particularly within a fixed-fee system) can be an elastic concept, subject to individuals' professional judgments. If 'need' is just defined as *whatever is needed in order to still get paid*, then it could be very little indeed, whereas if it is the more classic adversarial archetype of *win*

[23] J Campbell, 'The Quality of (In)justice in London's Magistrates' Courts' (2020) 36(5) *Anthropology Today* 3, 4.
[24] Welsh, *Access to Justice in Magistrates' Courts* (n 3) 137.
[25] ibid 136.

at all costs leaving no stone unturned, then it is not going to be particularly 'ruthless' efficiency. Realistically, such judgments on what really 'needs to be done' are not going to be totally neutral, as they will be made through the lens of one's *habitus*, reflecting the austere *field* if it is a well-attuned one (a 'feel for the game').[26] Certainly, some appear to take a restrictive view of what is really 'needed' or what one really has the time to do. Def-Sol-11's view was that:

> Magistrates' court cases by and large these days are just not prepared at all. They're just seen as, '£200 here, £300 there'. That's the legal aid cuts writ-large.

They went on to say preparation was:

> just lamentable … it is frightening that we've evolved to the stage where you're literally doing things on the day. There's no time to think and prepare and put things together and investigate, it's just literally bang bang bang on the day and the courts are encouraging that.

Whilst Def-Sol-11 found this standard lamentable and frightening, again, there is this tonal sense of inevitability. Def-Sol-03 stated their department is simply doing 'what we *have* to do'. In terms of *habitus*, one simply *has to* accept (or come to terms with) this 'lamentable' level of preparation time as just the way things are.

The situation for prosecutors was no better. Porter found that reduced staff (following budget cuts) had led to more work falling on those remaining. One interviewee explained the consequences thus: 'there just aren't enough hours in the day or enough prosecutors in the office to be doing the job that needs to be done'.[27] Pros-01 reported similarly on the problems lack of staffing from cuts causes:

> The volume of work is at the point now where, with the staff that we have, people are struggling to get through everything … we'll have a list of 32 [cases] or something, and we'll have to know everything about all of those 32 cases, and have no time to prep them.

The obvious consequence being:

> Pros-01: things get missed because there are so many, and we're only human at the end of the day.

This has a knock-on effect on agents given CPS magistrates' court work. Barrister interviewees speaking to Newman and Dehaghani reported receiving details very late or never, resulting in late nights, early starts and rushed preparation.[28] Beyond the immediate impact on the effective prosecution of offences, this also has consequences for (already time-poor) defence lawyers, with Nicklas-Carter's respondents stating that it was 'impossible to liaise with the Crown Prosecution Service in any meaningful way' outside of court hearings and, even in court,

[26] P Bourdieu, *The Logic of Practice* (R Nice tr, Polity Press, 1990) 66.

[27] A Porter, *Prosecuting Domestic Abuse in Neoliberal Times: Amplifying the Survivor's Voice* (Springer, 2020) Ch 4.

[28] Newman and Dehaghani, *Experiences of Criminal Justice* (n 19) 119.

'very, very difficult because they are pressed'.[29] Even some of my defence lawyer interviewees (whose clients' interests this could often benefit) viewed prosecution preparation as inadequate:

> Def-Sol-11: the number of times that the CPS turn up to court ill-prepared is just wrong and it's allowing defendants to walk out of cases that they should not be allowed to walk out from. The CPS and the police are not resourced properly.

Like defence, for prosecutors this view may be so ingrained by the *field* (into their *habitus*) that it is not necessarily going to be regarded as a free choice, but as a matter of common-sense that anyone who knows how it really works in practice must understand (or accept). As the above quote from Pros-01 illustrates, preparation time can come to be regarded more as a commodity that they simply do not possess (and mistakes a consequent fact of life), rather than there being a conscious decision to prepare poorly.

We shall examine some more specific examples of the consequences of this lack of preparation time for magistrates' court criminal lawyers next but, at this point, we should note the impacts of this for the logic of practice in this *field*. Interviewee comments here reflect the *habitus* necessary to survive in this *field*. Defence lawyers and prosecutors must prioritise speed at the cost of attention to detail. Those who do not will end up working overtime, perhaps at 4am at the end of their shift whilst it is quiet (per Def-Sol-10), or be in an even worse position for having spent too long on one case (out of eg 32, per Pros-01) at the expense of the others. Those that do work more 'efficiently' will earn their firm more money or the approval of their CPS supervisors.

C. Trial and Plea-hearing Preparation

The sorts of cutbacks and compromises this required in preparation for trial are illustrated by the following three examples of what Def-Sol-03 termed *ruthless efficiency*:

> Def-Sol-03: 15 years ago, I might have been able to go off and do a site visit on a case … spend a couple of hours with a client downstairs in the consultation room and go through all his papers. That site visit is now reduced to a Google Maps search, and that consultation is now reduced to a half-hour where we go through the case papers and pick out the absolute key points in order to raise a defence. It's had to be as ruthlessly efficient as that … we do what we need to do to advance the case properly. What we cannot do is go off chasing wild geese that might or might not yield something of a line of enquiry.

> Def-Sol-15: you don't get paid, as a defence lawyer, for going out and finding witnesses … money isn't the only thing that matters to criminal lawyers, but you've got to stack it

[29] C Nicklas-Carter, 'Efficiency of the English Criminal Courts in a Time of Austerity. Exploring Courtroom Lawyers' Assessment of Government Policy (2010–2017)' (DCrim Thesis, Keele University, 2019) 142.

up! At the end of the day you've got to pay the wages, the rent and all the rest of it, and if you don't make enough money then you will not remain in business.

Def-Sol-11: you say, 'right, you're accused of theft, what's your defence?' … there's no thinking about how you might prove the client's account or what you can do to mess the prosecution up. It's just, 'This is the accusation. This is the client's account. There you are.' Now that's something that didn't used to happen. There was a time when we were 'creative'. We were thinking more deeply about how we were going to defend our clients.

There is a sense of internal conflict here, which further demonstrates how 'need' can be elastic; mediated by the understanding of the world provided through a *habitus* structured by an austerity *field*. Things which were once considered necessary are apparently no longer needed to 'advance the case properly'. Yet, nor is investigating lines of inquiry (now just 'wild geese') or potential independent witnesses, despite the fact that they may provide useful evidence. Instead, as Def-Sol-11's quote illustrates, what really 'needs' to be done could be viewed as little more than preparing to summarise the defendant's own account in a more articulate manner.

Prosecutors found themselves in no better position. All of Nicklas-Carter's respondents noted that staff resourcing issues caused CPS shortcomings in preparation. This was to a severe extent: one defence lawyer remarked that they could not remember the last time they had lost a trial because prosecution cases were so frequently dismissed or lost due to poor and/or late preparation.[30] This view was reflected on the other side by prosecutors in my study:

Pros+Def-Bar-01: a lot of the time when these things settle, they settle at the day of trial. Largely because someone hasn't had necessarily the time … Not necessarily because the reviewing lawyer in any particular case is a bad lawyer, but a lot of the time they just have so many cases that things are going to get missed.

Similarly, Soubise noted that prosecution advocates in her study (chiefly associate prosecutors) rarely received the case management form, either because it was not done at all or not attached to the bundle by admin staff.[31] Certainly, cases arriving quite late on was not considered unusual. Pros+Def-Bar-01 got their magistrates' court files for trial from the CPS, at best, two days before (often, they could not start them until 6pm the day before). The result was:

I'm lucky if I spend 45 minutes preparing a trial, because you just don't have time if I'm going to get a decent sleep. There just isn't time to go through everything with a really, really fine-tooth comb, or have a very definite plan for cross examination, or your examination in chief. And you've got five, six, seven of them. That's a good number of hours. Sometimes it does feel like you just scratch the surface.

The position was just as bad when it came to preparing for remand or sentencing hearings:

Pros-01: remand courts [or] a [guilty anticipated plea] court: you'll need to open the facts to the Bench and know about any ancillary orders and whatever else. And you'll

[30] ibid 122–23.

[31] Soubise, 'Prosecuting in the Magistrates' Courts' (n 11) 856.

> have a list of maybe 25, and you'll have no prep time to do it. So you'll literally get into court in the morning, or like most of us do, sit there the night before, in our own time, reading them so that you know what to say when you get into court.

Again, the phrasing here is revealing. Pros+Def-Bar-01 and Pros-01 do not appear to view this as a choice to spend less time etc. Instead, they are beginning to internalise a view that time is a commodity they simply lack, without having any choice in the matter. It may be that, in due course, they will develop a more attuned *habitus*, and become even more inclined to see low levels of preparation as simply the way it is. Alternatively, they may continue to give up their evenings doing extra work but, like anyone else with a *habitus* out of sync with the *field*, they will suffer for that.

Hence, both prosecutors and defence lawyers must be 'ruthlessly efficient' in preparing for magistrates' court cases, whether that is the reviewing lawyer in the office or the advocate preparing for the day. This is the case for trials just as much as it is for traditionally swifter activities, like sentencing and remand. Again, this reflects the developing *habitus* we can see here. Lawyers must accept or come to terms with the need to be ruthlessly efficient (regardless of how much they would like to prepare/do the job properly).

D. Time for Prosecution Disclosure

Trial and hearing preparation is not just for one's own side's benefit. For prosecutors, there are due process obligations to disclose evidence to the defence, including evidence they do not intend to use, but which might reasonably be considered capable of undermining the prosecution or assisting the defence ('unused evidence').[32] Recent high-profile failures on this have arisen in very serious Crown Court cases, such as the collapse of Liam Allen's rape case.[33] Academic research[34] and reports from HMCPS Inspectorate[35] illustrate how problems with disclosure continue in Crown Court cases. Whilst magistrates' court prosecutions might be less high-profile, similar issues were identified in a less recent review: the prosecution were 'the primary cause' of most disclosure problems and 'resource implications' played 'a significant part'.[36]

Further difficulties were presented in the current study. Defence lawyers complained again and again about late or non-existent disclosure and failure to

[32] Criminal Procedure and Investigations Act 1996, s 3.

[33] BBC News, 'Met Police Apologise for Liam Allan Rape Case Errors' (30 January 2018) www.bbc.co.uk/news/uk-england-42873618.

[34] eg T Smith and E Johnstone (eds), *The Law of Disclosure: A Perennial Problem in Criminal Justice* (Routledge, 2020).

[35] HMCPSI, *Making it Fair: Disclosure of Unused Material in Volume Crown Court Cases* (Justice Inspectorates, 2017); HMCPSI, *Disclosure of Unused Materials in the Crown Court* (Justice Inspectorates, 2020); HMCPSI, *Disclosure of Unused Material in the Crown Court – A Follow-up* (Justice Inspectorates, 2020).

[36] DJ Riddle and HHJ Kinch, *Magistrates Court Disclosure Review* (Judicial Office, 2014).

comply with other deadlines in magistrates' court cases, sometimes with little consequence/sanction from courts. As Def-Bar-01 recalled:

> Your emails just go unanswered. So you arrive at court and say, 'well it's nice to meet you, nice to see a face', and you explain that you haven't received disclosure. And the Bench says, 'well she can send it to you now, and then we can crack on [with the trial]'. And then you get volumes and volumes of further disclosure, which under normal circumstances, you'd require quite a bit of time to consider, because it does affect your client's defence at the end of the day … At the worst, I've received about 200 further pages … 'We'll give you ten minutes' – I've had that before. And in that 10 minutes I'm supposed to read the papers, consider the law, consider the defence, speak with my client, explore defences and advise them to plead.

This reflects the experiences of interviewees in Helm et al[37] and Dehaghani and Newman.[38] Dehaghani and Newman argue that these prosecution failures to provide case information 'place the prosecution in an advantageous position (as the prosecution are met with a weakened opponent)' –[39] assuming that courts allow prosecutors to get away with this, as Def-Bar-01 reported. However, it is also true that this occurs even where disclosure might help secure convictions/guilty pleas. One of Nicklas-Carter's interviewees considered that prosecutions often failed due to disclosure: they were 'amazed' at some of the cases dropped against their clients, where there was 'every prospect of a conviction'.[40] Def-Sol-07 illustrates this issue:

> I said, 'give me the CCTV, this won't be a trial [because he will plead guilty if he sees a clear recording of himself committing the offence], but I need the CCTV' … and they didn't have it. I had another hearing today, and I said, 'have you got the CCTV yet?' Still not got it!

This suggests it is more likely a case of maladministration than malice. In fact, prosecution advocates reported receiving things not much sooner themselves:

> Pros+Def-Bar-01: I get to trial and find that the prosecution schedule of unused [evidence to potentially disclose] was just never served. It's just not been done and the first hearing on that matter was 18 months before. That schedule of unused should have been served within 28 days.

Again, this can operate to the detriment of the prosecution. The prosecutor may have to ask for an adjournment to serve the evidence in accordance with the law. This will often be refused by the court (for some time, case law and Criminal Practice Directions have encouraged an increasingly restrictive

[37] Helm et al, 'Guilty Plea Decisions' (n 19) 22.

[38] R Dehaghani and D Newman, 'Criminal Legal Aid and Access to Justice: An Empirical Account of a Reduction in Resilience' (2022) 29 *International Journal of the Legal Profession* 33, 44.

[39] ibid 46.

[40] Nicklas-Carter (n 29) 124.

approach to granting adjournments).[41] The case against the defendant might then collapse:

> Pros+Def-Bar-01: the magistrates rejected that application, because it just wasn't in the interests of justice … and so there was no option but to offer no evidence … I've only been doing this for [a few] months, but had dozens of cases where things like that have been missed. And I would put things being missed down to a lack of resources, a lack of staff.

Likewise, in Welsh's study both defence lawyers and prosecutors reported that the CPS 'either fails to comply with the required time limits for the service of case papers or simply fails to prepare cases thoroughly and in good time'.[42] One defence lawyer (in a view backed up by half the prosecutors) put it very bluntly: because of cuts 'The prosecution have no ability anymore to deal with summary only cases within the Criminal Procedure Rules.' Even explicit court directions 'have no bearing whatsoever in criminal trials'.[43] Pros-01 demonstrated a very similar approach in relation to magistrates' courts' directions:

> We would rather prioritise things like victim communications and the personal side of things, rather than a District Judge or a Bench saying, 'oh well you need to serve this by this day'. Well, it will get served, but it may not be by that date … I think it's a case of how serious is the offence, what's likely to be needed, are you going to get it in time? Kind of, as best you can, prioritise.

This apparent acceptance that directions need not be strictly complied with went as far as being resigned to the fact they would have to put up with a hard time from a judge in due course (having been asked by the judge to attend court to explain themselves in a current case). Again, we can see here the sort of *habitus* required to survive in this field requires accepting as normal things which to an outsider can appear 'unthinkable' (literally, according to Bourdieu). Ignoring a court direction so nonchalantly can sound quite shocking. However, for many practitioners these things must be come to terms with as just the way things are. If it were not, as Pros-01 points out, it might simply lead to problems in other areas, such as victim treatment. When faced with a number of competing demands on their time, and fewer prosecutors available to do the work due to budget cuts, successful prosecutors must 'as best you can, prioritise' (as Pros-01 puts it).

E. Time at Court

Time on the day of court hearings is of course impacted by many of the issues just considered, as a knock-on effect. In other words, if things that could (and should)

[41] See eg *CPS v Picton* [2006] EWHC 1108 (Admin); *DPP v Petrie* [2015] EWHC 48 (Admin); *R (Imbeah) v Willesden Magistrates' Court* [2016] EWHC 1760 (QB); and Criminal Practice Directions 2015, Consolidated with Amendment No 8 [2019] EWCA Crim 495 at [24C].

[42] Welsh, *Access to Justice in Magistrates' Courts* (n 3) 79.

[43] ibid 79–80.

have been done earlier end up needing to be done on the day instead, this reduces time available on the day for other things. As Pros+Def-Bar-04 noted: '[you] just muddle through as the trial's progressing … it's quite chaotic'.

However, austerity also presents great challenges when it comes to available time on the day of court in itself. For defence lawyers, the tight margins they operate under (many considered magistrates' court work as cashflow or loss-leading) serve to further encourage speed at all costs on the day of the hearing. As previously mentioned, volume of work is key to making any profit here. To accomplish this, first, multiple cases need to be stacked each day:

> Def-Sol-16: If I'm in my local magistrates' court on a Monday morning and I've got three cases to do, then I'll break even, but if I still have to be there for one case, then I won't. And one case can take as much time as three … You need to do volume and if there isn't volume then you're not going to make money, and if you don't make money, you go out of business.

Second, those cases need to be dealt with that same day. For example, once a guilty plea is secured, the incentive is to get the sentence done on the same day:

> Def-Sol-12: [Because] it's one fee, it costs you money if you have to go back … So let's imagine he's on a suspended sentence, he's done it again, he's probably gonna get a short prison sentence. I'm gonna encourage the magistrates to deal with it there and then.

Third, at the end of an (unsuccessful) day, any appeals also need to be dealt with briefly:

> Def-Sol-17: the whole system to some extent disincentivises doing the job properly. The fees for counsel on an appeal against conviction from the magistrates' court are ludicrously low: £130 for what is essentially a trial [a full re-hearing of the case by the Crown Court] and maybe someone's good name at stake.

Of course (as Def-Sol-12 went on to acknowledge) these strategies may not be in the client's interest. It may, for example, be more beneficial to the client to have their sentencing dealt with later, allowing more time for reports or other evidence on compliance with the suspended sentence order and their prospects for rehabilitation, as these are relevant to deciding whether to activate the suspended imprisonment term.[44] Newman and Dehaghani noted that practitioners were 'unhappy' with this lack of time on the day, but came to accept it as a 'pragmatic reality', to the point that, as one interviewee put it 'it's just a matter of going through the motions in terms of funding'. Another noted 'back-to-back cases' which they could not prepare to the standard they would like.[45] Once more, we have seen the *field* encouraging individuals to view such practices as inevitable or just 'reality', rather than an explicit choice. Def-Sol-16, above, framed volume working as

[44] Sentencing Council, 'Magistrates' Courts Sentencing Guidelines: Breach of a Suspended Sentence Order' (2018).

[45] Newman and Dehaghani, *Experiences of Criminal Justice* (n 19) 117.

something you 'need' to do, rather than something they had much choice about. If viewing things differently (with a different *habitus*) risks the firm going out of business, this disposition is likely to endure.

Whilst not operating under the same business/accounting incentives, prosecutors too suffered from lack of time on the day from their heavy and unpredictable workload:

> Pros-06: you can end up with 30 cases in a day … you can spend the evening prepping, late into the evening. You'll be shattered. And you'll [sometimes] turn up to court only to realise none of those cases are going ahead! And then you get, if you're lucky, 1–2 hours to prepare, or if you're unlucky you'll get 15 minutes, and if you're really unlucky, especially with District Judges, they'll just turn round and say, 'right, Prosecutor, are you ready to go?'

This is aggravated by the fact that, as McConville et al found in the 1990s, some prosecutors have never been all that prepared, or able to offer much scrutiny, at the best of times, giving the example of a suspect charged with theft, bailed and pleading guilty the next day. After asking the prosecutor what he made of the case against the defendant, he replied to the researcher that he had not had time to read the file, but it did not matter because the defendant was pleading guilty anyway.[46] This is then aggravated even further if, as Soubise found, these time-poor magistrates' court CPS staff are in practice being replaced by less-qualified associate prosecutors who, eg, struggle to make formal applications for special measures, when these are challenged by the judiciary (because they do not know the relevant law)[47] and exceed their powers to amend charges or accept pleas 'on a daily basis'.[48]

Further, beyond their own funding issues, both prosecution and defence must then operate in an environment which for some time has itself been critiqued for prioritising speed.[49] Def-Bar-01 gave the following example:

> The defendant had hearing loss and, [for legitimate reasons], they weren't able to get new and updated hearing aids. So, I asked for the matter to be adjourned until that could be done [but the court refused] … it was the magistrates' 'solution' that I act as an 'interpreter' and yell out what has been said … and that happens quite frequently, those kinds of things.

Hence, as with earlier in the process, in court, defence and prosecution lawyers must adopt a disposition that favours speed, with pressure to do so coming from all angles (from the court system, their own financial resources and their often equally-pressured opponent). It is all too easy to get swept along. Indeed, as we

[46] M McConville et al, *The Case for the Prosecution: Police Suspects and the Construction of Criminality* (first published 1991, Routledge, 2017) Ch 8.

[47] Soubise, 'Prosecuting in the Magistrates' Courts' (n 11) 854.

[48] ibid 855.

[49] P Carlen, *Magistrates' Justice* (Martin Robertson, 1976); A Bottoms and J McClean, *Defendants in the Criminal Process* (Routledge, 1976); D McBarnet, *Conviction: Law, the State and the Construction of Justice* (Macmillan, 1981); Welsh, *Access to Justice in Magistrates' Courts* (n 3).

have seen, these pressures become accepted (or resigned to) as a key part of an individual's *habitus* over time.

F. Time for TLC

The focus in this section is on defence lawyers. In the CPS, this issue of care (eg for complainants or witnesses) manifests itself most keenly when it comes up against targets and/or 'box-ticking', which we will consider afterwards. For defence layers, just as with police station work, lack of time also influences the logic of practice in terms of 'tender loving care' in magistrates' court work. Def-Sol-18 provides an example of this operating at guilty plea/trial verdict where an offender is committed to the Crown Court for sentencing and remanded in custody by magistrates, for the first time in their life. This is clearly a greatly distressing event, but:

> If they want visiting and they want to discuss their case in detail while they're in prison and they've never been in prison before, your fixed fee can be very easily eaten up as a result of doing those visits. Now, some people would say, 'well, no, you've been committed for sentence, we've seen you in the magistrates' court, you've been advised fully, you've entered your guilty plea, you're going to get a probation report, we've seen you, there's nothing more we need to say to you in the meantime so therefore we're not going to come to prison'.

Returning to the issue of lawyer perception of what is really 'needed' (and how elastic that concept can be), it is interesting to note from this example that this is one of those things which some would now not perceive as necessary ('there's nothing more we *need* to say to you'). No doubt a first-time prisoner might take a rather different view of what was necessary here. Nor is it purely about providing moral support: 'discussing their case' necessarily involves providing legal advice. Judgements of what is needed may not be neutral, but are instead seen through the lens of an austerity-driven *habitus*.

A similar way lack of time manifests in terms of client care is in continuity of representation:

> Def-Sol-13: in the perfect world, the lawyer who dealt with them at the police station would like to go to court with them because you know all about it, but the economic reality is we're gonna send one lawyer up to deal with all [of our court cases that day]. They'll know about it, we'll tell them about it, but we're now driven by the economic reality of life rather than necessarily what used to be called 'best practice'.

Dehaghani and Newman also noted this practice, with clients 'routinely passed between lawyers', sometimes swapping again on the same day in accordance with fluctuating workloads, rather than expertise or who had dealt with the same client previously.[50] Files 'would be read while walking to meet the client' and lawyers

[50] R Dehaghani and D Newman, '"We're Vulnerable Too": An (Alternative) Analysis of Vulnerability within English Criminal Legal Aid and Police Custody' (2017) 7 *Oñati Socio-legal Series* 1199, 1219.

described having 'winged it' in making it appear to clients that they knew the case. Conversely, this is something defendants and their families have complained about frequently when asked.[51] Again, whilst the limits of this were acknowledged by some, it was also accepted as 'business sense' and 'necessity'.[52] These sorts of practices come about as a result of the austerity-driven pressure to view clients as commodities rather than individuals:

> Def-Sol-17: there's real pressure and tendency to turn it into commodities. A lot of firms now, it's a factory concept of *get a lot of work in, put it through the sausage machine, get rid of it*. Because criminal clients – not all of them – but a lot of them tend to be quite needy, quite dependant. People will phone you up at all hours of the day or night. They'll often be asking hundreds of questions. Many will have mental health issues.

All those questions/issues, of course, take up time. Yet, as we have seen throughout this chapter, the effect of an austerity *field* is to engender a *habitus* in practitioners which views time as a commodity that criminal lawyers have very little of. Dedicated care can then be regarded as something which physically cannot be done, or, as Def-Sol-17 goes on to say, is 'inevitably' not going to happen, rather than a conscious practice/choice:

> Def-Sol-17: If you actually try and speak to people and maintain a service, that's different, so inevitably it means less time and care spent on individual cases. It's down to the bare bones.

Similarly, one lawyer told Dehaghani and Newman 'You used to be able to take longer on a case but not anymore. Some people say we need more time for certain clients who present with particular problems. Others say that you can make it work. You have to make it work.'[53] The juxtaposition by Def-Sol-17 here illustrates well the difference between the developing *habitus* in this field (that which is ruthlessly efficient, accepts turning clients into commodities as 'business sense' and 'necessity', is unempathetic, 'makes it work', etc) and the alternative approaches the interviewees here want to do, but struggle to. At best, providing that level of client support is very difficult; at worst it leads to being driven or burnt out of the market. Again, there is this sense of inevitability, also seen in Def-Sol-13's comment above (it's 'the economic reality of life') suggesting the influence of (and encouragement by these external pressures to develop) a *habitus* which cannot see beyond this approach.

i. *Prosecution Targets/Box-ticking*

In terms of prosecutors, similar issues arose due to the influence of targets or 'box-ticking'. This is not unique to the CPS of course. Newman and Dehaghani found

[51] Newman and Dehaghani, *Experiences of Criminal Justice* (n 19) 163.
[52] Dehaghani and Newman, '"We're Vulnerable Too"' (n 50) 1219.
[53] ibid 1217.

some defence firms using targets too.[54] Indeed, many publicly funded organisations and institutions outside of criminal justice have been critiqued for focusing on targets, metrics, league tables, etc to the detriment of actually doing the job well.[55] The CPS has embraced this, however. Porter argued this is manifested in the CPS by the adoption of a philosophy of 'New Public Management' (NPM):[56] a restructuring of public services, borne out of the 1960s and 70s global economic crisis, prioritising high output (but not necessarily quality).[57] As Porter put it: 'If neo-liberalism is an "art of governance" [Foucault], then, in the public sector, the tenets of NPM are its masterpiece and the CPS is, I suggest, its quintessence.'[58] The effects Porter observed of this were extreme: one prosecutor had 145 files that day on her digital caseload and a task list that was seven pages long in relation to cases appearing in court the next day.[59] Another was told that eight full reviews were expected each day and this was monitored by management. The result was prosecutors had to 'play' the system to achieve their targets, with one interviewee admitting the expected work could only be completed in the time allocated if she 'cut corners'.[60]

Porter was concerned in particular with (inappropriate) routine use of witness summonses in domestic abuse cases where the complainant has retracted their complaint, to save time by 'avoiding a thorough consideration of victim risk assessment from a variety of sources'.[61] Rather, as one prosecutor told Porter, it was all about targets:

> it is all becoming about targets and statistics and not about the individuals. There's not so much focus on victims. I've never been a manager, so I don't know what goes on in these management meetings and how much it is drummed into you but I always get the impression that it is very, very important that targets are met.[62]

Hence, targets and (for individuals) playing the game, in the absence of genuine success, become the focus. For example, in the domestic abuse cases context, the summons becomes little more than a shield from criticism for the prosecutor in the event of a case collapsing (as it is then on record that they at least did something).[63] However, I found that targets impacted well beyond the domestic abuse

[54] ibid.

[55] See generally M Power, *The Audit Society: Rituals of Verification* (Oxford University Press, 1997).

[56] Porter, 'Prosecuting Domestic Abuse in England and Wales' (n 20).

[57] See also H Sommerlad, '"I've Lost the Plot": An Everyday Story of the Political Legal Aid Lawyer' (2002) 28 *JLS* 335, 335–36.

[58] Porter, 'Prosecuting Domestic Abuse in England and Wales' (n 20) 496.

[59] Porter, *Prosecuting Domestic Abuse in Neoliberal Times* (n 27) Ch 4.

[60] ibid. In practice, this prosecutor said she did more work in her own time, but did not record this extra time spent, so as to look like she was hitting the targets.

[61] Porter, 'Prosecuting Domestic Abuse in England and Wales' (n 20) 505.

[62] ibid 507.

[63] ibid 508.

context. For example, Pros+Def-Bar-04 noted CPS instructions to run hopeless cases to trial if all the witnesses were there:

> It's got to the day of trial, if witnesses are there, they think ... *well we've come this far, everybody's at court, just run it.* It's a stats thing.

Alternatively, when key witnesses did *not* attend on the day and the prosecution is consequently no longer realistic, Pros+Def-Bar-01 reported still being instructed to go through the motions. Attempting further contact with such witnesses (which both they and their reviewing CPS lawyer considered inappropriate/pointless at such a late stage)[64] was required, for 'box-ticking' purposes:

> there are so many steps that I (as an agent) have to go through before I'm given authority to offer no evidence. Me and the reviewing lawyer may know exactly what the outcome's going to be, it's not going to make any difference. It's only done as a box-ticking exercise.

A similar example was provided where this was instead done to smooth inter-professional relations in a legally hopeless case:

> There was no way that we were going to [legally] succeed on that point ... and the instruction I was given was, 'well just run it, let the defence make their halftime submission of no case to answer so that we don't look bad to the police'.[65]

Targets are not necessarily a bad thing though. At best, they can provide a sense of purpose, motivation and achievement, or break a complex, overwhelming and nebulous task into something more manageable.[66] To return to the domestic abuse context, Pros-06 noted they could lead to this being (quite properly) treated seriously:

> when domestic violence cases come to the magistrates' court, everyone kind of collectively gets a bit more serious.

On the other hand, Porter notes the dangers in this context of domestic abuse work especially. A focus on targets, efficiency, etc can detach people from the reality of what they are dealing with:

> victim accounts feel unreal and the severity or even veracity of what has been experienced by the victim is diluted. ... routinely summonsing allows prosecutors to demonstrate a commitment to 'taking domestic abuse seriously' while ensuring a measure of emotional self-preservation ... Withdrawing emotionally from the details of the abuse therefore serves the prosecutor in effecting expeditious decisions and assists

[64] Even if such a witness picks up the phone and has got the dates wrong etc, there is still no right to an adjournment to allow them to attend later anyway. The starting point from case law and practice directions (see above n 41) is that the trial must go ahead as listed.

[65] Similar behaviour in terms of unquestionably backing up the police in hopeless cases was reported by McConville et al, *The Case for the Prosecution* (n 46) in the 1990s.

[66] See eg J Harackiewicz and A Elliot, 'The Joint Effects of Target and Purpose Goals on Intrinsic Motivation: A Mediational Analysis' (1998) 24 *Personality and Social Psychology Bulletin* 675.

> in managing the pressures of managerial targets, high workloads and the impacts of austerity.[67]

This has troubling echoes of the broader concerns made by Bauman in relation to the administration of the Holocaust and how so many seemingly ordinary people became complicit monsters. Bauman noted how many individuals involved, eg bureaucrats organising train timetables to concentration camps, were able to ignore or dissociate from the horrors that they were enabling. By focusing on processes and efficiency, they could disengage their humanity and avoid thinking through the consequences of what they were really doing:

> the result is the irrelevance of moral standards for the technical success of the bureaucratic operation … Once, thanks to the complex functional differentiation within bureaucracy, they have been distantiated from the ultimate outcomes of the operation to which they contribute, their moral concerns can concentrate fully on the good performance of the job at hand. Morality boils down to the commandment to be a good, efficient and diligent expert and worker.[68]

Or, to put it more bluntly: 'it is chemical plants that produce napalm, not any of their individual workers … '[69] I do not seek to suggest the gravity of these things are comparable. Rather, it is Bauman's more general point about human nature that is illuminating here: if it worked for some of those administering something as horrendous as the Holocaust, focus on targets and box-ticking is clearly an extremely effective way for individuals to detach themselves from challenging or difficult decisions and focuses any sense of agency towards meeting those targets and away from what might be the most appropriate decision in a given situation. For example (in our context), offering no evidence when success is legally impossible, or only summonsing alleged domestic abuse victims where that will provide genuine benefit.

All that said, some fought against targets to a greater or lesser extent. Whilst Pros-02 acknowledged targets existed ('you have lots of targets about cases to do, deadlines to meet, there's no end of them'), unlike others they did not worry too much about them and nor did it appear to affect the fundamental task of dealing with their cases properly:

> they don't annoy me yet, because I recognise that it's a big organisation, they need to keep a control of things somehow … the target speaks for itself every time you turn the computer on, you've got loads of cases to deal with. That's your target: it's to deal with all those without messing up.

Hence, for Pros-02, dealing with their cases properly ('without messing up') is still the real goal. Equally, targets can be opposed more actively, as with Pros-01's more blasé approach to court deadlines, etc (mentioned earlier), due to insistence on

[67] Porter, 'Prosecuting Domestic Abuse in England and Wales' (n 20) 510.
[68] Z Bauman, *Modernity and the Holocaust* (Polity Press, 1992) 86–87.
[69] ibid 85.

doing victim support properly. However, there are personal consequences. Pros-01 still worked late into the evening to get things done and received a telling off from a district judge. One also suspects that there are only so many times a prosecutor can be summoned for a judicial telling off before unwelcome questions are asked by their managers too.

In all these examples, it is the individual with a *habitus* which is focused on speed etc that will be the one that meets (or beats) the targets and progresses in their career. Others must stay up late, risk burnout, work for free in their own time, endure a hard time from judges, or their instructing CPS lawyer, etc. This means more than just saying speed and numerical output is strongly encouraged and that those who subscribe to a hit-the-target-at-all-costs philosophy will be rewarded. More than that, to say that the *habitus* is changed is to say that these dispositions are relentlessly drummed into prosecutors until they are no longer questioned. Over time, it becomes unquestioned 'common sense'.[70] It affects the way individuals perceive and understand their world, work, options and actions. This explains, eg, Pros+Def-Bar-01's incredulity at their instructions from their instructing CPS lawyer (a step removed, as both an independent agent and early career) and that CPS lawyer's brazenly cynical conduct in pursuing hopeless cases to improve targets and police relations. They have absorbed these targets into their habitus 'like air',[71] perhaps without even realising, and struggle to see beyond it.

ii. Defence Box-ticking and Undesirable Cases/Clients

Whilst, as noted, some defence lawyers have direct targets too, this is largely a decision for how particular firms are run, so can be quite inconsistent.[72] What was clear, as a more consistent theme amongst interviewees across various firms, was an absorption of a similar box-ticking mentality to that mentioned by CPS interviewees, due to the LAA's payment operations and audits. Some disputes with the LAA could be petty or technical:

> Def-Sol-03: they will pick up on things like mismatched codes … The fee is not affected, but human error meant that [xxxx] was put in instead of [yyyy].

The result was that, in a similar way to how CPS lawyers felt like they must chase targets at the expense of doing the job well, defence lawyers must 'paper push' at the expense of client care/TLC:

> Def-Sol-02: rather than providing that service, and enhancing your knowledge, and arguing the case better, you're paper pushing. Because if you don't put X, Y, Z down, then the LAA are going to refuse the funding.

[70] Bourdieu, *The Logic of Practice* (n 26) 58.
[71] Bourdieu and Eagleton, 'Doxa and Common Life' (n 22) 115.
[72] See also Dehaghani and Newman, '"We're Vulnerable Too"' (n 50) 1217.

One of the supposed benefits of a fixed-fee system is that it reduces administrative burdens on those claiming them (and indeed, on those administering them).[73] If, however, law firms are required to keep records that go into minute detail anyway (for audit purposes), this negates any such savings/convenience.

A further pervasive impact in terms of lack of time for care came from the perverse prioritisation of some cases or clients at the expense of more 'difficult' ones.[74] Some *offences*, regardless of facts, were regarded as not worth doing. For example, Def-Sol-07 (reflecting publicised complaints of solicitors)[75] viewed fees for burglary as particularly bad work: 'we lose money as soon as we touch a file for a burglary case'. Others could become better or worse, depending on the facts:

> Def-Sol-19: he's subject to several different ASBOs and he probably gets four to five cases a year now. Every now and again he'll try and get off one, but nine times out of ten, he's in the magistrates' court, Thursday night: offence, guilty plea: Friday morning. 15–30 minutes work, £190, so it came out well!

Undesirable *clients* were a similarly frequent complaint: essentially, anyone who required more hand-holding, care, etc or had unusual financial situations (harder to apply and prove earnings for the legal aid means test) takes up time that, as we have already seen, the magistrates' court defence lawyer on tight margins does not have.

> Def-Sol-20: often we're doing cases for free, in the hope that we will get legal aid sorted … I think people are less and less taking on self-employed people particularly, or anybody who's got what I would call 'out of the ordinary' income/finances.

Previous literature has also found that uncertainty of being granted legal aid is a common issue, with some cases being taken on as 'a wing and a prayer job' in the hope of eventually being paid.[76] The results of this for lawyer attitudes can be disquieting. Dehaghani and Newman found very unsympathetic (and disrespectful) views on difficult clients:

> I hate clients like this, waste your day having to deal with them. I have a list to do, I want to get back to the office [but] you get someone who can't string a sentence together and needs to be babied through the process and it wastes your time.[77]

As with other areas, some clearly fight against this tendency to turn difficult clients into undesirable commodities and prioritise speed. Def-Sol-21 said they did cases

[73] Bellamy, *CLAR* (n 8).

[74] See also my discussion of this in terms of 'junk' and 'golden' cases: J Thornton, 'The Way in Which Fee Reductions Influence Legal Aid Criminal Defence Lawyer Work: Insights from a Qualitative Study' (2019) 46 *JLS* 559.

[75] eg H Puri, 'Statement by LCCSA President' (London Criminal Courts Solicitors' Association, 5 September 2022) www.lccsa.org.uk/statement-by-lccsa-president-hesham-puri-voting-with-our-feet-5th-september-2022/: 'members have taken action in London courts too, refusing to take on low-paid burglary and stalking and harassment cases'.

[76] Welsh, *Access to Justice in Magistrates' Courts* (n 3) 131.

[77] Dehaghani and Newman, '"We're Vulnerable Too"' (n 50) 1217.

for free 'constantly' for regular clients who could not secure legal aid 'because we feel we should – we should help people'. However, as Def-Sol-01 points out, this feels unfair, makes the job harder and adds financial pressure:

> Why is it fair, that I'm dealing with a rape, involving an autistic person with severe learning difficulties, that I need an appropriate adult for, and it takes longer? Or I'm dealing with something that's more complex? I say this really respectfully of the clientele that I deal with, but anyone with mental health issues makes the job harder.

Certainly this reflects the latest review on neurodivergent people's treatment by the criminal justice system, which found they were poorly served 'at every stage' and noted the need for practitioners to use '"soft skills" – listening, empathy and compassion' to improve this.[78] Regrettably, we have seen here that it is these very things that many now struggle to do in the time available. As with prosecutor targets, it is the individual with a *habitus* which focuses on paper pushing, resists the urge to help vulnerable people and pushes them through as quickly as possible, who succeeds here. Others will lose on audits and fall behind as the financial stress levels ratchet up. Over time, such client commoditisation risks becoming unquestioned 'common sense'.[79]

G. Plea Advice

There have been overt incentives on defendants themselves to plead guilty for some time. The current scheme provides for a one third 'discount' on sentences (or a change in type of sentence, eg from imprisonment to community order), provided the plea comes at the first opportunity (the later the plea is, the smaller the discount).[80] Quite apart from any pressure or advice from the lawyer, this itself is highly coercive.[81] Indeed, it led Bottoms and McClean to take a charitable view of lawyers advising guilty pleas: because they operate within a system where 'their clients might indeed receive heavier penalties if they are found guilty rather than plead guilty'.[82]

Unfortunately, there are also personal/self-interested reasons for defence lawyers to tailor their plea advice and the effect of austerity can be to increase the stakes/temptation.[83] Some of these are very overt (and perverse) financial incentives in the fee system to encourage lawyers to secure early guilty pleas in the magistrates' courts. For example, 'elected' cases (where the defendant, charged

[78] HM Inspectorates, 'Neurodiversity in the Criminal Justice System' (2021) [1.6], [1.11].

[79] Bourdieu, *The Logic of Practice* (n 26) 58.

[80] Sentencing Council, 'Reduction in Sentence for a Guilty Plea – First Hearing on or after 1 June 2017' (2017); Sentencing Act 2020, s 73.

[81] R Helm, 'Conviction by Consent? Vulnerability, Autonomy and Conviction by Guilty Plea' (2019) 83(2) *Journal of Criminal Law* 161.

[82] Bottoms and McClean, *Defendants in the Criminal Process* (n 49) 231.

[83] See also Thornton, 'The Way in Which Fee Reductions Influence' (n 74).

with an either-way offence, initially exercises their right to elect trial by jury, despite magistrates being happy to try the case summarily, but then pleads guilty at the Crown Court later) used to attract a very small fixed fee indeed.[84] This was perceived as either an inducement to misadvise (to encourage/force an early guilty plea out of the client at the magistrates' court or, conversely, if it did reach the Crown Court, maintaining a not guilty plea) or, at best, a punishment for respecting the defendant's wishes and change of mind. Tight margins, lower fees and austerity meant this was not a theoretical risk:

> Def-Sol-20: I know a firm who, since that rule came in, have never elected a Crown Court case again. They'll just keep everything in the magistrates' court because it's not financially viable for them to do elected cases in case they crack [eg plead guilty later].

Belatedly (after almost a decade), the Government removed this particular financial incentive.[85] However, even if pursued less tardily, a strategy of trying to iron out all incentives has its limits. As Def-Sol-04 accepted:

> any half-decent lawyer, whatever system they come up with, will find a way round it to maximise what we get paid. I suppose my criticism of the system we've got at the moment is, we have to spend almost as much time working that out as we do doing our job as a lawyer.

Finances impact on plea advice more indirectly too. In some magistrates' court cases, such as more complex trials (one example being some kinds of benefit fraud), the lawyer's financial interest is best served by a trial, regardless of any direct incentives:

> Def-Sol-09: they can pay quite well because there's a lot of work to do, so you would be able to get into higher standard, or non-standard fees.

However, these are the exception. The vast majority of respondents felt financially pressured to advise guilty pleas with magistrates' court cases,[86] reflecting both recent and older research.[87] The reason for this is that pervasive issue of time. Guilty pleas are a way of ensuring cases are processed and finished quickly, in order to move on to the next one:

> Def-Sol-09: if you did four guilty pleas and they were all shoplifters, you're on £800. If you'd got to the magistrates' court and pleaded not guilty, and then gone to court and had a trial … a lot of simple trials will get paid £279.

[84] Criminal Legal Aid (Remuneration) Regulations 2013, Sch 1, Part 4 and Sch 2, Part 3.

[85] Criminal Legal Aid (Remuneration) (Amendment) Regulations 2022, SI 2022/848. Although note that whether a trial is 'cracked' will often still affect the classification of the lawyer's fee. A trial is said to have 'cracked' when it does not take place, despite the defendant initially pleading not guilty. Trials may crack because the defendant changes their plea to guilty or the prosecution drops the case by offering no evidence, etc. See Criminal Legal Aid (Remuneration) Regulations 2013, Sch 1 and 2, para 1(1).

[86] As we shall see, the situation is often the opposite in the Crown Court.

[87] Helm et al, 'Guilty Plea Decisions' (n 19) 24; M McConville et al, *Standing Accused: The Organisation and Practices of Criminal Defence Lawyers in Britain* (Oxford University Press, 1994) 210: 'for the most part, solicitors do not see magistrates' courts as trial venues but as places where defendants can be processed through guilty pleas'.

Hence, ignoring such incentives has (literal) costs (£800 as opposed to £279). Alternatively, others simply accept this as the reality of doing business:

> Def-Sol-15: [it goes on] all the time! People calculate that pleading guilty will benefit the lawyer best commercially and it gets justified on the basis that the evidence says that, despite his denials, he's probably guilty and even if he's not he's probably going to be convicted, so he'll do better with a third off for an early plea of guilty. I've seen it on a daily basis, that clients are pressured into pleading guilty where they say that's not what they want to do.

As with other contexts, we can see the emerging *habitus* here. Spending time on one trial case (if that is what the client wants) instead of a roughly equivalent amount of time on several guilty plea cases is (financially) punished. In Bourdieusian terms, those inclined to respect clients' wishes for trials have a *habitus* worth less *symbolic capital* and this nicely illustrates how such 'low value' *symbolic capital* can often equate to losing out on more traditional (financial) forms of *capital* in the field too. Conversely, those more inclined towards taking the approach reported by Def-Sol-15 have a *habitus* more attuned to the *field* and will financially benefit. Def-Sol-15's comment is particularly interesting, as it illustrates how such a *habitus* inclines people to behave in this way because it affects the way an individual understands their world. The lawyer here is not only thinking <I will do what makes me most money>, but, as first noted in the previous chapter, they are exercising a very human need to rationalise that choice too: <he is probably guilty anyway and even if he is not, he is likely to be convicted and therefore I am advising them well as they get one third off>. This helps to put aside any nagging moral concerns. As noted in Chapter 2, 'the nature of *illusio* … over time prevents the players from developing a healthy view of the game once they are heavily vested and entrenched in it'.[88] Individuals' *interests* can guide their interpretation of 'the facts', whether they appreciate this or not. Similarly, *conatus* relates to a set of dispositions 'which inclines agents to strive to reproduce … the properties constituting their social identity, without even needing to do this deliberately or consciously'.[89] People adjust their expectations to match their *field* conditions and therefore come to accept the way things are. Successes and failures (whether that individual's fault or not) are rationalised and this rationalisation implicitly accepts and is influenced by the financial (*field*) conditions being worked within.

Defence lawyers should be under no illusions that their advice on plea, in the context of the sentencing discount, can impact severely, even with what the lawyer themselves might perceive as very little pressure on their part. Psycho-legal analysis by Helm argues that the guilty plea discount is coercive, particularly where it is the difference between a custodial and community sentence,[90] or (and backed

[88] T Greenhalgh et al, 'Orthodoxy, *Illusio*, and Playing the Scientific Game: A Bourdieusian Analysis of Infection Control Science in the COVID-19 Pandemic' (2021) 6 *Wellcome Open Research* 126.
[89] P Bourdieu *Homo Academicus* (P Collier tr, Stanford University Press, 1988) 176.
[90] Helm 'Conviction by Consent?' (n 81) 161.

up by survey data) where it allows for release from custodial remand.[91] Similar concerns have been raised by Peay and Player.[92] The relevance of lawyer advice (among other pressures) to this is stark, as exemplified by one of Jones' interviews with female defendants:

> I'm innocent, but I pleaded guilty because my barrister advised me … 'If you plead you'll get a suspended sentence' and to me it was more important, rather than standing up for a principle, to be there for my daughter.[93]

When faced with such 'a gamble she cannot afford to lose', this is hardly surprising.[94] Even the Sentencing Council's own research (having interviewed offenders) acknowledges that lawyer advice is often 'pivotal' when it comes to determining plea.[95] The fact that, at magistrates' court level, such sentences are *relatively* trivial (absolute maximum of six months' imprisonment, which in practice equates to only three months actually inside a prison with the remainder spent on licence in the community),[96] should not be regarded as making such a discount unimportant here either. Defence lawyer interviewees in other studies have noted that if it is the difference between custody and a community order, it can be potent.[97] Indeed, some research even suggests that the guilty plea discount is *more* potent in the relatively trivial cases that are to be found in the magistrates' court: psychological tests have found sentence discounts can have a stronger effect when the stakes are lower because 'participants may not readily distinguish the objective difference in value between a "longer" and "shorter" sentence that are both subjectively quite long'.[98]

The above can then further interact with the previously noted late or minimal disclosure from the prosecution, leading to undue reliance on the police summary. Such undue reliance is not a recent problem. In the 1990s, McConville et al found that defence lawyer willingness to 'lean on' defendants was often down to uncritical acceptance of the prosecution case, giving an example of a defendant advised to plead guilty (by both the duty solicitor and his own solicitor). It was only when the Bench insisted that 'you must plead not guilty if you are in doubt', that he changed his mind, opted to represent himself and (to the surprise of his lawyers)

[91] R Helm, 'Constrained Waiver of Trial Rights? Incentives to Plead Guilty and the Right to a Fair Trial' (2019) 46 *JLS* 423.

[92] J Peay and E Player, 'Pleading Guilty: Why Vulnerability Matters' (2018) 81 *MLR* 929.

[93] S Jones, 'Under Pressure: Women Who Plead Guilty to Crimes They Have Not Committed' (2011) 11 *Criminology and Criminal Justice* 77, 82.

[94] Peay and Player, 'Pleading Guilty' (n 92) 954.

[95] Sentencing Council, 'Research to Support the Development of a Guideline for Reduction in Sentence for a Guilty Plea' (2017) 8, 9. It is worth noting that, having interviewed judges, the Sentencing Council also concluded that, whilst magistrates neither encouraged nor discouraged guilty pleas, District Judges 'gave the impression of proactively encouraging them'. Hence, any pressure from the defence lawyer may sometimes be all the more potent for being reinforced by the judiciary.

[96] Criminal Justice Act 2003, s 244. Under s 246, it could even be less than half if the offender is suitable for early release on home detention curfew.

[97] Helm et al, 'Guilty Plea Decisions' (n 19) 21–22.

[98] R Schneider and T Zottoli, 'Disentangling the Effects of Plea Discount and Potential Trial Sentence on Decisions to Plead Guilty' (2019) 24 *Legal and Criminological Psychology* 288, 298.

was acquitted.[99] However, the more recent disclosure problems certainly do not assist. As Johnstone notes, the position today is that 'pressure to enter a plea is often given in circumstances where the defence lawyer is not in full possession of the relevant evidence'.[100]

Some lawyers try to resist this, but again, over time it is all too easy to fall into the habit (or *habitus*) of relying on them and rationalising the decision to advise a guilty plea, on the basis that the summary is correct and the client is getting the benefit of the one-third discount and/or a lesser charge:

> Def-Sol-18: lots of people will dig their heels in and say, 'no, that's not acceptable', but I'm sure equally there are others that are just browbeaten into getting on with it and that's difficult … some people will just say 'yeah, okay, the evidence must be there if the police say it's there' and tell their client to plead guilty. [Although] I don't think there's many people that would.

Def-Sol-18 illustrates again the operation of *conatus*. Over a period of time, on the same trajectory, individuals' *habitus* is moulded so that they get a feel for the game, a stake, such that they simply become browbeaten into accepting the way things are in the *field*. They 'tend to rationalise both personal failure and personal success so as to uphold the overall logic of the social order … they come to accept their fate as how it was meant to be'.[101] However, this rationalisation is dangerous. The police summary is not necessarily a remotely accurate portrayal of the evidence or what happened. Def-Sol-11 provided an extreme example of the dangers of relying on it:

> The prosecution case summary indicated that they had three independent witnesses to what happened and the client was advised, on the basis of three independent witnesses, to plead guilty. I [then] found those three independent witnesses outside court and they told me they hadn't spoken to the police officer … at all and the case summary form was a – shall we say – *oversimplification* of the conversation the three had had. That's the most vivid example, but there's many more. Case summaries are prepared by police officers. They omit the parts of the evidence or the case that doesn't assist them.

It is all too easy to speculate on what would have occurred had Def-Sol-11 not been lucky enough (or, given the time-poor nature of many defence lawyers, diligent enough) to find those witnesses outside court.

H. Less Experienced Lawyers

As with the police station, another area where austerity bites in magistrates' court criminal practice is the experience of the lawyers involved and their training. This

[99] McConville et al, *The Case for the Prosecution* (n 46) Ch 8.

[100] E Johnston, 'The Adversarial Defence Lawyer: Myths, Disclosure and Efficiency – A Contemporary Analysis of the Role in the Era of the Criminal Procedure Rules' (2020) 24 *International Journal of Evidence & Proof* 35, 49–50.

[101] S Fuller, 'Conatus' in M Grenfell (ed), *Pierre Bourdieu: Key Concepts*, 2nd edn (Acumen, 2012) 173.

problem is particularly notable in relation to youth court work (a youth court being a specialist magistrates' court for defendants who are under 18).[102] Despite the quite serious offences involved (eg robbery, which, for an adult, would always result in a Crown Court appearance and fees) and the skills required to deal with vulnerable children, more senior counsel may avoid the work due its low fees. For some, youth court work is only done until one is experienced enough to be instructed in more remunerative things:

> Pros+Def-Bar-02: junior people seem to get quite a lot of youth court work, even though it's a really highly specialised arena and the rules, it's almost a jurisdiction in its own right … Even though quite often, you're dealing with vulnerable children, and really quite serious things. So that's probably one of the main difficulties in getting more experienced people into that arena. The payment I think … For senior people, compared to a Crown Court brief it's just no contest.

The exception to this was where a certificate for counsel is granted (which provides greater fees), but these were considered very difficult to get.[103] In the absence of them, the rates are the same as the adult magistrates' court, even though, for an adult, that offence may in practice have been sent to Crown Court due to its seriousness (or even being indictable only – though this would at least push the youth fee up to the magistrates' court higher 1A standard fee if not a trial: equivalent to adults' either way offences guilty pleas). Further, as Pros+Def-Bar-05 points out, applying for certificates for counsel can itself be ethically hazardous:

> often what you're trying to argue is that their case isn't very serious, but if you are (in the same hearing) trying to argue that it's serious enough for you to be paid all of this extra money, it can be quite problematic.

They also agreed with Pros+Def-Bar-02 that:

> people who would be experienced to deal with serious sex matters wouldn't go to the youth court to deal with them … partly [because they are just not paid enough] I think, but it's partly because it's just not seen as particularly prestigious work.

These echo comments made by respondents to the Criminal Legal Aid Review (reflected in its overall conclusions) that youth court work was 'seriously undervalued'.[104] Likewise, earlier research for the BSB and CILEX found it to be perceived as 'low status' and as a 'training ground' for newly qualified barristers.[105]

[102] Children and Young Persons Act 1933, s 45(1) and s 46(1).

[103] See Criminal Legal Aid (Determinations by a Court and Choice of Representative) Regulations 2013, SI 2013/614, reg 16: certificates for council may be granted "because there are circumstances which make the proceedings unusually grave or difficult".

[104] Bellamy, *CLAR* (n 8) Ch 10.

[105] A Wigzell et al, *The Youth Proceedings Advocacy Review: Final Report* (Institute for Criminal Policy Research, 2015) 54.

In terms of adults (as noted previously), the same issue of some seeing cases as a loss-leader (for more profitable Crown Court work) was present as it was for police station work. This meant that there was little incentive for firms to send particularly experienced lawyers to the magistrates' court:

> Def-Sol-04: the argument is of course, that those cases go up to the Crown Court, and therefore they feed into the fees at the Crown Court, and there is force in that argument, but there's force in that argument if you pay them £20,000 [salary] and have a child doing it … it's a loss-leader.

Of course, this is not to say that all (or even most) lawyers who do magistrates' (including youth) court work are inexperienced. Likewise, even those who are inexperienced may nonetheless be trying their hardest to provide a good service; we all must start somewhere. The point is that the incentive to send cheap (in terms of salary) or inexperienced lawyers is there and those firms who do so may benefit at the expense of those who provide more experienced (and therefore expensive) staff. Equally, the work of those more experienced lawyers who nonetheless attend is undervalued. It all feeds into a theme we have seen throughout this chapter, that austerity encourages this sort of work to be regarded as unimportant. As Def-Sol-11 put it earlier 'just seen as "£200 here, £300 there"'.

Similar issues arise in terms of investing in staff. Def-Sol-20 noted cutbacks they had had to introduce in terms of training provision due to tight margins:

> Back in the day I'd probably have just said, 'oh, there's a trial course here, go on that'. But now I feel like I've got to do it myself … and of course, I've got targets to reach every month and that doesn't help me get to them.

Nor was it possible to observe new colleagues in court for mentoring purposes:

> There's just not the money! I can't justify a day going to watch [Name] do something in court because the funds have been cut so badly that that's a whole day and we just can't afford it.

Equally, Pros-01 made similar points about lack of time for training on the other side:

> We have a lot of mandated learning that we have to do by particular dates, but frankly that goes by the wayside a lot of the time, and ends up getting done at a weekend or an evening or something … it's literally in your own time, or maybe when you're sat eating a sandwich if you get five minutes to actually get lunch at court. Or we get shouted at, at team meetings.

Hence, whilst a sense of professionalism (or at least fear of getting into trouble) keeps some on both sides going in terms of training, even then this has to be pared down or done in their own time. Those who simply don't care, or put on the bare minimum training, or send inexperienced lawyers out will profit at the expense of those who do.

I. Burnout/Demoralisation

Just as with police station work, a common theme thus far is of some lawyers or firms giving in to financial pressure (and eg preparing very little if at all for the magistrates' court) whereas others disregard this in the name of good service ideals, no matter the cost and terrible hourly rates it equates to (eg working late into the night to prepare properly). We could conclude, therefore, that some lawyers just need to be more dedicated. However, just as with the police station work, such idealism, suggestive of an out-of-sync *habitus*, can be exhausting and demoralising. Previous literature suggests that burnout and morale have been issues for defence lawyers for some time[106] and the Law Society has noted the dwindling numbers and high average age of duty solicitors (who spend time on-call at magistrates' courts).[107] In some ways burnout and demoralisation come directly from low fees themselves/profitability and the impact this has on professional self-worth:

> Def-Sol-20: It's tough when we look at our figures and our property department's made five times the amount we have in one month. It's a bit soul destroying.

I also found both defence lawyers and prosecutors suffered high stress, in a less direct fashion, due to the long days and heavy workloads that the already seen austerity imperative for a high volume of work demands:

> Def-Sol-03: as somebody that's worked in this for [near 20] years, I've never known it as hard and as gruelling as it's been for the last 16 months. I know of very few who aren't working at home in their evenings to try and keep up with workloads. The sustainability of the profession as a whole has gone beyond breaking point.
>
> Pros-01: we've just been left with what feels like skeleton staff. It's literally burnout.
>
> Pros+Def-Bar-01: you get so exhausted and so burnt-out, to the point of being worried about actually being safe when I'm driving home from court [after my day of prosecuting]. To then get home, have something to eat, and crack on with the next day's prep.

Some were more blunt:

> Def-Sol-01: we are effectively running on adrenaline and coffee, and alcohol.

As with police station defence, working hard to provide good service in spite of incentives and workload takes its toll over time and is arguably unsustainable. For some, both defence and prosecution, this can go beyond simple exhaustion and into illness:

> Def-Sol-02: there's a lot of mental health issues because it just gets a bit much. There's only so much you can do, and in order for it to be profitable, you want to make sure that

[106] Dehaghani and Newman, '"We're Vulnerable Too"' (n 50) 1217; J Thornton, 'Is Publicly Funded Criminal Defence Sustainable? Legal Aid Cuts, Morale, Retention and Recruitment in the English Criminal Law Professions' (2020) 40 *Legal Studies* 230.

[107] 'Criminal Duty Solicitors: a Looming Crisis' (The Law Society, 1 September 2022) www.lawsociety.org.uk/campaigns/criminal-justice/criminal-duty-solicitors.

> your staff are all working streamlined, that you haven't got any 'unnecessary' support staff that take the burden off the practitioners. But actually, you do need that extra support.
>
> Pros-01: I think a lot of people are struggling. I think wellbeing and mental health is a really big issue at the minute … I think they're already miserable, a lot of people. I think there'll be a lot of sickness. I think people will end up having to take time off work, and potentially moving onto other things. Because they can't cope with it the same way that they used to be able to.

This is compounded by the emotionally challenging nature of criminal law work and the issues and themes it deals with:[108]

> Pros-01: there's an underestimation of the type of work we do as well, in terms of how that impacts upon people. The cases we see and the victims that we deal with and the offences have a bigger impact than people might imagine.

Equally though, even the less factually unpleasant cases take their toll:

> Pros-06: your wellbeing struggles. I know recently qualified prosecutors who struggle. I think some of them really slip into a kind of depression, but it's a depression with a kind of mundanity of it.

This is not necessarily because management do not care. Indeed, Pros-06 noted that the CPS was 'particularly good with work/life balance' and that there had been recent 'pushback' by management against people overworking, especially remotely. However, in the magistrates' court team, they found such edicts to be unrealistic and ineffective:

> If you get a case at 4.30, and it's a domestic abuse trial, what are you going to say? [Chuckle] stand up in court and go, 'sorry Your Worships, I've hit my flexitime limit'! [Laughs], you have to work it. And you'll come home at 7pm or whatever and then you will probably have to prep for the next day, then you wake up in the morning and you prep for the two hours before you go in … in the magistrates' team, work/life balance is a problem.

This is then all aggravated by an overall sense of decline in the magistrates' court system as a whole:

> Def-Sol-11: they've got chairs that are broken, they've got things that don't work, issues with flooding. No one's investing in the courts themselves, so no one's investing in the court staff who are demoralised and don't answer the phone.

Hence, as with police station work, it would not be all that surprising if even the most committed lawyers were to reluctantly come to accept some of the poor practices detailed elsewhere in this chapter, or, alternatively, just burnout and/or quit. The result is that the *habitus* required to adapt (or survive) in the *field* contributes to a practical logic that accepts little preparation, disclosure failures, lack of

[108] See also J Fleck and R Francis, *Vicarious Trauma in the Legal Profession* (Legal Action Group, 2021).

TLC, etc as simply the way it is. Pros+Def-Bar-06 provides a vivid example of the hazards for such disillusion in terms of lawyer behaviour when it comes to the sorts of less serious offences magistrates' courts deal with:

> The advocate has been paid so piss poorly, is having such a shit time, that he or she just wants to go home. You throw up your hands, giving the impression that you know the system better than the client – which you probably do – and say 'well it's all looking very negative isn't it? Perhaps you should reconsider your plea'. And that happens at the margin cases, the pickpocketing or the low-lying Public Order Act offence. Where the junior advocate, who's thinking <fuck this, I've lept across [City] to do this brief, I dunno if I'm ever gonna get paid for it, when I started this brief was worth £150, now it's worth £75> [says] 'you should just plead guilty I think.' Now *that* is the sort of culture, the early cynicism instilled in advocates which, yes, I definitely *did* see a bit of: these prematurely war-weary and cynical late 20-somethings who were just knackered and disillusioned. And they're a real danger to their clients at that point. Because of course to the client they look like they know what they're doing, they're professional and so forth, but it could be the difference for example between having a criminal record or not. Yes it might be a low-lying offence, but if it's one of these marginal things – which may not matter very much to the advocate – but make a huge difference to the life of that person.

Not everyone behaves like this of course, but, as we have seen, the mental consequences for going against this can be severe exhaustion or even mental illness. Bourdieu's concept of *hysteresis*, where one's *habitus* is poorly adapted to a particular *field*, resulting in distress and disorientation, is alive and well here for magistrates' court lawyers on both sides, just as it was for defence lawyers in the police station.

III. The Logic of Criminal Prosecution and Defence Practice in Magistrates' Courts

We have seen that, for defence lawyers, magistrates' court work is so poorly remunerated that it can be regarded by some as a loss-leader and that, for prosecutors, it is likewise poorly resourced. This austerity in the funding of magistrates' court work manifests as a lack of time, on the part of both prosecutors and defence lawyers (much as it did for defence lawyers in the police station). Time before court, time to prepare for court, time on the day in court and time afterwards are all in short supply. The findings in this chapter thus suggest Newman and Dehaghani's argument in relation to defence lawyers in Wales (that '"time" and "money" – are inextricably linked')[109] applies much more widely and to prosecution as much as defence (albeit more indirectly). It also provides further evidence for Welsh's

[109] Newman and Dehaghani, *Experiences of Criminal Justice* (n 19) 111.

argument (which itself built upon my own in earlier work) that 'practices that encourage standardisation become an important part of the habitus, providing actors with a sense of appropriate actions to take in particular circumstances'.[110]

In particular, what this chapter's analysis demonstrates is a logic of practice that is, perhaps surprisingly, quite consistent between defence and prosecution. Whilst Dehaghani and Newman argue that defence fee cuts and stagnation have 'allowed the resilience of police officers and the prosecution to increase',[111] the present study suggests prosecution resilience in magistrates' courts has been significantly reduced too.[112] Whilst it is true that prosecutors 'reactively benefit (whatever their own challenges faced by, for example, austerity cuts and staffing reductions) by the retreat and dilution of the defence lawyer from their role as zealous advocate',[113] what we have seen here is that poor preparation by prosecution, disclosure failures, missed deadlines, etc can equally result in refused adjournments and prosecutions collapsing. Resourcing issues cut both ways (badly). Hence, whilst both sides might take different routes to get there, ultimately, we have seen that practising in this *field* encourages and develops a disposition of wearied acceptance of the 'fact' (which those of the high *capital*/dominant *habitus* will perceive as 'common sense')[114] that speed or being 'ruthlessly efficient' must be prioritised. Little time can be spent on preparation, clients and victims must unfortunately be turned into commodities (to facilitate speed), swift guilty pleas and sentencing (as another way of ensuring speed and volume) must be encouraged robustly, highly restrictive interpretations of what is 'really needed' must be developed (indeed are reinforced/incorporated into the subconscious world-view from such a *habitus*), targets must be met and boxes ticked, the game must be played.[115] All this may be viewed by some individuals involved as regrettable, but crucially it must also be accepted (albeit sometimes wearily) as a 'fact of life', 'business necessity', 'just the way things are', etc to succeed. As we saw, such a *habitus*, tailored to this environment, assists individuals to rationalise this: <he is probably guilty and even if he is not, he is likely to be convicted and anyway, the police summary suggests a very strong case, so he may as well benefit from the discount and save us all some time>. The absorption of this disposition over time ('like air', without necessarily noticing)[116] is difficult to resist. As the previously discussed concepts of *illusio*/*interest*, *conatus* and *symbolic violence* demonstrate, even the well-meaning may adapt their dispositions and behaviour to benefit themselves (their *interests*) or

[110] Welsh, *Access to Justice in Magistrates' Courts* (n 3) 74, citing Thornton, 'The Way in Which Fee Reductions Influence' (n 74).

[111] Dehaghani and Newman, 'Criminal Legal Aid and Access to Justice' (n 38) 1.

[112] ibid. They did acknowledge this as a potential issue at fn 11.

[113] ibid 15.

[114] Bourdieu, *The Logic of Practice* (n 26) 58.

[115] I do not use this metaphor flippantly. Bourdieu regarded all *fields* as a site of struggle, where a game is played and those with the most well-adapted *habitus* (here, those willing to accept and not fight against the incentives seen in this chapter) have 'a feel for the game' (ibid 66).

[116] Bourdieu and Eagleton, 'Doxa and Common Life' (n 22) 115.

uphold the status quo without necessarily appreciating this, or when trying to do the opposite, or even (*symbolic violence*) where it operates to their detriment. Those who do not accept this or whose *habitus* does not accord with this *field* (like many of the interviewees here) are therefore to be commended, but, just like defence lawyers in the police station, pay a price in the form of Bourdieu's *hysteresis*, as the foregoing section on burnout illustrates vividly.

5

Crown Court Defence and Prosecution Practice in Austerity

I. Introduction and Context

The Crown Court[1] deals with a minority of cases (around 5 per cent).[2] This consists of offences so serious they can only be tried on indictment and those triable either way which magistrates have sent for trial (potentially at the defendant's request/election) or committed for sentence (beyond their six-month sentencing powers).[3] In mid-2022, this amounted to around 60,000 outstanding cases.[4] After a brief introduction to the system of defence and prosecution in the Crown Court, we shall then examine the implications of austerity for the logic of criminal legal practice here across four key themes emerging from the interview data and relevant literature:

(1) time (generally and in a number of key areas/moments);
(2) inexperience;
(3) plea advice; and
(4) burnout.

That said, as with previous settings, it should always be borne in mind that these themes operate in addition to the systemic challenges of the setting, already established by broader literature.[5] Further, in addition to legal aid and prosecution service austerity, the Court itself has suffered direct austerity measures, which

[1] Whilst there are many magistrates' courts, strictly speaking there is only one 'Crown Court', which sits in various cities: Courts Act 1971, s 4.

[2] 'About Magistrates' Courts' (Courts and Tribunals Judiciary) www.judiciary.uk/courts-and-tribunals/magistrates-courts/magistrates-court/.

[3] Sentencing Council, 'Allocation Overarching Guideline' (2016). The Crown Court will also deal with more serious youth cases, but there is greater potential/imperative to keep these in the (youth) magistrates' courts and increased maximum sentencing powers of two years' detention also assist with this. See Judicial College, *Youth Court Bench Book* (2020) 72–74.

[4] MoJ, 'Criminal Court Statistics' (Gov.UK) www.gov.uk/government/collections/criminal-court-statistics.

[5] For recent appraisal, see eg J Jacobson et al, *Inside Crown Court Personal Experiences and Questions of Legitimacy* (Policy Press, 2016), who branded it 'structured mayhem' and, from the same authors, *Briefing: Structured Mayhem: Personal Experiences of the Crown Court* (Criminal Justice Alliance, 2015).

it is important to understand at the outset. For several years, there has been a 'backlog' of cases in the Crown Court. This was, initially, a matter of fiscal choice: the number of 'sitting days' (ie days where a courtroom with a judge, etc would be available) was capped by the 2010–2015 coalition Government at a significantly lower number than the court estate could have physically delivered (a policy continued by subsequent Conservative Governments).[6] These Governments also sold off parts of the court estate.[7] This reduced expenditure, but meant fewer cases could be dealt with in a given year. During the COVID-19 pandemic, the number of sitting days collapsed due to physical limitations of court buildings to eg allow for social distancing of juries. The backlog then ceased to be a matter of choice, with physical capacity becoming the limiting factor.[8] Since then, the Government has promised no limit to sitting days, to get the backlog under control, but it is unclear how long this will last.[9] Prior to the pandemic, the Government apparently considered a (growing) backlog in eg 2019 of around 38,000 cases as acceptable.[10] Quarter 2 (2022) figures suggested a growing average waiting time for trial of 293 days (compared to 189 in 2019).[11] Although none of this has a direct effect on lawyers' working practices, it does mean they suffer cashflow problems. Fees are generally paid at the conclusion of the case and if the case does not conclude until much later due to lack of space, then this can become a significant problem. More generally, many court buildings themselves are showing their age, needing maintenance and investment in new infrastructure.[12]

Prosecution and defence interviewees provided many examples of this in action, eg on delays:

> Def-Sol-01: I've just come from [Prison] this morning, dealing with a client who's accused of attempted murder. He's been on remand since [early] 2020, and his trial date is [mid] 2022.
>
> Pros-02: The courts are just over-listed. Trials are listed for fraud in 2–3 years' time. You've got victims hanging on for 2–3 years. The whole system's rubbish because it doesn't have money.

[6] J Slingo, 'No Cap on Judicial Sitting Days Next Year' (*Law Society Gazette*, 23 April 2021).

[7] O Bowcott, '77 More Courts in England and Wales to Close' (*The Guardian*, 13 September 2019). This was also the position in magistrates' courts, which have their own backlog, but not to as severe an extent.

[8] Burnett CJ, *Lord Chief Justice's Report 2022* (Judicial Office, 2022) 18. The Government attempted to mitigate this by running 'Nightingale courts' during the pandemic, but these were relatively few and unsuitable for defendants considered an escape risk etc.

[9] ibid.

[10] MoJ, 'Criminal Court Statistics' (n 4).

[11] ibid.

[12] J Hyde, 'Crumbling Crown Courts: Running Repair Bill Tops £35m' (*Law Society Gazette*, 25 July 2022) www.lawgazette.co.uk/news/crumbling-crown-courts-running-repair-bill-tops-35m/5113214.article. Eg, in late 2022, Nottingham Crown Court was brought to a halt for weeks because of one broken door part in the cell block: R Sherdley, 'Cases Adjourned at "Crumbling" Nottingham Crown Court as Wait on for 6-inch Part' (*Nottingham Post*, 7 October 2022) www.nottinghampost.com/news/nottingham-news/cases-adjourned-crumbling-nottingham-crown-7676397.

There were also strong feelings on the physical state of the courts:

> Def-Bar-02: they're disgusting and I think it's a bit of an embarrassment. If you go to [three London Crown Courts]. God! Some of those places I don't think have ever been cleaned. The lifts don't work, the bathrooms are broken.

> Pros-03: Most of the Crown Court Estate was built in the 70s and 80s. [City] Crown Court, you very much feel like you're in a 1970s council leisure centre … regardless of its inherent grimness, and darkness, it's not fit for the modern age.

All of this operates in addition to the direct financial challenges considered in this chapter that criminal lawyers must contend with.

A. Legal Aid in the Crown Court

Unlike the magistrates' courts, there is no Crown Court duty solicitor scheme (as a defendant would not find themselves there without first appearing in a magistrates' court, where they can receive advice and representation from the duty solicitor and then arrange their own lawyer for the future). Defendants (in practice, their lawyer) must apply to the LAA for a Representation Order. Whilst (unlike the magistrates' court) the 'interests of justice' test is automatically passed for almost all Crown Court work,[13] there are still restrictions on means: those with a *disposable* income above £37,500 are ineligible.[14] Further, (unless the defendant's income is very low) a Representation Order is usually subject to a Contribution Order. This requires the defendant to pay contributions to the LAA towards their representation (which are reimbursed if subsequently acquitted).

From the lawyer perspective (litigator and advocate), Crown Court fees are often 'graduated' – meaning that, whilst payment is largely by fixed fee (according to type/severity of offence), this can increase incrementally in accordance with other proxies for complexity, such as the number of pages of prosecution evidence (PPE) and number of hearing/trial days.[15] There are still purely fixed fees for some hearings. There are then a very small number of highly complex cases which operate outside this scheme (Very High Cost Cases, VHCCs). These are dealt with on a case-by-case basis via a negotiated contract.[16]

[13] Legal Aid Agency (LAA), 'Standard Crime Contract 2022 Documents' (Gov.uk, 19 October 2021) www.gov.uk/government/publications/standard-crime-contract-2022.

[14] LAA, *Criminal Legal Aid Manual* (MoJ, 2022) although, as of May 2023, MoJ has committed to abolishing this restriction.

[15] See Criminal Legal Aid (Remuneration) Regulations 2013, SI 2013/435, Sch 1 (for litigators) and Sch 2 (for advocates). See also V Ling and S James, *Legal Aid Handbook* (Legal Action Group, 2022) and previous years' editions.

[16] See LAA, 'Crime High Cost Case Arrangements and Contract Documents' (Gov.UK, 22 March 2017) www.gov.uk/government/publications/high-cost-case-arrangements-and-contract-documents.

B. Crown Prosecution in the Crown Court

Crown Court prosecution advocates are qualified lawyers (with Crown Court rights of audience) either working in-house for the CPS (Crown Advocates),[17] or independent advocates instructed by the CPS for particular cases.[18] As in the magistrates' court, the latter must take instructions from the CPS and therefore cannot (for example) decide unilaterally to drop or reduce charges.[19] Currently, the CPS's professed strategy is to use both in-house and instructed advocates, based on the principle of 'the right advocate for the right case', regardless of employment status.[20] Litigation work is conducted by in-house staff: paralegal officers, paralegal assistants, etc led by CPS lawyer/s (the precise human resourcing obviously depends upon work complexity). This is organised across 14 regional offices/Areas, with two further specialist national teams: (1) Serious Economic, Organised Crime and International Directorate; and (2) Special Crime and Counter Terrorism Division.[21]

II. Financial Challenges of Crown Court Practice

Unlike magistrates' courts and police stations, nobody regarded Crown Court work as a loss-leader. Quite the opposite:

> Def-Sol-11: if you had no Crown Court cases in a six-month period you would go out of business. I can tell you that now. I say that as someone who ran a firm for 11 years, so I've got a pretty good handle on cash flow … ideally you're looking for cases with high page counts, but if a case is at the Crown Court and if it goes to trial, by and large it's gonna be worth some money.

Nonetheless, whilst the financial challenges for lawyers working in this setting are more nuanced, as we shall see, they are no less significant. Like previous settings, one of them (for both prosecution and defence) is the effect of financial resources on the use and perception (and lack) of time. First therefore, we turn to this fundamental issue.

A. Money and its Connection with Time

As previously mentioned, Morison and Leith, commenting on barristers working in the Crown Court, noted that time 'dictates much in the life of the barrister'.

[17] Prosecution of Offences Act 1985, s 1(3).
[18] ibid s 5.
[19] ibid s 5(2).
[20] CPS, *2025 Advocacy Strategy* (2021).
[21] See CPS, 'About CPS' www.cps.gov.uk/about-cps.

Managed properly, a barrister can 'cover enough cases to be busy and successful'.[22] However, in 'the hostile barristerial world … time is short and pressures are constant'.[23] Likewise, Newman and Dehaghani have argued that '"time" and "money" – are inextricably linked'. Their research participants had very limited financial resources or (consequently) time, and felt 'pressure' to compensate for this by working faster.[24] Chapter 4 argued that this inextricable link was the case for both defence and prosecution lawyers in magistrates' courts. Here, I build on this further to argue that it is equally true of defence and prosecution work in the Crown Court. Therefore, Morison and Leith's comment is all the more apt in today's austere environment. As in other settings, this issue arose in various specific contexts (in the sections below), but was a frequent theme in general in terms of volume/workload too. Volume was also an issue in Crown Court for Dehaghani and Newman, with their interviewees reporting 'back-to-back cases' and a consequent inability to put as much work into each as they would like.[25] Whilst I heard similar from defence too, my data also suggests prosecutors felt the pressure:

> Interviewer: With all that said, do you think mistakes get made because of the [time] pressures that people are under?
>
> Pros-03: Yes definitely, without question.

Even defence lawyers (who in some ways might benefit) noted this pressure on their opponents:

> Def-Sol-01: I'm a defence lawyer, but they've savaged the CPS and we are in this position whereby there could not be a better time in England and Wales to commit serious crime.

We now consider more detailed and specific consequences of this lack of time for Crown Court work in their chronological context, starting with preparation for court.

B. Lack of Time to Prepare before Court

As with magistrates' court work, the first thing this lack of time impacts is court preparation. Unfortunately, this is arguably the most important time. Hunter et al, in interviews with judges, found that 'thorough preparation is a necessary precondition for 'good' advocacy'. Indeed, one judge considered that: 'The battle is won

[22] J Morison and P Leith, *The Barristers World and the Nature of Law* (Open University Press, 1992) 19.

[23] ibid 91.

[24] D Newman and R Dehaghani, *Experiences of Criminal Justice: Perspectives From Wales on a System in Crisis*, Kindle edn (Bristol University Press, 2022) 111.

[25] ibid.

or lost before the court doors are unlocked.'[26] Austerity plays its part here. Over half of their interviewees blamed 'declining levels of remuneration' for negative impacts on advocacy quality.[27] In the current study, both prosecutors and defence lawyers reported great difficulties.

In terms of prosecutors, both established and recent literature have not been kind. McConville et al's seminal study found 'the CPS playing an essentially subordinate and reactive role' to the police.[28] Given the above resource constraints, we may note that it is hardly surprising if such a subordinate role is still played. Certainly, HMCPS Inspectorate's recent findings on preparation were damning:

> Many CPS Areas were lacking grip on casework: the core function of the CPS … in too many cases, in the period between first appearance and trial, the CPS appeared to do little to review the case or progress work that needed to be done. Too much was left to be done at a late stage, if it was done at all.[29]

The key impact here of 'the challenges of resourcing' was acknowledged: 'budget and staff reductions have had an impact on delivery'. The report went on to state that managers were forced to make difficult resourcing decisions, which had impacted service provided.[30] In relation to charging, for example, they found a minority (around 45 per cent) of charging decisions fully met expectations for case analysis and trial strategy. Around 40 per cent partially met the standard and around 16 per cent did not meet it at all. Issues were not minor or inconsequential, but related to fundamental matters, such as 'meaningful analysis' of how to prove the offence and strategy for dealing with the defence case, or addressing weaknesses in the prosecution case.[31] My own data reflects these concerns and illustrates how some have come about in the context of austerity. For my prosecutor interviewees, the sheer number of cases they were required to work on speak for themselves:

> Pros-02: the challenges at the CPS are the volume of work … [in my specialism] you might have 5/10/20 very big cases when you're defending. And now, I have probably 100 files that I'm working on at any one time. So I'm working on a lot more files, perhaps less work on each of them.

Pros-04 went further. It was not just a case of 'less work on each' case, but rather 'firefighting' from the very start every day if caseloads were to be kept on top of:

> When I log on in the morning, you will have a list of coloured tasks and you're firefighting to try and keep as many of the red numbers down as much as you possibly

[26] G Hunter et al, *Judicial Perceptions of the Quality of Criminal Advocacy* (University of London, 2018) 11.

[27] ibid 29.

[28] M McConville et al, *The Case for the Prosecution: Police Suspects and the Construction of Criminality* (first published 1991, Routledge, 2017).

[29] HMCPSI, *Annual Report 2019–20* (Justice Inspectorates, 2020) [1.21].

[30] ibid.

[31] HMCPSI, *2020 Charging Inspection* (Justice Inspectorates, 2020) [1.28].

> can. In the same day, you can be trying to work on loads of those at the same time, and also have other stuff coming in. [Eg] your charging day: none of that's [extremely] urgent, but you've got to have it done because all the police will say, 'where's my charging decision?' Sometimes you get your facts mixed up! I ring an officer and say, 'what's happened with this witness?' And he says, 'what witness is that?' I think, <oh shit, it's the other bloody case I've got open on this system!>

Hence, the volume of cases is such that they can even blur into one another. Similar issues presented with the more junior staff that people like Pros-02 and Pros-04 end up supervising. As Pros-03 noted, this combines with the natural increase in case complexity from modern technology:

> Pros-03: The caseloads have got massive. And things haven't got simpler, they've got more difficult, because there is not a case now that does not have some element of phone data in it, which complicates things massively. Same with any kind of sexual offence, you've not just got phone *data* [as a means of proving someone's location at a particular time], but with a RASSO [rape and serious sexual offences] case, you've then got the [defendant's and complainant's] phone downloads … So everybody has been facing a massive increase in the number of cases, combined with (just as important) a massive increase in the complexity.

There was some awareness of these issues in the sense that more people were being recruited,[32] but this was insufficient in Pros-03's experience:

> Not in numbers that will make real differences to our caseloads. All they're doing is stopping them rising faster.

This reflects the fact that, whilst CPS budgets have increased somewhat since coalition Government cuts, they are still far off even 2009 levels in numerical terms (and even further off in real terms).[33] The above comments suggest the situation in relation to Crown Court preparation for prosecutors is as bad or worse than it was for magistrates' courts. Even those working on the serious offences dealt with here must 'firefight' and spend less time on each case (sometimes to the point that they confuse one case with another). Prosecutors appear to have (or feel that they have) no choice but to ruthlessly manage time, to the detriment of quality of work.

Closer to the court date, barristers also recognised CPS lawyers' invidious position in having to 'firefight' and how this made their own preparation for court more difficult:

> Pros+Def-Bar-07: They end up firefighting. They haven't got time to answer letters because they're just jumping from case to case dealing with problems and it's not their fault because they're being effectively set up to fail.

One result of the above was that they would be briefed at the last minute and only then could notice flaws, missed deadlines, etc. For example, Pros+Def-Bar-03 did

[32] See CPS, *Annual Report and Accounts 2020–21* (House of Commons, 2021) 10.

[33] The CPS budget was cut by 26% (£185m) from 2009–2016 before an £85m increase in 2019–20: CPS, *Annual Report and Accounts 2019–20* (2020).

not get a clear picture of the case (or documentation) until the night before, or even the morning of the hearing for various applications, with them being served late 'in nearly every case'. At such a late stage, as Pros+Def-Bar-02 notes, there is often very little that can be done:

> you see the case the night before, there really isn't a great deal you can do to compel a deadline to be complied with … Some judges are more forgiving than others, and more realistic about the pressures that the CPS are under with the caseloads that they manage.

Pros+Def-Bar-02's comment in relation to judges (and being somewhat resigned to suffering their displeasure) chimes well with what we saw one prosecutor noted in the previous chapter in relation to magistrates' courts and Pros-03 noted in relation to their Crown Court preparation: 'We try and deviate [from standard deadlines] wherever we can, because [in] all our cases we just won't be able to meet it. No-one's interested, to arbitrarily stick to it.' For these interviewees, it is just the way it is. In terms of *habitus*, one has to come to terms with this level of preparation time as the reality of life in order to get a proper 'feel for the game' of Crown Court criminal practice.[34]

Quite apart from missing deadlines, insufficient time for CPS office lawyers also affected the quality of those applications that *were* sent to their advocates on time.

> Pros+Def-Bar-03: they just don't have the time to devote to cases …
>
> bad character applications are nearly always one-liners. They don't serve the material or understand what material might assist the application, in nearly all cases.

At best, this puts more pressure on advocates, who must then spend time fixing this (assuming it is not too late):

> Pros+Def-Bar-08: if I get a prosecution case, I will sit down with all the papers, go through every page and send an advice to the officer saying 'this is what's missing, you need to ask the victim this, would the victim like a screen in court? I notice that the victim hurt her leg, does she need a special chair in court? Does she need breaks when she gives her evidence?'

However, self-employed advocates themselves are equally subject to the general imperative we have seen throughout to do high volume work. Having to, on top of that, sort out prosecution cases, heightens the potential for mistakes:

> Pros+Def-Bar-02: It's tough to keep on top of everything. It really is. And you can see how things slip though occasionally.

Of course, those less inclined to be as thorough as Pros+Def-Bar-08 in sorting out these problems are likely to be able to complete greater volumes of work, demonstrating a similar *habitus* to that developing amongst magistrates' court advocates, prioritising speed at the expense of avoiding mistakes. Certainly, similar recent

[34] P Bourdieu, *The Logic of Practice* (R Nice tr, Polity Press, 1990) 66.

qualitative work found that judges were expected to accept evidence on the morning of the hearing, without which the prosecution could not proceed effectively.[35]

The defence suffer from similar issues in terms of preparation for Crown Court, to which we now turn. Principally, low fees and the imperative for volume impact on the time available for solicitors to prepare a Crown Court case. As Def-Sol-20 explains:

> a lot of firms now … you're talking minimal work on it. They're not really looking at any of the legal issues, they're just sending all the papers to the barrister: 'you sort it out'. The barristers? It's going from one to the other to the other and no-one's *really* getting to grips sometimes with the very important issues that are going on.

This was not necessarily to the benefit of prosecution either. As Pros-05 notes, lack of time to consider the case beforehand can mean early plea negotiations (which may have avoided a trial completely) are undermined:

> Pros-05: we would send an open letter out … to have a meeting with defence solicitors to explore what their client may be prepared to accept … The major problem with that is there's no legal aid funding for that work. It's a good thing in principle, but as soon as you write to the defence, pre-charge, they'll say 'well, there's no legal aid for us'.[36]

Similarly, barristers told Newman and Dehaghani that they would often receive cases and documents very late from solicitors, even for very serious crimes.[37] Indeed, lack of time to prepare appeared to be an issue across the board. Even for the most complex (and highest fee) cases, volume was still an imperative, which in turn impacts available time:

> Def-Sol-05: the hourly rate on a VHCC is despicable, in my view. It's halved at least in the last 10 years, but obviously if there's a lot of volume, then you can make it work.

For advocates, in much the same way as it did for prosecution (and defence solicitors, as Def-Sol-20 noted above) this then places pressure on the barrister, when they eventually get the case, to remedy things:

> Def-Bar-03: if your solicitors don't have the resources to do what needs to be done, then you'll turn out to do a case without the proper preparation.

That said, remedying things is not always viewed as possible. Def-Bar-03 did not appear to consider that they could pick up the slack here, perhaps suggesting (as we have seen elsewhere) a similar sense of viewing these matters as the inevitable reality, rather than choice.

Added to that, and again much like when prosecuting, defence barristers themselves must prioritise volume of work in response to low fees, reducing

[35] V Kemp, 'Bridewell Legal Advice Study: Adopting a "Whole Systems" Approach to Police Station Legal Advice' (Legal Services Research Centre, 2013) Appendix A, 59.

[36] See also E Johnstone, 'Pre-charge (Lack of) Engagement: An Empty Gesture?' [2022] Crim LR 737 and HC Justice Select Committee, *Fraud and the Justice System* (HC12, 2022) [115], which found legal aid to be a 'key barrier' to early engagement in fraud cases.

[37] Newman and Dehaghani, *Experiences of Criminal Justice* (n 24) 120.

available preparation time for each case even further. Indeed, systemically, one of the *Criminal Legal Aid Review* (*CLAR*)'s critiques was that the advocates' graduated fee scheme focused too much on the trial, at the expense of pre-trial work.[38] Likewise, the Westminster Commission on Legal Aid found that low fees meant lawyers took on a high volume of work, impacting wellbeing, preparation time and (potentially therefore) quality.[39] This was borne out by interviewees here too:

> Pros+Def-Bar-02: if you want a good hourly rate, you need to do the least work possible, or you need to work as efficiently as possible … it's always a factor that you think, <am I spending too much time on this, to the point where I've wasted time doing it, because I'm not going to be paid for it?>

For Pros+Def-Bar-02, reluctance to be embarrassed was the chief motivation against this:

> What drives a lot of people in this job is not wanting to stand up and look stupid. It certainly is for me. I'd spend hours on it just so I didn't look like a fool.

Although we can note here: (1) their other comment above in being resigned to sometimes earning displeasure from judges due to lack of preparation (even when not their fault); and (2) that in terms of *habitus*, those predisposed towards being less professional (or more shameless) will be financially rewarded.

Equally, as with defence solicitors, even the highly complex and seemingly desirable cases outside the fixed-fee system (VHCCs) have similar problems. As Def-Bar-04 noted, there are assumptions about how much work/time ought to be spent and by whom.

> Def-Bar-04: There were many times where there was work I felt should be done, but legal aid wouldn't pay. Eg, I wanted to look at some evidence and the LAA felt this was something that could be done by [a junior solicitor]. I know something that's suspicious when I see it because I've had 20 years of experience and skill, so I insisted on doing the work, even though it wasn't paid.

This was not perfectionism. Def-Bar-04 went on to explain how this and similar issues that would have otherwise been left unexplored ultimately resulted in permission being given to appeal. In other words, Def-Bar-04 recognised the importance of these lines of enquiry and was ultimately backed up by the Court of Appeal. Such diligence (essentially doing lots of work that the LAA refused to fund) might be laudable, but should not be assumed or expected vis-à-vis general practice. Again, in terms of *habitus*, those inclined towards Def-Bar-04's

[38] C Bellamy, *Independent Review of Criminal Legal Aid (CLAR)* (November 2021) [13.108].

[39] Westminster Commission on Legal Aid, 'Inquiry into the Sustainability and Recovery of the Legal Aid Sector' (All-Party Parliamentary Group on Legal Aid, 2021) [208].

approach are going to be disadvantaged compared to those who are not so inclined.

C. Time at Court and Appeals

All the above then impacts on available time at court too. As Def-Sol-10 notes, things which should have been done much earlier then need to be done at the last minute:

> we'd get the witness statement, you'd read through it, and then you'd go to court, and only then you interview the witness. Because everyone would simply not have time to do that. And you would be getting instructions from your client who's on remand, on the morning of the trial.

The results of this are demonstrated by the following revealing quotes from two barristers, explaining how they sometimes had to catch up with the case as it went along or 'wing it':

> Pros+Def-Bar-09: I got a call at 4.30pm to say 'you've got a trial in [City] tomorrow and it's a [GBH with intent] and the brief is being emailed through'. There was no proof of evidence from the defendant. They had given a no comment interview. There was no defence statement ever served. I therefore had to go to court, grab my chap in the cell, find out what his defence was and make my own notes, which is not ideal … I found out what his defence was and then I could cross-examine the first prosecution witness and catch up with the case as I went.

> Def-Bar-03: if you're unlucky, you'll be winging it at the court trying to get 15 minutes here or there to ask questions to try and make sure you're able to ask the right questions of the witness and keep the trial on track. Things get done, but just not done properly [laughs], or sometimes not done … people are trying to cut all the corners they can.

Equally, as with their preparation beforehand, regardless of their instructing solicitors' time for preparation, barristers themselves also have less time to focus on each case at court, given the imperative for volume work. Pros+Def-Bar-10 provides an example of this, compared to what a private paying client could expect:

> the fact that I was privately funded meant I got the papers at the first appearance. I could meet the client for a conference. We could prepare a proper defence. The prosecution barrister, who was very experienced, got the papers the night before and hadn't been able to look through them, hadn't been able to plug any of the gaps in his case, and it was that that made the difference. It wasn't my brilliant advocacy … mostly it was the fact that I'd been able to prepare the case properly and that was all I was doing on that day. I wasn't running around trying to make ends meet by doing 16 other things – because that's how barristers keep doing legal aid work.

It has also been noted that appeals work in particular is very poorly remunerated, meaning it is either not done by firms at all or, if it is (potentially as a loss-leader), little time is spent.[40] Other research has already considered austerity and appeals in depth,[41] but it is worth noting briefly how this is backed up here:

> Def-Sol-20: I get a file this big [brings hands over half a meter above the table] and I've got to read it, review it, listen to the client, speak to them, for £270 ... it means you have to do a very quick nip into the case to try and find the relevant issues.

Hence, as with preparation time, at court it is those who are more inclined to cut corners, who take on volumes and volumes of cases, try and do 16 things at once etc, that will do well (or survive) here. This is all the more effective for, as part of *habitus*, it being difficult for those involved to fully appreciate. For example, in relation to the 'winging it' comment above, Def-Bar-03 struggled to explain how this could happen: 'it's difficult to put in to a sort of a sense, rather than just, sort of, experiencing it and seeing it, sort of, describe it'. It is probably less of a conscious choice and more the perceived 'fact' that time (as a matter of common sense or the feel for the game that an experienced criminal lawyer gets) comes to be seen as a possession that one simply does not have. That sort of *habitus* is encouraged in this *field*, whilst a more diligent one is discouraged.

D. Time for Prosecution Disclosure

As noted in the previous chapter, trial preparation for prosecutors also involves due process obligations in relation to disclosing evidence they find which undermines their case or assists the defence.[42] We saw the problems austerity caused to this process in relation to magistrates' court work and the situation in Crown Court is similar. This is not a new problem. In 2006, Quirk noted the issue of inadequate human resources for disclosure work and a corresponding tendency for prosecutors to examine schedules (ie a descriptive list) of unused evidence rather than the materials themselves, to keep workloads manageable.[43] As noted, the CPS has suffered plenty of cuts to resourcing since then. To truly appreciate the scale and severity of the problem, it is therefore worth considering the recent literature in some detail before examining how these issues play out in the work of interviewees from the current study.

Initially, it must be appreciated that the police and their associated workload constraints play a key role here too.[44] Indeed, one of the most high-profile disclosure failures, Liam Allen, came about due to police failures and was ultimately

[40] A Clarke and L Welsh, 'United by Cuts: Exploring the Symmetry between How Lawyers and Expert Witnesses Experience Funding Cuts' (2022) 4 *Amicus Curiae* 455, 460.

[41] Eg A Clarke and L Welsh, '"F**k This Game ... I'm Off": Financial and Emotional Factors in Declining Legal Representation in Miscarriage of Justice Cases' (2022) 49 *JLS* 518.

[42] Criminal Procedure and Investigations Act 1996, s 3.

[43] H Quirk, 'The Significance of Culture in Criminal Procedure Reform: Why the Revised Disclosure Scheme Cannot Work' (2006) 10 *Journal of Evidence & Proof* 42, 52.

[44] Beyond the scope of this work, given our focus on criminal *lawyers*.

rescued/revealed by the prosecution's instructed barrister. Hence, whilst Johnstone notes there was a 53 per cent increase in discontinued cases due to prosecution disclosure failures when all of 2014 is compared even with just part (Jan–Sept) of 2018, he goes on to argue that this may be as much a result of police failures as prosecution (who can be 'boxed in' by earlier police failures).[45] For Johnstone, whilst funding certainly exacerbates these issues, it is also a 'frequently cited excuse' which ignores an adversarial 'occupational culture' towards defence on the part of police and prosecutors.[46] There are problems with such an analysis in relation to prosecutors, however. First, as Smith notes, an adversarial culture has its strengths and it may even be required 'in light of the dangerous and emotionally taxing work' for the police to have that sense of 'mission' to get through a challenging shift.[47] Whilst Smith was concerned with the police, one can readily imagine prosecutors relying on a similar sense of 'mission' to get through the day too. Second, though, this simply did not reflect the attitude of my prosecutor interviewees, regardless of whether they were 'home-grown' CPS or also had experience of defending. They were not indifferent about their jobs, but they tended to perceive their work (and any sense of 'mission') in terms of acting in the public interest, rather than an unduly adversarial convictions-at-all-costs attitude.[48] Third, as I have argued throughout this book and potentially contrary to Johnstone, we need not (and ought not to) consider funding and culture in isolation. The former, as a *field* condition, influences the other potently through *habitus* formation – although the favoured *habitus* presented by prosecutors in this study does not appear to be *unduly* adversarial (for an adversarial-style system). Indeed, Smith ultimately lays the blame with 'adversarial culture *within policing*' (emphasis added) rather than prosecution.[49]

Nonetheless, prosecutors clearly do struggle. As Smith notes, the police excuse/blame only goes so far: prosecutors have a duty to consider and ensure they have all the relevant information before making charging decisions and, under the Attorney General's guidelines on disclosure, are expected to challenge police where insufficient information is supplied.[50] Hence, for Smith, whilst austerity is not directly responsible for individuals' errors, it significantly raises the risk due to reduced scrutiny and investigation.[51] Both constabulary and CPS inspectorates have arrived at similar conclusions. Whilst they critique police *scheduling* (listing

[45] E Johnstone, 'The Rise of Managerialism' in E Johnstone and T Smith (eds), *The Law of Disclosure: A Perennial Problem in Criminal Justice* (Taylor and Francis, 2020) 3, 17.

[46] ibid 17–18.

[47] T Smith, 'Changing Culture? Thinking Differently about Police and Prosecution Disclosure' in Johnstone and Smith, *The Law of Disclosure: A Perennial Problem* (n 45) 32, 36.

[48] Allowing of course for, like anyone else, self-selection bias and the fact that there may be a difference between 'talk' and 'walk'. See D Newman, *Legal Aid Lawyers and the Quest for Justice* (Hart Publishing, 2013).

[49] Smith, 'Changing Culture?' (n 47) 32.

[50] T Smith 'The "Near Miss" of Liam Allan: Critical Problems in Police Disclosure, Investigation Culture and the Resourcing of Criminal Justice' [2018] Crim LR 711, 728–29.

[51] ibid 729.

all the unused pieces of evidence and summarising what each is) as 'routinely poor', equally 'prosecutors fail to challenge' this. The result is 'chaotic scenes' outside the courtroom and 'last minute and often unauthorised disclosure between counsel, unnecessary adjournments and – ultimately – discontinued cases' being 'common occurrences'.[52] In statistical terms, just 22 per cent of files examined by HMCPSI showed adequate initial disclosure and correctly endorsed disclosure schedules by prosecutors.[53] HMCPSI has been clear that lack of resources plays its part: 'almost without exception', disclosure faults were 'caused or exacerbated by the problem of too few legal staff being spread too thinly over a volume of work of ever increasing complexity'.[54]

It is difficult to find much positive comment anywhere. HMCPSI did at least claim that issues 'rarely arise' in serious and complex casework, such as homicide, terrorism or complex fraud, as these are dealt with by better-resourced and specialist teams.[55] However, even this limited claim to success can be critiqued. Dargue, in a review of 58 murder/inchoate murder appeals between 2006–2018, found (in terms of disclosure) 'lax control of prosecution evidence and seemingly a disregard of procedural rules'.[56] Likewise, things do not appear to be getting better, with a later report finding decline when compared to the January 2020 report.[57] For example, sufficient instructions and identification of disclosable unused material were provided by the charging lawyer in circa 56 per cent and circa 51 per cent of cases respectively.[58] Even the DPP is somewhat defeatist, having argued that 'the reality is we will never be able to promise that no case will ever fail because of disclosure issues'.[59]

We will now consider how the data suggests all of this impacts the work of prosecutors and their *habitus*. The first thing to say is that these issues, combined with austerity-driven lack of time, make for a highly stressful task. As Pros-03 notes:

> If we're going to make a mistake, chances are it's in the disclosure. We will have people come over from defence; they will spend a bit of time [chuckle]. Once they realise the responsibility and pressure, and what is expected of them, but at the same time, how little time they're given to do it, they go back!

[52] HMCPSI and HMICFRS, *Making it Fair: A Joint Inspection of the Disclosure of Unused Material in Volume Crown Court Cases* (2017) 3.

[53] ibid 16.

[54] HMCPSI, *Disclosure of Unused Material in the Crown Court* (2020) [1.6]–[1.7].

[55] ibid.

[56] P Dargue, 'An Analysis of Disclosure Failings in Murder Appeals against Conviction 2006–2018' [2020] Crim LR 707. This represented all the relevant appeals found on Westlaw/LexisLibrary during that period, although not all cases with disclosure issues are necessarily appealed, or reported if they are.

[57] HMCPSI, *Disclosure of Unused Material in the Crown Court: A Follow-up of the January 2020 Review* (December 2020) [1.16].

[58] ibid [4.10]. See also Tables 5 and 6.

[59] M Hill, 'Disclosure – A Response from the CPS' [2019] Crim LR 611, 616.

Pros-03 noted how unacceptably generic police descriptions on schedules could be signed off as not being relevant to disclose nonetheless. For example, the description 'papers found in room' – it is impossible for anyone to make a judgment of whether these might undermine the prosecution or assist the defence without even knowing what sort of papers they are (newspapers, personal letters, bank statements, a diary?), let alone what is written in them. They went on to describe how high workloads operated to encourage this:

> [disclosure] schedules on a relatively small case have hundreds of items. Schedules on one of our cases will be hundreds of pages featuring thousands and thousands of items and a lawyer has to sit there and make a decision for every single item and endorse every single page. You're looking at the same things again, and again, and again, and again, and again. Your attention wavers. If you're doing that in a very pressured time sensitive way, between tiredness, fatigue, boredom – or conversely slight panic – the potential for mistakes is massive.

Such pressure perhaps explains why HMCPSI found 'blanket non-disclosure' where descriptions on the police schedule were 'plainly inadequate and the reviewing prosecutor could not have known what the item contained'.[60] There simply is not the time and the schedule needs to be ticked off the ever-growing task list.

Pros-06 noted similar in relation to rape and serious sexual offences (RASSO):

> [in the past 6 months] I have sat on more than one trial that has disintegrated because of disclosure going wrong. This is not any criticism of any personnel, but what it goes to show is the system that's struggling. The police are struggling with the material, then the reviewing/charging lawyers struggle with the material, and it's just a snowball of cracks isn't it? Everything just starts to tumble. And workload, especially in RASSO, is quite bad. You have reviewing lawyers who have 10 cases going on side-by-side, and mountains and mountains of disclosure exercises to conduct … So in those circumstances when everyone's pushed to their limits, everyone's overworked, underpaid, and being pushed to the very limits, errors *will* happen.

Similarly, Pros-04 considered that 'It will always happen'. They went on to note that there were two types of case. The obvious mistakes like Liam Allen's case (where it is difficult to understand how they were missed in the first place) and the more discreet but equally problematic case collapses (eg several frauds) due to issues which are less obvious, 'but amongst the absolute volume of material that you get, it's more easy to miss'. Pros-04 provided an example, which aptly demonstrates the impact of high volume/workload:

> if [a witness's] first account is at odds in some way to their actual statement to the police, but you don't spot it and you end up not disclosing it, it's an inconsistent statement which might [collapse] the case. I had that happen once, but it was [luckily spotted], and it was disclosed. But if you think how many of these you might have … you think <Christ Almighty! There aren't enough hours in the day to do this!>

[60] HMCPSI and HMICFRS, *Making it Fair* (n 52) 15.

It is worth noting that the above interviewees had all worked on serious and complex cases, which bolsters Dargue's point above and further undermines the above blanket claim from HMCPSI that these areas at least are better. Again, we see even here this sense of resignation that, in the current environment, these things will just happen. Pros-06's example is particularly concerning given that RASSO was also the context in *Allen*: resourcing lessons may not have been learnt. Prosecutors might be deeply unhappy with the situation (Pros-04 said risk of significant disclosure failure was what frightened them 'more than anything else') but, as we have seen with other austerity driven issues in this field, they must accept it as just the way things are if they are to continue in the *field*. Those with a *habitus* a bit more blasé (or, perhaps more accurately, reluctantly at peace) with such a state of affairs are likely to be better off. Those who spend time trying to fix (or just agonising over) these things (arguably a form of *hysteresis* from their out-of-synch, quality-focused *habitus*) are worse off financially and emotionally.

As in the magistrates' courts, whilst this is clearly of great concern in terms of miscarriages of justice, failures or delays in disclosing evidence can operate to the detriment of the prosecution advocate's case too. At best, their own case preparation is hindered:

> Pros-04: [the defence lawyer] said, 'have you got the CCTV?'
>
> [I said], 'no I haven't got it. Six days to the Plea and Trial Preparation Hearing, I'd like to have a look at it, I'd like to see whether he's done it as well!'

At worst, cases collapse:

> Pros-03: more often than that [miscarriages of justice], cases get kicked out or [offences] get kicked out, or evidence becomes inadmissible.

As with other more general issues with preparation, externally instructed advocates could sometimes fix some of this, but this brings its own problems:

> Pros+Def-Bar-07: I don't think it's [the CPS's] fault. They just don't have the resources to deal with all this, so we do it … And this is increasingly prevalent: there are cases I've done where everything's done as it should have been and they are now unusual.

Whilst it is obviously preferable that disaster is averted, even at a late stage, this will aggravate advocates' own lack of time to prepare, which we have already considered, and is a competing demand on their time, which some may not feel able to justify. Indeed, as we have seen, the *habitus* encouraged in this *field* is likely that which pre-disposes individuals to not do so.

E. Time for TLC

The last issue where lack of time caused by the high-volume working imperative affects the logic of criminal lawyer practice is lack of time for what might be termed 'tender loving care', as we also saw with magistrates' court and police station work. Def-Sol-20 gave an example of support, explanation (and commiseration) regarding appeal options at the end of the case:

> He's had his advice and the case is finished and I've run out of funding, but I feel for the guy. He doesn't understand why I'm saying there's no grounds of appeal, so I've taken the call and I've spent 45 minutes on the phone that I can't bill for because I just feel I've gotta explain to him.

Similar concerns were raised by Pros-03 in terms of time allocated for prosecution witness support:

> [support staff] are expected to attend the first two days of trial or, if it's complex or RASSO, you will be expected to attend trial until the conclusion of the first victim's evidence … but that's nonsense … it can take two days for us to finish going through all the preliminary matters that have been raised … And if it's a difficult case, eg we deal with a lot of historic sex cases, people trafficking cases, modern slavery cases, dealing with the first [vulnerable witness], and then going afterwards is nonsense.

Advocates similarly felt the tension between providing that extra level of support (which may make the whole process of going to court easier and less alienating) and the time available:

> Pros+Def Bar-05: pre-trial visits etc with CPS advocates and defence advocates. Realistically, if you're not going to get paid to be involved in that then it's going to be very difficult for barristers to actually go along.

These add to the examples that Newman and Dehaghani found (from interviewing clients and clients' families) in terms of negative impacts of resourcing for client care. For them, lack of time to build a rapport with clients (eg a barrister meeting them for the first time on the day of trial)[61] and lack of continuity of representation (an issue for both solicitors and barristers)[62] were other consequences of the requirement for high volume and time pressures caused by legal aid cuts. Lawyers viewed such things as 'an organisational necessity' in response to funding.[63] Just like in the magistrates' court then, we can see the difference between the developing *habitus* in this field (that which accepts some levels of support are simply not possible or unjustifiable on the basis of 'organisational necessity') and the alternative approaches that eg Def-Sol-20 and Pros-03 want to do, but struggle to fulfil. At best, this means they have even less time to do the many other things on their list/firefighting; at worst it leads to being driven or burnt out of the market.

[61] Newman and Dehaghani, *Experiences of Criminal Justice* (n 24) 160.
[62] ibid 163.
[63] ibid.

F. Prosecution Targets/Box-ticking

In relation to magistrates' court work, we previously saw that targets and box-ticking had a strong influence on prosecutors, reflecting previous literature. For example, one of Welsh's prosecutor interviewee's views that 'it's all statistics driven … you just want to get a guilty plea, a good result on the file'.[64] They went on to note that these 'tick the right boxes for the CPS' in spite of victim interests.[65] Hence, McConville et al have argued that prosecutors generally do not seek 'a plea to what they can *prove*, but to what they can bluff or "arm-twist" defendants into'.[66] For magistrates' court work, we saw the ultimate result was the promotion of a *habitus* focused on speed etc in order to meet (or beat) the austerity/efficiency-driven targets. These dispositions were relentlessly drummed into prosecutors until they were no longer questioned. Over time, they become unquestioned 'common sense'.[67] The alternative is staying up late, risking burnout, etc. A very similar picture emerged in relation to Crown Court work.

At the heart of this is a reasonable question of how to best manage public resources. However, as we have seen, part of the problem is that those resources have been cut. The consequences are that, even for serious offences (for example, serious fraud), difficult decisions have to be made:

> Pros-05: sometimes they will drop a case, or at least trim the case maybe from seven suspects down to three to make it more manageable and also mean that it can be done more quickly … if we can get a reasonable outcome within 12–18 months by investigating that section, and that is going to give a reasonable return to justice in terms of reflecting the criminality and get sensible sentences, then that's better to do. The problem with that approach is that of course, you are then cutting off some victims from your case.

It is interesting to note, however, how Pros-05's conceptualisation of 'reasonable outcomes' and 'reasonable returns' is focused on the context of available resources/speed. They went on to explain how this affects the question of whether it is within the public interest to prosecute, within the Code for Crown Prosecutors:

> [it's] trying to build the case within a reasonable timescale, that is a fair reflection of the criminality involved. It might not be all of it, but it will yield, within the public interest test, a sufficient outcome.

Whilst it is true that 'cost can be a relevant factor when making an overall assessment of the public interest' and 'in a case involving multiple suspects, prosecution might be reserved for the main participants in order to avoid excessively long and

[64] L Welsh, *Access to Justice in Magistrates' Courts: A Study of Defendant Marginalisation*, Kindle edn (Hart Publishing, 2021) 83.

[65] ibid 85.

[66] McConville et al, *The Case for the Prosecution* (n 28) 156.

[67] Bourdieu, *The Logic of Practice* (n 34) 58.

complex proceedings',[68] Pros-05's view of what was insufficiently serious suggests an interesting prosecution *habitus*:

> If the 18 people are all involved in a £10m fraud, the answer will be yes. If the last six to seven of them are money launderers and the quantum is £50k or less … I think really, if you apply the code, you probably shouldn't have put that amount before the court. If you've got people whose criminality is at that level, you almost have to take the view that those people have got lucky. You can't prosecute everyone: it's just finite resources.

On its face, this might sound a reasonable argument. However, juxtaposed against eg the (in comparison) extremely low-value shoplifting etc that is prosecuted every day in the magistrates' court, it becomes harder to justify £50k money laundering as insignificant. Instead, we can see that financial and resourcing concerns in terms of what is and is not worth prosecuting have become a key part of the Crown Court prosecutor's *habitus* – one which might not have been the case a few years ago, when cuts were less severe and (Pros-05 went on to note) 18-hander prosecutions were more frequent.

More overt targets exist here too, which have consequences for how resources are allocated:

> Pros-03: it's more process-driven rather than quality-driven. We have a case management system where theoretically every case that's registered on there, goes towards budget projections, every case that's finalised, we get paid for. And some of those financial dynamics extend to how some of the staff theoretically are justified.

Hence, much like in the magistrates' court, the imperative becomes getting a case 'finalised' rather than necessarily the most appropriate offence, sentence, etc. The amount of time spent at various junctures is then also strictly controlled and reviewed:

> Pros-03: You've got these arbitrary seven, 21, or 28 days [internal deadlines]. Otherwise, we don't meet performance targets locally, which means we don't meet performance targets nationally, which then means emails have to be sent and questions asked why.

As Pros-03 went on to explain, the workload management model did not reflect the reality of the work the CPS had to do, eg in supporting witnesses:

> You can't put any kind of performance target, or economic value to that, because you met the witness and they were upset, so you didn't just go into your usual spiel that you would give a witness. You sat there and you talked to them, you got them straight and you sorted them out. And *then* you went into, 'right this is what's going to happen today, this is what we need from you today, this is what you're going to do today'. But that whole process could take an hour.
>
> Interviewer: And the way your work is defined, it's assuming that that's going to take, what? 20 minutes?
>
> Pros-03: Yeah exactly and then of course you are expected to keep on top of all your other work. You've [still] got the deadlines. You can't pass on your work to anyone else, because they too are subject to the same sort of pressured deadline.

[68] CPS, *Code for Crown Prosecutors* (2018) [4.14](f).

Unfortunately, prosecution barristers did not have much chance to do this either:

> Pros+Def-Bar-05: as an advocate you don't really have the time to sit down and talk to the victim, particularly if they're a vulnerable victim or witness, they may need quite a lot of time. It's difficult to find that.

Targets and box-ticking also extended to prosecution barristers. Pros+Def-Bar-03 gave the example of announcing custody time limit (CTL) dates:[69]

> The CPS want you to announce in open court, at every hearing, the CTL date. It's completely irrelevant at many hearings, but they just want it to be announced. They have a target and a tick box about it being announced … I have known of people that have got an email from a District Crown Prosecutor saying, 'I have found out that you didn't announce the custody time limit at ['Pointless Hearing'], on X date. I would like to know why?'

Hence, in much the same way as we have seen in other contexts, the prosecutor here who, for example, is inclined to spend time providing the support the witness needs, which ultimately supports the public interest and overall goals of the CPS, falls behind with their work compared to those inclined to just give the usual 'spiel' and move on. A *habitus* focused on time, targets and box-ticking is prioritised and, eventually, as Pros+Def-Bar-03 noted in relation to the District Crown Prosecutor, internalised.

Similarly, having internalised the absolute importance of such targets and performance measures, some become highly risk-averse or adopt strategies to cover their backs for fear of missing them, and higher workloads aggravate this further:

> Pros-03: the pressure is such, they've got so many of these … the culture is now to be risk adverse, to flag that up to someone at the next level, who will then flag it up to the next level. And that way, if you have missed something, someone else has signed off on it.

Pros-02 reported similarly on their own practice, noting that part of this was formalised. Some things were required (by policy) to be approved from higher up:

> Anything that looks a bit scary, you would tend to get approved, and have to get approved. The negative is that you can't just get on with your work. You have to wait for various approval levels.

[69] Under Prosecution of Offences Act 1985, s 22, those remanded in custody prior to trial are subject to time limits. If the CPS are not ready for trial by then they must apply to court to extend the limit. Announcing the CTL date reflects guidance to prosecution advocates on the basis of agreed protocols with the CPS and HMCTS: CPS, *Custody Time Limits National Standard for the Effective Management of Prosecution Cases Involving Custody Time Limits* (2020) and CPS, *Handling Cases with Custody Time Limits: A Guide for Advocates Representing the Prosecution* (2014) 2. Failure to do so is regarded by the CPS as a 'significant failing' by the advocate. As this guidance suggests, there are benefits to announcing CTL dates in court (for listing purposes). However, the risk (as illustrated by Pros+Def-Bar-03) is that having a target to do so at every single hearing can become a 'tick-box' process and (as an important metric) be given undue prominence by advocates at the expense of the other important prosecution work discussed in this chapter that they perceive they are unable to find time to do.

Again, something which starts out formal eventually becomes ingrained and spreads to practices and dispositions generally.[70] It is absorbed like air and becomes 'common sense': of *course* I would seek approval.[71] Unfortunately, as Hodgson notes of such fragmented approaches to case ownership, whilst 'in theory, this looks to provide additional guarantees' through checks and balances, in reality the opposite occurs: 'case preparation and prosecution is fragmented, with no case ownership, and so no clear point of responsibility'.[72]

Of course, targets and box-ticking can be fought against in just the same way as we saw in the previous chapter in relation to CPS targets with magistrates' court work. Pros-04 did not think much of league tables for area performance etc:

> There are league tables etc like you wouldn't believe … there are league tables for [charging decision turnaround times] as well and you might get an angry email saying, 'this officer's waited more than 28 days for his charging decision'… we've got a bloody table for how often you go to the toilet!

Hence, they did not pay much attention to them:

> I don't see them; I'm not interested in seeing them quite frankly. It's just more stuff to worry about if you do that.

However, this is not without consequence. Those who focus on meeting targets are more likely to secure promotion etc. Equally, even just surviving where you are requires some engagement with eg those CTL targets, even for Pros-04:

> I've just had an email ping in about a custody case [from my manager]. They're saying, 'what's happening with it?' So that gives you an idea of how seriously it's taken. It's not for trial for about 40 days …
>
> Interviewer: so even though you say you don't pay too much attention to them, it still impacts on you, because the people above you are?
>
> Pros-04: Yeah that's right and they are assessed in it as well … how they are managing those beneath them in terms of those key performance indicators, and they pass them onto you.

In order to survive (never mind thrive) at the CPS, such targets cannot be completely ignored, even if arbitrary. Hence, just as with targets in relation to magistrates' court work, interviews suggest that it is the individual with a *habitus* which focuses on these who will survive and progress in their career. Others must catch up in their own time, endure a hard time from management, their instructing

[70] Similar to what Porter found in relation to issuing witness summonses (to cover the prosecutor's back). Even those who ultimately become trusted with discretion on this will very rarely exercise it. In order to get that discretion in the first place, they must embrace the very working practices which discourage using it: A Porter, 'Prosecuting Domestic Abuse in England and Wales: Crown Prosecution Service "Working Practice" and New Public Managerialism' (2019) 28 *Social & Legal Studies* 493, 505.

[71] P Bourdieu and T Eagleton, 'In Conversation: Doxa and Common Life' (1992) 191 *New Left Review* 111, 115.

[72] J Hodgson, *The Metamorphosis of Criminal Justice: A Comparative Account* (Oxford University Press, 2020) 165.

CPS lawyer, etc. These dispositions are relentlessly drummed into prosecutors until they are no longer questioned. The target then risks being perceived as an end in itself (or at least a shield from criticism, rather like the summonses in domestic abuse cases discussed in the previous chapter), rather than just an analysis tool. Over time, Bourdieu's work would suggest this becomes unquestioned 'common sense'.[73] It affects the way individuals perceive and understand their world, work, options and actions. It colours the way they interpret and apply the Code for charging decisions. Such targets are absorbed into the dominant and successful *habitus* 'like air',[74] perhaps without even realising, and are then difficult to see beyond.

G. Gold Dust and Loss-making Defence Cases

As noted initially, Crown Court work, particularly trials, was generally considered worthwhile in a way that police station and magistrates' court work was not:

> Pros+Def-Bar-02: trials are a good way to get paid, and they obviously command the biggest fee.

Nonetheless, not all Crown Court work was and the effect of austerity is to heighten the stakes such that only the profitable parts are prioritised. As *CLAR* found, cases without a high PPE count were of little value to solicitors (given that is the main proxy for complexity under the Litigators' Graduated Fee Scheme, LGFS).[75] For this reason, *CLAR* recommended replacing the scheme with one similar to magistrates' court fees.[76] Hence, the stakes for securing those trials with eg a large PPE count are extremely high for solicitors. Def-Sol-04 noted that it was the only thing which kept firms going:

> They are gold dust. If we can get one of those, that is pay day … most small firms are kept afloat by those.

On the other hand, like in the magistrates' courts, burglary was frequently cited as an example that was not worth having:

> Def-Sol-01: two-day burglary in the Crown Court will bill jack shit.
>
> … you're relying on getting that big work in. It's a gamble. It's a lottery.

There are many other examples and nor did this necessarily operate in the way one might expect: more serious = more valuable. For example, fraud was considered better than murder, due to the likelihood of higher PPE counts:

> Def-Sol-15: fraud pays better than murder, because fraud you've got lots of pages. The fact that there's 25,000 pages of bank accounts which you skim through because that's

[73] Bourdieu, *The Logic of Practice* (n 34) 58.
[74] Bourdieu and Eagleton, 'Doxa and Common Life' (n 71) 115.
[75] Bellamy, *CLAR* (n 38) [12.21].
[76] ibid [12.24].

> not really where the eye of the storm is, that's treated as a measure of how you should be paid.

Similar was said in relation to child sexual offences, which were very serious, taxing and complicated, but had a comparatively small PPE count (and therefore, fee) when compared to fraud:

> Def-Sol-06: the fee for a five-day trial, for a sexual offence with a child complainant was £3200. Now you just have to think how much work is involved in that with 200 pages of evidence. Because some cases, like big fraud cases have got huge amounts of pages, and that's where firms can actually make some money.

Equally, despite less emphasis on PPE for the Advocates' Graduated Fee Scheme (AGFS), similar criticisms were made by barristers in relation to very serious, difficult, cases having relatively low fees:

> Def-Bar-04: It doesn't pay to be in a long murder. The level of responsibility and stress is considerable, with relatives all around on both sides and the seriousness of the consequences: life imprisonment or a person walking free … I prefer fraud cases because fraud cases continue to be remunerated at a higher rate or similar rates to murder.

Another issue, as Def-Bar-04 notes, is that such cases are more unpleasant to do for lawyers, regardless of the monetary value. As noted above in relation to TLC, the emotional labour is not accounted for.

Hence, in terms of *habitus*, we can at this point conclude that those predisposed towards chasing those 'gold dust' cases, at the expense of the 'jack shit' (as Def-Sol-01 put it) ones, will survive or make money and those who are not, will not. A common-sense emerges that these cases are valuable and others are not. How does this work in practice? For those who are more senior, it is possible to focus on the gold dust cases. For example, fraud VHCCs and privately funded work:

> Def-Sol-05: Since I've left [Firm], I've survived from private work more than legal aid [but] my legal aid work is going to be fruitful soon, because of the VHCCs.

At the same time, these people can eliminate or cut down on the poorly paying (although, as we have seen, not necessarily less serious) cases:

> Def-Bar-04: I haven't done burglary for a long time [or] lower levels of assault below wounding with intent
>
> Def-Sol-21: I'm sure there are lawyers out there who say 'I'm not going to do [burglary]'… If somebody came to my door and said 'could you represent me on this?', I could say 'no, I'm really busy at the moment; I can't', but we've never done that.

Often the result is that somebody less experienced does the work instead. The case gets:

> Pros+Def-Bar-07: knocked down from someone who's more senior all the way down to someone who's low enough on the ladder that they need the experience and they'll take the case no matter what.

The less experienced taking on such matters is all very well, even natural, if the case is not that serious/complicated. However, as we saw above, there is not always a logic (in terms of seriousness/complexity) to what pays well and what does not, even for extremely complicated cases such as murder and child sexual offences. The results are therefore unsettling:

> Def-Bar-02: I have had a few cases where I'm sure that they were innocent and they probably needed, in a couple of cases, more senior counsel than me and because of legal aid … I don't know if those kinds of counsel are going to get the case.

Alternatively, others grit their teeth and do the case regardless, often at a loss.

> Def-Sol-20: I'm probably going to be paid an absolute pittance for it and that is all because of cuts really … when the boss comes and goes 'right, why have you only made this amount this month?', you have to face up to the fact that it's because you've had cases like that … the case will be a massive loss.

Like prosecution targets/box-ticking, it is the individual with a *habitus* which focuses on chasing the good cases and avoiding the bad ones who succeeds here. Others will lose money, get awkward questions from managers and fall behind as the financial stress levels ratchet up. Just as we saw in the magistrates' court, over time, such client commoditisation becomes unquestioned 'common sense'.[77]

H. Less Experienced and Reduced Staff

We saw that austerity also bites in magistrates' court criminal practice via the experience of the lawyers involved and their training. This was equally a problem for Crown Court work, despite it being more serious.

In terms of defence, Def-Sol-06 spoke of paralegals and clerks being left with 'hundreds of pages of evidence over a weekend', after it was served late. They went on to explain that having more experienced lawyers working on these (in order to prepare them 'properly') could not be financially justified:

> It doesn't pay for somebody with my experience to be doing Crown Court work. I would usually keep hold of one or two Crown Court files, maybe three or four at a max, but just the amount of work that's involved to prepare them properly, is just not worth it.

Partly, this is a result of prioritising work, but cuts also lead to workforce reductions, which likely aggravates the problem:

> Def-Sol-22: four to three years ago, we had 45 people in this business. We've now got 20.
>
> Interviewer: Okay. So, how do you cope then if you've lost all that staff and fees are down?
>
> Def-Sol-22: You do more work, each fee earner.

[77] Bourdieu, *The Logic of Practice* (n 34) 58.

This has a knock-on effect on the advocates presenting the case when it gets to court:

> Pros+Def-Bar-03: they have very junior people doing some legal work, like drafting applications and so on. Not up to it. Not qualified enough. Not even solicitors. The bad character applications and hearsay applications are drafted by caseworkers. They may be very experienced (and so *some* of them are very good at it), but the base level is quite low.

Relatedly, the support of expert witnesses was also impacted, both in terms of time available for solicitors to source them and the limited rates paid by the LAA for them.

> Def-Sol-20: we went through about five psychologists before I had someone who would do it for the money that the LAA are offering. So what's happening there? I'm spending loads more time – which is unprofitable out of my fixed fee – finding an expert.

Def-Bar-05 noted the consequences this had on their own practice:

> The case I've literally just finished today, which is a sentence on a robbery case where the client is 16 … to be honest I would have liked to have got a psychological report on my defendant, but it's one of those where it would have been very difficult.

Other research suggests that prosecution has also suffered in terms of staffing and support.[78] Beyond raw numbers, Quirk noted a loss of experience/qualifications of staff even in 2006: legally qualified staff were doing less, with greater reliance on executive officers.[79] This accords with what interviewees reported in the current study. Pros-03 considered the police and CPS to have similar issues in this regard. The problem is both quantity and experience of staff:

> we've lost a lot of good staff, a lot of experienced staff [and] even where they have been replaced in number, you've lost the most experienced staff … it isn't an equivalent replacement. Experience counts for almost everything in the criminal justice system.

This is made worse by, as we saw in relation to magistrates' court work, a corresponding reduction in ability to provide training:

> Pros-03: because we're so desperate, you join, and you are thrown in at the deep end … the CPS will say 'this is what you need to know to do your job, so this is what we will teach you'. They don't teach you, or expect you to learn anything around that … that made you better at your job, made you more experienced at your job.

Staffing levels then have impacts later in the process at court, even for seemingly basic things:

> Pros-05: We do have resourcing problems with paralegal officers … the last thing counsel can afford to do is say to the judge, I'm sorry Your Honour, I'm going to have

[78] Newman and Dehaghani, *Experiences of Criminal Justice* (n 24) 61.

[79] Quirk, 'The Significance of Culture' (n 43) 53.

> to go and do some printing myself and I'll come back in the court room with sixteen copies of what I need to print in 40 minutes time'!

These concerns were reflected by prosecution barristers, who reported how such basic issues could cause substantial problems for themselves, the case and victims:

> Pros+Def-Bar-07: little things make a huge difference. If there's no one in the CPS room because they haven't got enough people and the photocopier is broken, then the case you're trying to present comes to a halt. I prosecuted on my own a five-handed drugs case some years ago, and it was five weeks of sheer unadulterated hell with the judge giving me a hard time in circumstances where I had no support.

As with this issue in relation to magistrates' court work, this is not a criticism of inexperienced prosecution or defence staff, many of whom I am sure do their best. It is not their fault if they are required to do too much too soon and without much training; and we all have to start somewhere anyway. The point is that the incentive to use cheap (in terms of salary) or inexperienced staff exists and those who do so may benefit (for defence, in terms of profits and, for prosecution Areas, in terms of budget targets and league tables) at the expense of those who provide more experienced (and therefore expensive) staff. Equally, the work of those more experienced lawyers who nonetheless do this work is undervalued. It all feeds into a theme we have seen throughout this book: that austerity encourages some kinds of work to be regarded (arbitrarily) as unimportant. Those who simply don't care, put on the bare minimum training, or send inexperienced lawyers out will profit at the expense of those who do.

I. Plea Advice

i. Guilty Plea Incentives

Just like in magistrates' courts, there are overt incentives for defendants themselves to plead guilty in Crown Court, with a one third 'discount' on sentences (provided the plea comes at the first opportunity, otherwise it is less), or a change in type of sentence, from custody to community order, for example.[80] Quite apart from any pressure or advice from the lawyer, this itself can be criticised for being highly coercive.[81] It is also ignorant of the fact that individuals are capable of admitting things they have not done in response to such incentives.[82] In psychological tests, Schneider and Zottoli found 'a false guilty plea rate just over 11 per cent, with

[80] Sentencing Council, 'Reduction in Sentence for a Guilty Plea – First Hearing on or after 1 June 2017' (2017); Sentencing Act 2020, s 73.

[81] R Helm, 'Conviction by Consent? Vulnerability, Autonomy and Conviction by Guilty Plea' (2019) 83(2) *Journal of Criminal Law* 161.

[82] R Schneider and T Zottoli, 'Disentangling the Effects of Plea Discount and Potential Trial Sentence on Decisions to Plead Guilty' (2019) 24 *Legal and Criminological Psychology* 288.

nearly a fifth of innocent participants pleading guilty in some conditions'.[83] Recall also the empirical example from Jones in the previous chapter illustrating this:

> I'm saying to you now I'm innocent, but I pleaded guilty because my barrister advised me if I did that, and that the police came forward with an offer at the last minute and he said 'If you plead you'll get a suspended sentence', and to me it was more important, rather than standing up for a principle, to be there for my daughter.[84]

Not much pressure may in practice be required. As McConville et al highlighted: 'the fact that defence lawyers, objectively viewed, may not have to employ great pressure on defendants does not undermine the power of the subjectively experienced pressure'.[85] These systemic pressures may also be greater in Crown Court. Research by the Sentencing Council with judges found that, whilst magistrates neither encouraged nor discouraged guilty pleas, several Crown Court and district judges 'gave the impression of proactively encouraging them', for example emphasising potential difference in sentence type and duration.[86] Problems in other areas can then further compound these pressures. As Newman and Dehaghani found, 'lack of disclosure renders more difficult the task of ascertaining whether a guilty plea is the best possible option'.[87]

As a starting point therefore, the ethics are muddied. As Barry notes, if lawyers work in a coercive system they do their clients a disservice by pretending otherwise: 'one would not expect a patient to take choices about their care without knowing the risks that they exposed themselves to'.[88] The problem is that there are also personal/self-interested reasons for defence lawyers to tailor their plea advice, and tight margins aggravate this. Given research from the Sentencing Council that 'the main factor determining plea' was perceived likelihood of conviction and that 'weight of the evidence against them and their representatives' legal advice on this point were pivotal to this judgement'[89] the potential for manipulation is clear. Barristers at both a junior and senior level acknowledged such pressure to selfishly advise guilty pleas existed at Crown Court, and was aggravated by cuts, but did not consider it was necessarily given in to:

> Def-Bar-04: There are always instances where you could capitulate, advise a client to plead guilty and it would be better for your bottom line, but your professional integrity says you just don't do that. I'm not just saying this is something that's recent in terms of the dilemma itself – it's always been there – but these further cuts in legal aid have made it more likely.

[83] ibid 297.

[84] S Jones, 'Under Pressure: Women Who Plead Guilty to Crimes They Have Not Committed' (2011) 11 *Criminology & Criminal Justice* 82.

[85] McConville et al, *The Case for the Prosecution* (n 28) Ch 8.

[86] Sentencing Council, 'Research to Support the Development of a Guideline for Reduction in Sentence for a Guilty Plea' (2017) 1.

[87] Newman and Dehaghani, *Experiences of Criminal Justice* (n 24) 168.

[88] J Barry, 'A Barrister's Role in the Plea Decision: An Analysis of Drivers Affecting Advice in the Crown Court' (PhD Thesis, University of London, 2010) 108.

[89] Sentencing Council, 'Research on Guilty Plea Guideline' (n 86) 8.

On the other hand, the literature is full of examples of manipulation. Eg, Newman and Dehaghani were told that easily confused clients could be manipulated more easily.[90] Similarly, commenting on a barrister interviewee who said 'I would crack it early enough so I could guarantee I'd have more work', Alge notes this suggests the barrister regarded 'cracking a trial' in his financial interests 'as something he could actively seek to achieve, rather than the decision to plead guilty being solely the defendant's'.[91]

However, there is also much to suggest that, in relation to Crown Court, if this is done, it is out of a belief that it is for the defendant's own good rather than the lawyer's interest. For example, Barry split interviewees into those who tended towards a 'persuasive approach' as opposed to a 'facilitative approach'. The persuaders felt duty-bound to encourage those with a hopeless case to plead guilty: 'giving advice is persuading them to my view. I accept that and that is in fact what I'm doing'.[92] Even the 'facilitators' believed barristers should 'not pull any punches' in advising on plea. The difference was that facilitators would (eventually) agree to go along with a hopeless case.[93] As Alge notes, if defendants are perceived as 'inept and incapable of making rational decisions', lawyers may consider it ethical to impose their own view of what is best on clients.[94] The problem, as we also saw in relation to guilty pleas in the magistrates' court, is one's perception of what is likely to occur at trial or what is in a client's best interests can be influenced by one's own *interest*/*illusio*. Those willing to follow financial incentives have a more attuned *habitus* to the *field* and will financially benefit. Such a *habitus* inclines people to behave in this way because it affects the way an individual understands their world. The lawyer here is not necessarily thinking <I will advise what makes me most money>, but, where it happens to be financially advantageous too, that choice can be rationalised: <pleading guilty is for his own good anyway>. As noted in Chapter 2, 'the nature of *illusio* … over time prevents the players from developing a healthy view of the game once they are heavily vested and entrenched in it'.[95] Individuals' *interests* can guide their interpretation of 'the facts', whether they appreciate this or not. Similarly, *conatus* suggests *habitus* operates to ensure that people adjust their expectations to match their *field* conditions and therefore come to accept the way things are. This need not be deliberately or consciously; rather, it is simply social momentum keeping us on the same trajectory.[96] Successes and failures (whether

[90] Newman and Dehaghani, *Experiences of Criminal Justice* (n 24) 169.

[91] D Alge, 'The Effectiveness of Incentives to Reduce the Risk of Moral Hazard in the Defence Barrister's Role in Plea Bargaining' (2013) 16 *Legal Ethics* 162, 172. NB: a trial is said to have 'cracked' when it does not take place, despite the defendant initially pleading not guilty. Trials may crack because the defendant changes their plea to guilty or the prosecution drops the case by offering no evidence, etc. See Criminal Legal Aid (Remuneration) Regulations 2013, Sch 1 and 2, para 1(1). Whether a trial is considered 'cracked' will often affect the classification of the lawyer's fee under the Regulations.

[92] Barry 'A Barrister's Role in the Plea Decision' (n 88) 118–20.

[93] ibid 123, 149.

[94] Alge, 'The Effectiveness of Incentives' (n 91) 175.

[95] T Greenhalgh et al, 'Orthodoxy, *Illusio*, and Playing the Scientific Game: A Bourdieusian Analysis of Infection Control Science in the COVID-19 Pandemic' (2021) 6 *Wellcome Open Research* 126.

[96] P Bourdieu, *Homo Academicus* (P Collier tr, Stanford University Press, 1988) 176.

that individual's fault or not) are rationalised and this rationalisation implicitly accepts and is influenced by the financial (*field*) conditions being worked within.

ii. Not Guilty Plea Incentives

However, what is interesting is that, unlike the magistrates' court, financial incentives often tend to point towards not guilty pleas in the Crown Court. Despite the above large volume of commentary and understandable concern about forcing guilty pleas and the undeniable systemic pressures on defendants to do so, if lawyers *were* being selfish, the above examples would be the exception rather than the rule. *CLAR* found that, mechanically/financially, the LGFS usually incentivises *against* advising early guilty pleas.[97] *CLAR* considered the focus on PPE as the LGFS's 'central weakness', which 'incentivises firms to try to obtain cases with a large amount of served material, and then delay the outcome until the trial begins'.[98] Likewise, for advocates, it found: 'the AGFS is geared to the concept of the trial, with the consequence that a trial is paid considerably better than a guilty plea'.[99]

There are also practical reasons why not guilty pleas may be preferable.[100] Many noted how difficult it was to get across to clients the strength of the evidence against them. In contrast, accepting or encouraging not guilty pleas was easy:

> Def-Sol-19: it's not a very difficult exercise to persuade a client, to say 'well, it looks a bit difficult, but I think we've got a good run here! I think we should run it!' Even though it might be very much in [clients'] interests to say 'early guilty plea, first opportunity in the Crown Court, maximum mitigation and maximum discount on the sentence', but it means a reduction in fee to the solicitor.

Pros+Def-Bar-11 agreed from the advocate perspective:

> you can really sit someone down and go through the evidence with a fine-toothed comb [or] you can just turn to the client and say 'well did you do it?' they'll say 'no of course not' and you go 'right, well you've just given me not guilty instructions, so we'll crack on'.

Hence, even ignoring finance, the easiest course can be to tell clients what they want to hear. Further, as some told Barry, there can be reputational benefits from being known by clients as a fighter.[101] When the above financial incentives (noted by *CLAR*) are added to the mix, literature suggests advice is influenced. For example, one barrister told Newman and Dehaghani that, whilst barristers would never 'advise not to plead guilty in a hopeless case just because he wanted to earn more money', they had 'seen that happen from solicitors'.[102] Contrary to this, Barry's

[97] Bellamy, *CLAR* (n 38) [12.8].
[98] ibid [12.9].
[99] ibid [13.3].
[100] See also Newman and Dehaghani, *Experiences of Criminal Justice* (n 24) 165.
[101] Barry, 'A Barrister's Role in the Plea Decision' (n 88) 227.
[102] Newman and Dehaghani, *Experiences of Criminal Justice* (n 24) 115.

respondents suggested barristers are not excepted: 'some cases crack later than they should because counsel want a cracked trial fee. No question about it'.[103] Inter-professional mudslinging aside, Stephen et al's quantitative economic research on changes to fees in Scotland found a statistically significant increase in not guilty pleas following changes to payment arrangements there, thus concluding: lawyers respond to financial incentives.[104] The qualitative data here bears this out. Most were under no illusions about the financial advantages of Crown Court trials, even if this did not impact their own advice:

> Def-Sol-10: We certainly never advise our clients to take a not guilty plea if they were guilty, because of financial … encouragement for us to do so … but if the clients would plead not guilty there would certainly be cheers [chuckle] in the office.

Def-Sol-11 provided an example of how high the stakes could be:

> For the best part of 12 months, we prepared a case. The page count was extremely high, the effort needed to prepare it was extremely intense, and we literally prepared that case to the door of court. On the day of trial, we were confronted with the Crown offering a deal that was so good no solicitor in the world in good conscience could possibly have turned it down. He didn't even go to jail, he was given a suspended sentence, when he was looking at four or five years! … we pleaded at the door of court and were paid £12,000. If the case had gone to trial, we would have been paid £40,000. So we lost £28,000 having prepared the case to the door of court. 2 months of work. And that happens all too frequently. I have a case starting at the Crown Court at [City] tomorrow and we've been told it's going to fold, which means I'm gonna lose £12,000 tomorrow, even though in that instance, we've had the case for two years.

The financial reality is clearly keenly appreciated here: the potential money from the trial fees is not regarded as an impossibility, but something clearly achievable that has been 'lost' by acting ethically. Whilst Def-Sol-11 insisted this did not impact on advice given (by any firm) in those sorts of circumstances, they did acknowledge that pleas could be delayed by other firms: 'firms are telling their clients not to plead guilty at the PTPH, so they get a cracked trial fee [later]. Now that I do know is happening'. Others were even more candid:

> Def-Sol-07: there are some solicitors that I know do this (not in [City] thankfully) … who will advise their clients to take it to trial, and probably it's not the right thing to do, so they end up benefitting from it for giving poor advice.

Def-Sol-04 provides an illuminating illustration of how these incentives can operate:

> I decide that maybe I'm not happy with the state of the evidence, and I can't really advise my client to plead guilty [at the magistrates' court], so we withhold our plea, but we get

[103] Barry, 'A Barrister's Role in the Plea Decision' (n 88) 203.

[104] F Stephen et al, 'Incentives, Criminal Defence Lawyers and Plea Bargaining' (2008) 28 *International Review of Law and Economics* 212, 218.

> to the Crown Court, and we plead at the Crown Court instead. So, exactly the same number of hearings, suddenly I get a litigator fee of £500, and an advocacy fee of £500. So suddenly I've made £1000 instead of £400. Which am I going to do? Now what's the dis-benefit? Well, my client doesn't get his full credit for his guilty plea. Do I really care about that? I don't [care] because I know that I need to be in business next week and the week after, and the week after that. So yeah, he loses a bit of credit, but I can probably make up for that in my speech. One third credit's a notional thing; it depends on where you start. If I can persuade the judge the starting point's lower, well it doesn't matter that he only gets 25 per cent credit. So we're using financial decisions like that to decide how we advise clients.

Like others, Def-Sol-04 did not foresee any difficulty in getting most clients to play along:

> Most of them are just content to let you make the decision, and sometimes it *is* the right decision, because I might be able to negotiate with the prosecution a better basis [for the plea]. In which case, OK, I've lost the one third credit; I've got a 25 per cent credit. But suddenly, if the Crown accept that he had a 'lesser role', because I've got that bargaining chip of a not guilty, which I've thrown away if I plead guilty … So there is that as well, it's not all down to money, but trust me, a lot of it is.
>
> Interviewer: And if they both point in the same direction, that's … ?
>
> Def-Sol-04: It's a happy coincidence.

Just like with the guilty plea incentives, this illustrates again how the defence lawyer *habitus* is moulded in an austere field. Goriely et al called these situations *ethically indeterminate*:

> where the choice is between two courses of action, both of which have advantages and disadvantages, and where ethical practitioners genuinely differ about which is the better. In making difficult and evenly-balanced judgements, greater weight is placed on the advantages that flow from a course of action that is in one's own interests. Less weight is placed on those that flow from actions that run contrary to one's interests.[105]

Hence, it is not always as simple as saying that the defence lawyer here calculates what is most financially beneficial to them and then follows that course regardless of client interest. Equally though, as Def-Sol-04 hints at, the situation is not always indeterminate. It might not all be down to money, but 'a lot of it is'. Instead, it is more accurate to say that practitioners' understanding of what 'the facts' actually *are* can be moulded by their *habitus*, which tends towards their own *interest*/*illusio* (in Bourdieusian terms): 'the nature of *illusio* … over time prevents the players from developing a healthy view of the game once they are heavily vested and entrenched in it'.[106] In other words, my argument here goes further than Goriely et al: whether a given situation is or is not ethically indeterminate can itself be a matter of opinion, and practitioners with the *habitus* structured and rewarded by an

[105] T Goriely et al, 'The Public Defence Solicitors' Office: An Independent Evaluation' (Scottish Central Research Unit 2001) 69.
[106] Greenhalgh et al, 'Orthodoxy, *Illusio*, and Playing the Scientific Game' (n 95) 16.

austerity *field* will be more inclined to perceive a given situation as such. Their own and the client's interests can then (as far as the lawyer is concerned) align in a 'happy coincidence'. The *field* encourages and rewards such a disposition via financial gain/survival. Defence lawyers can rationalise their interests with their clients' by taking the view that they will get a better basis of plea by delaying/using it as a bargaining chip, or that they can argue that the facts are less serious, etc. Individuals' interests can guide their interpretation of 'the facts', whether they appreciate this or not.

The position for advocates was similar:

> Pros+Def-Bar-03: You get a case. Defendant looks very guilty. You have two options. You can either give them very, very firm advice, and they plead: you don't earn an awful lot. You don't give that very, very firm advice, you have a trial: you earn lots of money.

Def-Bar-05: considered financial incentives a 'daily problem' for criminal legal aid advocates, which austerity aggravates:

> the less money there is, exacerbates that particular problem and you're conscious when you've got a case which represents a certain sum of money, and there aren't that many cases like that around anymore, because of the cuts … you're less willing to give up what that case might be should it go to trial.

Def-Bar-05 was very conflicted as to whether advocates resisted this pressure or not, reflecting how *habitus* has a more sub-conscious rather than conscious influence on the way one perceives of the world (and is all the more effective for that):

> they'll be just a sort of unconscious working for something like that where you probably don't do as good a job as you might otherwise do when there is a financial incentive working against you. It shouldn't, but of course, you get paid much more money if the case goes to trial than if they plead guilty and of course no-one does that but the way that it's set up doesn't assist.

Others, such as Pros+Def-Bar-09, were more resigned to the matter:

> You can't avoid it. You know in your soul [laughs]. You know exactly what everything's worth and there are times – well, put it this way – there's someone who says they want to plead guilty. I would never persuade them to plead not guilty, even if it was in my financial interest. But if they're not very sure, I will outline the two scenarios, but I probably wouldn't seek to persuade them to plead one way or the other if it wasn't in my financial interest. Although I would never persuade anyone out of acting against my interests, I probably wouldn't persuade them into it.

However, as with previously considered incentives, the ethics here are debateable. For example, in the early 2000s, having interviewed barristers about their work, Tague concluded that it may sometimes be in a barrister's self-interest to get their client to plead not guilty in the Crown Court (for both financial and career development reasons),[107] but *equally* sometimes advantageous to the defendant

[107] P Tague, 'Barristers' Selfish Incentives in Counselling Clients' [2008] Crim LR 3, 6, 12.

as well. Tague provided three examples: likelihood of acquittal (in that statistics suggest trying one's luck with the jury can be fruitful); comparative sanction (in that sentences at the end of trial might be lighter if more mitigating evidence can emerge during the trial); and that it is harder to appeal against conviction following a guilty plea.[108] Agreeing with Tague, Barry found that some barristers saw benefit from running trials for the defendant, regardless of financial interest, eg sometimes during a trial 'the judge will see the defendant for the person he really is, and by the same token will see the prosecution witnesses for the people that they are', such that 'the whole complexion of the case' will have changed dramatically enough to make it worth the loss of discount.[109] Nicklas-Carter found similar justifications from interviewees for advising not guilty pleas, for clients' benefit, eg in the absence of adequate disclosure.[110]

Hence, presenting this as a binary choice between prioritising one's own interests or those of one's client is often too simplistic. We have seen many ways here for barristers to justify (to interviewers and, in some cases I suspect, to themselves) courses of action which (just like with their solicitor colleagues) by 'a happy coincidence' (as Def-Sol-04 put it) also follow their own financial interests. As has been a running theme throughout this book, I am sure there are some who simply do not care and follow their own interests all the time (every profession has bad apples). Equally I expect some ignore all financial incentives and only ever act in the client's interests (although, with such a *habitus*, they will be unsuited to an austerity-based *field* and will frequently feel frustrated, burnt out and uncomfortable). Between these poles, it is the group in the middle that is often forgotten (despite the fact that, realistically, they are probably the largest group in most professions/jobs). The group that, by a natural interaction between their *habitus* and their *field* are more and more inclined to see what they want to see. To interpret 'the facts' so that that 'happy coincidence' where everyone wins can be found. Just like the well-intentioned medical scientists who ended up acting unethically (first considered in Greenhalgh et al's work in Chapter 2),[111] the *habitus* conditioned to this field will affect the way 'the facts' are perceived. By operation of *interest/illusio*, those most inclined to view them in such a way as to find that 'happy coincidence' are more likely to stay in business, survive, or even thrive in an austerity *field*.

It should also therefore be apparent why I do not consider that simply tweaking or changing incentives (as the Government belatedly did with incentives in

[108] P Tague, 'Tactical Reasons for Recommending Trials Rather Than Guilty Pleas in the Crown Court' [2006] Crim LR 23, 25.

[109] Barry, 'A Barrister's Role in the Plea Decision' (n 88) 89.

[110] C Nicklas-Carter, 'Efficiency of the English Criminal Courts in a Time of Austerity. Exploring Courtroom Lawyers' Assessment of Government Policy (2010–2017)' (DCrim Thesis, Keele University, 2019) 173.

[111] Greenhalgh et al, 'Orthodoxy, *Illusio*, and Playing the Scientific Game' (n 95).

relation to the fixed fees for electing jury trial and then pleading guilty later)[112] to be sufficient. The dominant *habitus* which survives and thrives in such a field will simply adapt to the new lie of the land unless the more fundamental features of that *field* (including the focus of this book – austerity) are altered. As Bellamy in *CLAR* noted: 'if one tweaks one fee, some other fee will seem out of line. It is almost impossible to avoid anomalies'.[113] Recall also Def-Sol-04's perspective as a practitioner:

> any half decent lawyer, whatever system they come up, will find a way round it to maximise what we get paid. I suppose my criticism of the system we've got at the moment is we have to spend almost as much time working that out as we do doing our job as a lawyer.

The final point to note here is the effect all this has even on those who do not follow the financial incentive (or do not always do so). Every time one does not, (in addition to what is often experienced as direct financial penalties) there is a personal cost in terms of frustration, morale and (ultimately) burnout. Naturally, this makes one less and less inclined to go against such incentives (or even leave the *field* entirely). We now turn to consider this important final issue.

J. Burnout/Demoralisation

Just like with the magistrates' court and police station, a common theme thus far is of some lawyers or firms giving in to financial pressures whereas others disregard them, no matter the cost and terrible hourly rates it equates to. We could conclude, therefore, that lawyers just need to be more dedicated. However, as with other areas already considered, such idealism can be exhausting and demoralising. Previous literature suggests burnout and morale has been an issue for defence lawyers for some time.[114] Additionally, as Harris has noted, the nature of this kind of work is tiring at the best of times.[115] Def-Sol-01 provides an example of the stressful nature of the work for solicitors (aggravated by the imperative for volume from austerity-practice, increasing the numbers of such clients):

> I'm getting calls at 8 o'clock, people stressed, literally losing their shit:
>
> 'I'm going to kill myself [Name], I didn't commit that offence, I've lost everything, everyone's calling me a rapist.'
>
> 'I'm, scared to go out there, I've been accused of this attempted murder, I was at the scene, someone [else] stabbed him, I don't want to be called a grass, if I say anything, I'm scared for my life. The gangs are knocking on my door giving me shit.'

[112] Criminal Legal Aid (Remuneration) (Amendment) Regulations 2022, SI 2022/848.

[113] Bellamy, *CLAR* (n 38) [13.2].

[114] See further discussion in J Thornton, 'Is Publicly Funded Criminal Defence Sustainable? Legal Aid Cuts, Morale, Recruitment and Retention in the English Criminal Law Professions' (2020) 40 *Legal Studies* 230.

[115] L Harris, 'The Emotional Labour of Barristers: An Exploration of Emotional Labour by Status Professionals' (2002) 39 *Journal of Management Studies* 553, 572.

> '[Name], I've been charged with possession with intent to supply class A. I'm a victim of modern slavery; I'm scared to talk to you about it. I didn't tell the police because I'm scared.'
>
> I'm getting these phone calls all the time.

Pros+Def-Bar-09 noted a similar example from an advocate's perspective:

> It's absolutely ghastly. It's very stressful work. I mean, to have to cross-examine a seven-year-old about why she's making up these wicked stories is no joke.

Austerity-driven practices from others (eg prosecution and courts) then worsen this further:

> Pros+Def-Bar-09: I find working like this, always at the last minute, really, pretty unbearable … the whole thing is just like it's tied together with string and you just wait for some moment where something is going to go terribly wrong and you will somehow be left holding that particular parcel as it all goes off in your face … you realise that actually the work itself is just turning into such shit that you're losing the will to live.

Additionally, more bureaucratic concerns, such as the required approvals from the LAA and mechanics of payment can add to personal stress, irrespective of what the rate is (although these will assume greater significance on tighter margins). Solicitors and barristers both noted the frustration caused by, in their view, obstructive behaviour from the LAA:

> Def-Sol-01: we have to justify reviewing the evidence. But … I'm a defence lawyer and I've been served with evidence. In one way or another, I'm going to have to read it.
>
> Def-Bar-06: If there's anything that [the LAA] can quibble about, they will. If there's any problem at all you have to try and speak to them on the telephone. They will only answer their telephone for a certain number of hours per day and they will only deal with a certain number of cases per day … I mean to be honest, they're a bit like a shady backstreet garage!

As Def-Sol-01 implies, some of these issues can seem paradoxical or contradictory: basic logic suggests it is very difficult to know whether evidence needed reviewing or not before one found out what it contained (ie reviewed it). Similar frustration arose from *delayed* payment, both by design (Def-Sol-06) and in practice (Pros+Def-Bar-06):

> Def-Sol-06: you would get paid absolutely nothing between this very measly police station fixed fee and the very conclusion of a Crown Court case, unless you did some sort of interim bill. Everything: reading the case papers, working out whether or not there is any further enquiries that you should be doing, obtaining CCTV, advising the client, speaking to all their members of family who are ringing you up every two minutes, trying to liaise with the prison, going to see them, going to court, bail applications, you've got to start doing your defence case statements and considering unused material, and asking for further evidence, and starting to have conferences in order to prepare the defence case statements. All of that's really front loaded.
>
> Pros+Def-Bar-06: if you're struggling to make a rent payment or if you're trying to plot month-to-month how you're going to run your household budget. The fact the fee

might be a bit lower is probably a bit less important than the fact that you may or may not get it.

Hence, even before considering the effect of fees in numerical terms, the context is frustrating and stressful. In terms of low fees themselves, Harris has noted the way tight financial margins and dedication can grind people down, although interviewees in that study said: 'you always struggle on', even through illness.[116] Can such dedication be sustained? As with other areas we have considered, the data here suggests not, or at least not without cost.

Like the magistrates' court, low morale and burnout can come directly from low fees themselves/profitability and the constant negative impact this has on professional self-worth:

> Def-Sol-20: It's tough, when we look at our figures and our property department's made five times the amount we have in one month. It's a bit soul destroying.

Lack of motivation also comes from the disillusion of (again, due to having to work on high volume) not feeling like one can really make a difference anyway:

> Def-Sol-10: It was very difficult to stay motivated … You wouldn't have time to actually spend some time with a client, or spend some time analysing the evidence properly. You'd ship it off to counsel, and then you'd hope that counsel's good enough to actually deal with a case … And you're not enjoying what you do, because it was effectively a white-collar factory.

Alternatively, one can work into the night most days to provide the service believed to be necessary:

> Def-Sol-08 we all work beyond what our salary, always … me personally, on average, I prepare until 10.30pm.
>
> Interviewer: What, every night?
>
> Def-Sol-08: Almost.
>
> Interviewer: And weekend, or … ?
>
> Def-Sol-08: It depends, but on Sunday night, I would always be preparing for the week ahead/Monday. I think I can cope with it because I love my job so much and I know that if I didn't feel prepared I'm not doing my job properly, and I wouldn't deliver what I wanted to deliver, and I wouldn't get the results that I otherwise would get. But it is a choice. I mean I suppose it is difficult, but you can't do this job if you're not 100 per cent in it … if you're a lawyer or a doctor and you're not tired, you're not doing your job properly. It has to be that way.

Hence, for some, this state of affairs is so ingrained as to just be viewed as natural: it 'has to' be this way. Of course, it does not *have* to be this way at all: resourcing policy and its implementation are not inevitable. It does perhaps *have* to be this way if one wants to prepare thoroughly in the *field* as it stands though and this illustrates how simply expecting lawyers to be more dedicated, ignore financial incentives, etc may not be sustainable. Certainly, Def-Sol-08 was very dedicated,

[116] Harris, 'Emotional Labour' (n 115) 569.

but they were also at an earlier career stage. Def-Sol-15, who was equally committed to good service, but had been in the job much longer, ultimately took a different view on working late into the night:

> You either do the job properly and lose money or you don't do the job properly and the alternative perhaps for some is to work evenings and weekends as a matter of ordinary routine, but you end up so tired that you can't really do it.

As with other areas, the lawyers who reported working late into the night etc and being really dedicated tended to be either early in their career or reflecting on previous practice before they moved away from criminal legal aid (as Def-Sol-15 eventually did). Admirable though it is, it is difficult to see how such an approach can be sustained in the long term.

Defence barristers painted a similar picture. Again, low fees themselves can have a potent impact on people's motivation and sense of self-worth:

> Pros+Def-Bar-07: if you're repeatedly told you are worthless, eventually one's enthusiasm for getting up in the morning and going to do that which is 'worthless' wanes somewhat.

Similarly, struggling to make ends meet on low rates is itself highly stressful:

> Pros+Def-Bar-09: people are all really, really close to the line financially. They won't admit it because it's so humiliating, but it's true … The fees are so low that the financial anxiety is now impossible. It was difficult before and now it's impossible because you're always living – I used to live with this knot of tension in my chest, which was always really about money and <would be I be paid then?> and <did I dare go on holiday at that point because in the summer a lot of very good briefs come through because a lot of other people are on holiday?> and it's not a very nice way to live and it's very stressful.

It also makes people doubt whether they can continue in the long term:

> Pros+Def-Bar-11: everyone continuously contemplates leaving. I don't know anyone who's adamant they're gonna stay.

This is all aggravated by the working practices already considered, which are necessitated by the imperative for high volume and (if motivated) what it takes to do all that to a satisfactory standard:

> Def-Bar-03: people look at their lifestyle and think, <well, I'm still working on a Sunday getting ready for a trial, I work each evening of the week, and I get to Friday and I've got a stressed and tiredness headache, and yet my income has gone down 20 per cent this year, or down 30 per cent this year>.

Nor was prosecution much better. In the first instance, it suffers from the similarly emotionally challenging nature of the work as defence does, which makes higher volumes of work and admin all the more difficult to manage:

> Pros-01: the Crown Court team especially, you were dealing with witnesses, so you would literally know every intimate detail of the offence that was committed against them, because you'd hear them giving their evidence and re-living it and then have to deal with the fallout afterwards when they're finished. It's just the very human aspect of

> it. And unless you physically do that yourself, it's very hard to comprehend what sort of an impact that has when you're already under so much pressure with the admin side of things as well.

Beyond feeling demotivated by the salary, the ways of working necessitated by reductions in human resources caused further stress for Crown Court teams:

> Pros-03: job satisfaction is a lot less. Our pay obviously hasn't increased for some years – not in any measurable way. It's certainly not increased with the increase in productivity that we have had to meet in order to discharge our responsibilities with the changing nature of prosecution, all the usual stuff you would expect to have: work/life balance, etc, stress levels.

Barristers could also see the impact of this by the time they got hold of the case:

> Pros+Def-Bar-05: The CPS in particular really struggle with the fee cuts on their side, so they now have a lack of bodies to do the work, but also a lack of incentive to do it properly and that is partly because they're stretched so thin, it's partly because there's just not enough money and that all takes its toll on people just not feeling terribly enthusiastic about the job; not truly caring if they are going to stay late and do something that really needs doing, making sure that disclosure gets out on time etc.

Hence, as with police station and magistrates' court work, it is not all that surprising if even the most committed lawyers, on both sides, eventually come to accept some of the poor practices detailed elsewhere in this chapter, or, alternatively, just burnout and/or quit. The result is that the *habitus* required to adapt (or survive) in the *field* contributes to a practical logic that accepts little preparation, disclosure failures, lack of TLC, etc as simply the way it has to be. As Pros+Def-Bar-05 went on to note (in relation to both prosecution and defence), this can lead to resigned acceptance of poor conduct as somewhat inevitable:

> You don't feel like the work you're doing is valued and so, like you say, when practitioners are faced with a decision: A is in my client's interest, B is in my financial interest. A lot of people might say 'B', unfortunately. Simply because you don't get the recognition for the fact that you have sat up all night to prepare a particular case in a particular way or gone out of your way to do something that other people wouldn't necessarily do.

Not everyone behaves like this, of course, but, as we have seen, the mental consequences for fighting this can be severe. Bourdieu's concept of *hysteresis* – where one's *habitus* is poorly adapted to a particular field, resulting in distress and disorientation – is alive and well here for Crown Court lawyers on both sides, just as it was for lawyers in the magistrates' courts and police stations.

III. The Logic of Criminal Prosecution and Defence Practice in the Crown Court

Whilst Crown Court work is regarded by many defence lawyers as the only place where money/profits can be made (and therefore upon which police station and magistrates' court work depends), this does not mean the pressures of austerity decrease. If anything, they are worse, as the financial stakes are extremely high: the Crown Court is the difference between having a profit and not. Hence, whilst we see similar issues to magistrates' court work in relation to available time (both to prepare and on the day of court), client support/TLC and staff experience or numbers, this all comes to its head at the highly pressurised point where lawyers advise on pleas – where the difference between a client pleading one way or the other can be between financial survival and liquidation. The temptation to hope, aspire to, or even engineer that 'happy coincidence' where client and lawyer interests combine, in the right sort of 'gold dust' case, is potent.

Prosecutors similarly struggle with budget cuts, even in very serious cases. Time at all stages remains in short supply and this can lead to mistakes, eg with disclosure, like we saw in the magistrates' courts, but with higher stakes. At the same time, in the fight over increasingly limited resources, targets and box-ticking become more important in order to justify a larger portion of the ever-shrinking pie. Meanwhile, report after report from HMCPS Inspectorate suggests a poorer reality. Further, as Welsh, Skinns and Sanders have recently pointed out, post-trial acquittals by jury represent just 36 per cent of Crown Court acquittals.[117] The majority are instead judge-directed/ordered, suggesting inadequate application of the 'evidential test' under the CPS Code.[118] They blame 'bureaucratic pressures', 'professional misjudgement' (which, as we have seen, is more likely with austerity-driven lack of time), or that prosecutors are simply hoping the defendant will plead guilty[119] (perhaps an increasingly vain hope given the findings above in section II.I.ii).

The findings in this chapter thus suggest Newman and Dehaghani's view in relation to defence lawyers in Wales, that '"time" and "money" – are inextricably linked',[120] applies just as much to English Crown Courts and to prosecution as much as defence. Likewise, this chapter also demonstrates that Welsh's argument in relation to magistrates' courts (which itself built upon my own in earlier work) that 'practices that encourage standardisation become an important part of the habitus, providing actors with a sense of appropriate actions to take in particular circumstances'[121] applies very much to Crown Court work by prosecution and defence lawyers too.

Above and beyond that, what the data and Bourdieusian analysis in this chapter demonstrate is a logic of practice for Crown Court work which, just like the magistrates' courts, is (counterintuitively) consistent between the opposing sides of defence and prosecution. Austerity does not necessarily favour one side over

[117] L Welsh et al, *Sanders & Young's Criminal Justice*, 5th edn (Oxford University Press, 2021) 433.
[118] ibid.
[119] ibid.
[120] Newman and Dehaghani, *Experiences of Criminal Justice* (n 24) 111.
[121] Welsh, *Access to Justice in Magistrates' Courts* (n 64) 74, citing J Thornton, 'The Way in Which Fee Reductions Influence Legal Aid Criminal Defence Lawyer Work: Insights from a Qualitative Study' (2019) 46 *JLS* 559.

another. Prosecution disclosure failure might result in a miscarriage of justice, or it might result in a case collapsing. Forceful defence advice on plea may result in a miscarriage of justice, or it may result in a factually guilty defendant pleading (or even being found) guilty at a later stage than they otherwise would have. Ultimately, just like the magistrates' courts, practising in this field encourages and develops a disposition of wearied acceptance of the 'fact' (which those of the high *capital*/dominant *habitus* will perceive as 'common sense')[122] that certain things must be prioritised. Defence lawyers can financially justify little time on anything other than those 'gold dust' cases. Prosecutors must meet targets, process cases at volume and tick the boxes just to firefight through the day. To succeed, this must be accepted (albeit sometimes reluctantly) as 'the way things are'. However, as we saw, the effect of a *habitus* tailored to this environment is more insidious than that. It also assists individuals to manipulate/rationalise this to themselves, perhaps without realising: <it's just 'happy coincidence' that this favours my financial interests too>. The absorption of this 'like air', is very difficult to escape.[123] Even the well-meaning can adapt their dispositions and behaviour to benefit themselves or uphold the status quo without necessarily appreciating this, or when trying to do the opposite.[124] Those who still resist are commendable, but pay a heavy price, demonstrated in the previous section on burnout.

[122] Bourdieu, *The Logic of Practice* (n 34) 58.
[123] Bourdieu and Eagleton, 'Doxa and Common Life' (n 71) 115.
[124] Greenhalgh et al, 'Orthodoxy, *Illusio*, and Playing the Scientific Game' (n 95).

6

The Future of Criminal Court Practice in Austerity

I. Introduction

This chapter considers two key elements of 'the future' and its implications for the logic of criminal court practice. First, the success (or otherwise) of courtroom mitigations that were put in place in response to the COVID-19 pandemic, and to what extent these might mitigate (or aggravate) the effects of austerity we have seen in previous chapters. Second, in the context of austerity, the broader question of sustainability of the criminal law professions in terms of recruitment, retention, etc. I first provide an overview of technology changes in response to COVID-19, before considering these across each stage of the court process (initial hearings, sentencing and trials). I then examine the implications of austerity for sustainability in each profession (solicitors and then barristers) across four key themes emerging from the interview data and relevant literature:

(1) recruitment, retention and (for solicitors) firm solvency;
(2) diversity;
(3) private work; and
(4) hobbyists and altruists.

In terms of sustainability, burnout and demoralisation also play their part. However, whilst this should always be borne in mind, the focus here is on broader/systemic issues of sustainability, given the extensive consideration of burnout and demoralisation in earlier chapters.

II. Measures from COVID-19

A. Summary of Criminal Courts' COVID-19 Mitigations

We have already considered some COVID-19 mitigations in relation to police station advice (Chapter 3). In terms of the courts, the Coronavirus Act 2020 greatly enhanced the scope of what was previously a limited scheme for online work.[1]

[1] Coronavirus Act 2020, Schs 23–24.

Prior to that, there was provision for vulnerable and/or intimidated witnesses to give evidence via video-link where this would improve their evidence[2] and for, in some cases, witnesses abroad to give evidence remotely.[3] There was also scope for other witnesses to give evidence remotely 'in the interests of the efficient or effective administration of justice'[4] and for those in custody to appear from prison via video-link in some ancillary hearings. Whilst these have been permitted for some time, even such limited measures were (and are) not immune from stringent criticism in terms of fairness and effectiveness. For example, a survey, interviews and roundtable discussion with practitioners (and judges) concluded tentatively that (pre-COVID) 'video hearings are prejudicial'.[5] One prosecutor told the researchers: '[p]sychologically, it is easier to do something negative to someone when they are not physically present. When I prosecute a bail matter, I prefer the defendant to be on the [video] link'.[6]

Likewise, both defence and prosecution respondents (and researchers' observations) to Terry et al (reporting on a 2010 pilot of remote courts from police stations) found that the 'physical separation' made communication between prosecution and defence advocates harder, leading to delays and adjournments.[7] Judges equally reported it was sometimes difficult to impose 'authority' remotely and that defendants therefore took the process less seriously.[8] More recently, a 2017 survey of around 200 court workers and users (lawyers, magistrates, defendants, etc) by Transform Justice found that most considered video-link appearances had a negative impact on defendants' ability to communicate (with their lawyer, the Bench, probation, etc) and participate in proceedings. Similarly, most also stated that it was quite or very difficult to discern whether a defendant/offender may have a physical or mental disability if workers were in the courtroom and the defendant/offender appeared by video-link from prison or the police station.[9] The Equality and Human Rights Commission (EHRC), having interviewed and/or surveyed the judiciary, lawyers and defendants similarly found that opportunities to identify impairments and make adjustments are lost or reduced when a defendant appears in court by video-link rather than in person.[10] Lawyers noted 'the separation between the defendant and their solicitor and/or court'.[11] In terms of defendants, the EHRC was so concerned that it concluded video hearings were

[2] Subject to statutory criteria. See Youth Justice and Criminal Evidence Act 1999, Part II.

[3] Criminal Justice Act 1988, s 32(1)(a). See also (and since amended further) the Criminal Justice Act 2003, s 51. In *Kadir* [2022] EWCA Crim 1244 [39], the Court took the view that even giving evidence from abroad via WhatsApp could be permitted in appropriate circumstances today.

[4] Criminal Justice Act 2003, s 51(4).

[5] P Gibbs, 'Defendants on Video – Conveyor Belt Justice or a Revolution in Access?' (Transform Justice, 2017).

[6] ibid.

[7] M Terry et al, 'Virtual Court Pilot Outcome Evaluation' (Ministry of Justice, 2010) 21.

[8] ibid 22.

[9] P Gibbs, 'Vulnerable Defendants and Virtual Justice – A Survey' (Transform Justice, 2017).

[10] Equality and Human Rights Commission, *Inclusive Justice: A System Designed for All* (2020) 208.

[11] ibid 9.

generally unsuitable for many neurodivergent defendants and those with cognitive impairments or mental illness.[12]

Nonetheless, scope for online, video and audio hearings increased dramatically at the height of the pandemic. There was even statutory provision to hold summary trial entirely online by video[13] and online jury trials were seriously considered.[14] Replacement of jury trial with routine trial by judge was also suggested,[15] but ultimately neither measure was used to replace traditional jury trial.[16] However, lawyers (both prosecution and defence) did appear remotely for various hearings, including bail, trials and sentencing.[17] In such cases, the courtroom was open, with judges and staff present, but lawyers, witnesses and defendants potentially appearing via video-link.[18] Given this book's focus on the work of the legal professions, it is these measures that we shall consider in depth here. They provide an interesting illustration of the operation of austerity and what its influence might be as technology continues to change the criminal justice system in future. Indeed, whilst (anecdotally) this practice may have reduced, the COVID-19 power for lawyers and others to appear remotely upon application to the court was permanently retained.[19]

B. Basic Technology Enhancements

To begin with, it is worth noting the general positives for individuals that can flow from more remote/flexible/online working. Many industries discovered the advantages of doing so during the pandemic and criminal law is no exception. For those that embraced it, even something as basic as increased use of videoconferencing made a big difference:

> Def-Sol-05: I've not been into a physical office now to do a day's work for a year and a half. And I never will again. Clients either see me at court or they see me at the police station …

[12] ibid 10.

[13] Coronavirus Act 2020, Sch 23, para 8. To my knowledge, this power was never used in practice, as it is considerably easier for 2–3 magistrates (or one district judge) to social distance between themselves and other court users than it is for a jury of 12.

[14] eg L Mulcahy et al, 'Exploring the Case for Virtual Jury Trials during the COVID 19 Crisis. An Evaluation of a Pilot Study Conducted by JUSTICE' (Oxford Brookes University and University of Oxford, 2020).

[15] eg Henriques J (retired), 'Judge-Only Trials Would Let Courts Get Back to Work' (*The Times*, 1 May 2020), a view which was defended by former Law Lords Mackay and ('to the hilt') Brown, 'Letters' (*The Times*, 2 May 2020). Funnily enough, the most enthusiastic advocates for this were judges ….

[16] Coronavirus Act 2020, Sch 23, para 2 expressly prohibited jury members from participation via live-link.

[17] ibid, Sch 23, para 2, permitted *anyone* (as opposed to, pre-2020, 'a witness (other than the defendant)') to take part in criminal proceedings via live-link if the court permitted it and the proceedings were not excluded by para 8.

[18] See Magistrates Association (MA), 'Magistrates' Courts and Covid-19' (2022) 20 for an indication of prevalence of various parties appearing remotely in magistrates' courts.

[19] Police, Crime, Sentencing and Courts Act 2022, s 200.

This applied to all cases, big or small:

> all of the meetings and all of the preparation, and all of the instruction-taking, basically, I did it online. Big VHCC money laundering case, my client's in [other City]. I've only met him [in-person] once.
>
> On the smaller ones, where I've maybe represented someone for a road traffic even, I've done a couple of those, and that's been great.

One can question how happy the clients are with this arrangement of course (although for Def-Sol-05's private practice, they could go elsewhere fairly easily if they were unhappy). However, such arrangements may operate to clients' benefit too in terms of time spent on their cases, as Pros+Def-Bar-03 noted in relation to prison visits:

> You can probably only travel to a prison once or twice in the preparation for a case … more often than not, you are spending twice as long travelling than you are actually in the conference … you've wasted effectively half a day in just travel and waiting and that's under-productive. Under-productive time means you're not really preparing that person's case for that time.

On the other hand, we should bear in mind the imperative for volume discussed in previous chapters. Time gained from not having to travel might be used to prepare that client's case more thoroughly or, with the extremely tight margins of criminal defence work, it might be spent packing in more cases. Certainly those with the austerity *habitus* we noted in previous chapters are likely to see this as an opportunity for the latter. There is also the fact that such efficiency depends upon the prison service itself being adequately resourced and set-up for it. For Def-Sol-09, this had yet to occur:

> somebody will appear in court one day, can be remanded in custody to the Crown Court for four or five weeks later, and I can't get a prison visit for seven weeks … the Ministry of Justice, the prisons, they haven't kept up with that side of technology.

Others reported more fundamental communication difficulties with defendants when giving advice/conferences online rather than in-person:

> Def-Bar-01: face-to-face contact is invaluable if I have to explain to my client, the severity of the offence, or the potential outcome in terms of sentencing. It hits home if I'm there. I don't think it seems real if I'm on a screen.
>
> Def-Sol-06: quite a lot of it is about working out how people are going to react to the evidence that's put to them and getting the measure of that. I think most of the time it's fine, but it really is very helpful if at least once you get to see your client [in-person before the trial].

Going beyond miscommunication, Def-Sol-09 noted the dangers of people being coerced where the lawyer had only met them online before court:

> You do get people who put pressure on people, either defendants or witnesses, to plead guilty or not to complain, or to say particular things. And of course, if you're having a

> meeting with somebody [online], and they're a witness, and they provide you with all these instructions, and you then go to trial, you're hanging your hat on their version of events until the day they turn up at trial. And if they've been coached, or if they've said something that wasn't actually what they thought was going on, it's a bit late on the day of trial to try and unpick it. The last thing you need is for them to go into the witness box and give evidence that was completely different to what you thought they were going to say.

Technical literacy is also an issue for some clients. Not everyone is set up for video-conferencing, particularly those who live chaotic lives or are homeless (as, sadly, many defendants are):[20]

> Def-Sol-06: There are a lot of firms out there where a good portion of their work is from people who haven't got a phone, haven't got an internet connection, haven't got an email, or are off their faces on something, are in a very difficult situation mentally, and just can't get themselves together to organise that type of thing.

Perhaps less controversially, many CPS interviewees found similar advantages in their work too:

> Pros-05: to be able to have Teams meetings with the police[etc] without having them travel to us in [City], or us having to go to their office, is a revelation, saving us time.

Similarly, others noted how it meant extra contact with their advocates and that this could help with noticing mistakes:

> Pros-06: reviewing lawyers are finding that they're able to have more contact with their counsel [etc] because they don't have to travel to get all these various people in one room … It's faster and conversations are happening more. So things like, going back to the disclosure obligations, you're more likely to have those conversations early on and in the long run avoid tragedy.

As with defence, there may of course be temptation to use this extra 'free' time to pack in more cases, rather than spend more time on each one (for individual prosecutors, to get through the day's 'firefighting' as we saw in Chapters 4 and 5, or, at macro-level, to justify employing fewer staff). However, for now, Pros-06 is suggesting conversations are genuinely happening more.

Hence, at this stage, basic technology enhancements appear principally to have benefits in terms of time (although not without hazards for some clients and witnesses in terms of communication difficulties and coercion). This is particularly important given the significance of time (or lack of it) demonstrated in previous chapters as an issue across all areas of austerity criminal legal practice. The danger, however, is how this time is used and in particular, how a *field* and its associated practitioner *habitus* is inclined to view any bonus time: is it a way to redress

[20] For an overview, see V Cooper, 'No Fixed Abode: The Implications for Homeless People in the Criminal Justice System' (Howard League for Penal Reform, 2013).

the balance towards quality work, or is it an opportunity to achieve the volume working imperative we have seen in previous chapters?

C. Online Hearings (CVP)

For this study, the most substantial (and divisive) COVID-19 mitigation was use of online or semi-online/blended court hearings (principally via the 'cloud video platform' – CVP). This reflects a similar division in broader literature. A general interim report by HMCTS (across all jurisdictions, not just crime) was mixed. Many respondents (lawyers and clients) had positive overall views and levels of satisfaction. However, others noted difficulties in communication/rapport with clients (especially, but not exclusively, with vulnerable people), communication between lawyers and technology problems.[21]

In the current study, views and experiences generally differed depending on the nature of the hearing. However, before exploring these in more detail, it is important to bear in mind some basic technical issues too,[22] such as:

> Def-Sol-02: sometimes you can't hear what the prosecution are saying or whether anything else is being asked of us.

Whilst mundane, this is important. It can even lead to inequality of arms in relation to available technology:

> Def-Sol-04: Especially young barristers … They're calling in from their poxy flat with all the street noise and everything coming in the background and then you'll get the older barristers from their study, and it's not fair.

Similar issues arose in relation to courts' technology, quality, range and positioning of cameras, etc. Def-Sol-07 and 09 noted how 'reactions' could be lost over video:

> Def-Sol-07: The nod, to know if you're doing alright, or if you've just annoyed the magistrates … You can't get those types of cues … because sometimes you're not even seeing the person you're talking to, or you're seeing one of the magistrates rather than three.
>
> Def-Sol-09: the technology at the moment … you wouldn't be able to pick up on how a witness would give their evidence. Perhaps because the camera is one side of the room, and you can only see just … you can see what's going on, but you can't see the nitty gritty of it, the intimate detail.

On the other hand, many defence respondents (both solicitor and barrister) noted positive development in terms of court management/logistics, as a knock-on effect of the move to CVP:

> Def-Sol-08: before the pandemic there were a number of cases listed, starting at 10:30. You could estimate when case number seven would be heard, but it would not be sure,

[21] J Clark, 'Evaluation of Remote Hearings during the COVID 19 Pandemic: Research Report' (HMCTS, 2019).

[22] ibid. This also reflects comments from magistrates, who noted that court IT problems were 'enormous' and led to frequent and lengthy delays: MA, 'Magistrates' Courts and Covid-19' (n 18) 19.

> so it may be the case that they were late, you are waiting … Whereas now, because of the CVP system, there is 10:30, 10:45, 11:00, 11:15, 11:30, and of course longer slots when cases are listed for longer by the court. And I think this is extremely valuable.

Hence, any improvements noted later in this section are dependent upon some basic/fundamental technical and logistical issues being (or remaining) fixed. Some might be sorted without much investment (such as listing practices), but others will require greater investment in technology by HMCTS (and in practice by Government) than is currently the case.

i. *First Appearance, Bail and Intermittent Hearings*

Interviewees (from both sides) were generally very positive about hearings outside of trials. The expenses and efficiency savings of having lawyers appear remotely are significant:

> Def-Sol-01: If you're based in [City X], and you've got a trial in [City Y], and you need to go before [City Y] Crown Court for a mention, to resolve a case management issue, then why am I going to pay £100 on the train to go [there] for a 10-minute hearing when I can just dial into it?
>
> Pros-03: The ability for [barristers] to be able to dial into a non-contentious hearing, without having to travel is a massive benefit. Not just to them, but the criminal justice system and the public purse. You're saving the train fare and they can do other work.

For defence, there are also potential benefits in terms of continuity of representation, the absence of which (as noted in previous chapters) is something lawyers have come to accept as business necessity, but defendants and families have frequently complained about:[23]

> Def-Sol-07: it would be much better for me to do the case by CVP, who knows everything about the case from start to finish, than my colleague take it on.

The option to appear remotely provided similar benefits to defendants in terms of convenience and accessibility:

> Def-Sol-08: an all-day [bus] ticket for a big portion of our clients is what they would spend on a meal. So CVP is an extremely valuable service, because it allows people to attend court without needing to afford childcare, without the bus fare, the train fare or whatever, and they're still a part of their case.

Clearly, most lawyers saw significant benefits, both for their own convenience and finances, as well as those of their clients. However, there is a danger here if these personal benefits ever conflict with client or wider public interests. Other interviewees (again, from each side and role) recognised how such remote/online

[23] D Newman and R Dehaghani, *Experiences of Criminal Justice*, Kindle edn (Bristol University Press, 2022) 163.

hearings were not always to the benefit of defendants, particularly in terms of confidence, communication and feeling looked after:

> Def-Sol-02: They're in a vulnerable position, and there's uncertainty, and sometimes by you speaking to them in-person, they feel that level of confidence. From the ones I've dealt with more recently, that's what I feel.
>
> Pros+Def-Bar-02: If you're dealing with someone who's mentally ill, you can have a really hard time connecting with them. Sometimes you can't, but I think you stand a better chance in person ... defendants feel uneasy about not having a barrister in person.
>
> Pros-02: There is a slight downside I can see for the defendants, because you do get a greater degree of interaction when you're in a room with people and so they can probably interact more in the proceedings if you're there in person. But, selfishly, I think it works fine.

Pros-02's comment reflects that of the prosecutor in the aforementioned pre-COVID study of video hearings: they can work well for prosecutors, but sometimes at the cost (or even because) of working less well for defendants.[24] After all, the less chance a defendant has to 'interact' in the proceedings, the quicker and easier those proceedings are likely to be for the prosecutor. As Pros+Def-Bar-02's comment illustrates, these issues can be particularly so for more vulnerable clients.[25] Hence, whilst running intermittent hearings online is undoubtedly extremely convenient for lawyers, it is not without risk. In particular, the danger is that it will exacerbate the negative impacts on client care documented in previous chapters.

Indeed, whilst most positive commentary related to quasi-administrative hearings, several even considered contested bail applications (where decisions in relation to an individual's liberty are made) to be suitable for CVP too:

> Def-Sol-09: I could do the remand court by sitting at home and just phone the cells, speak to the client on the phone, and then appear on video.

Many other defence lawyers, however, viewed these hearings as something lawyers 'needed' to attend. Prosecutors also expressed a preference for appearing in-person for bail applications (although, institutionally, this was obviously not always up to them as individuals). Pros-01, for example, found it more efficient to be present. Pros-03 went further, considering anything contentious to be better off in-person, as it was both more persuasive and made communicating with the other side easier:[26]

> anything we were obstructing, we would want the advocate to be there in-person, we want them to be as persuasive as possible. I think the same for [Plea and Trial Preparation Hearings] PTPHs. We'll want time to talk to the defence ... we can look at

[24] Gibbs, 'Defendants on Video' (n 5).

[25] In accordance with Clark, 'Evaluation of Remote Hearings during the COVID 19 Pandemic' (n 21).

[26] Pros-04 said very similar in relation to negotiating guilty pleas: 'Far easier if lawyers are in the same room, and in the next room is their client who they can go and speak to, or the officer is in the next room, who the prosecutor can speak to.'

> whether or not a plea is acceptable. You can't do that over a video link, because a lot of that is done in the Robing Room.

As with the pre-COVID literature,[27] there is a sense from prosecutors that they recognise the benefits for their side of being in-person (more persuasive, etc). Whilst there are also benefits in terms of being able to communicate with the defence, this view also suggests other potential benefits to prosecutors if the defence does not appear in-person. If, as Pros-03 argues, it is necessary to appear in-person 'to be as persuasive as possible', then implicitly that suggests appearing remotely is less persuasive and therefore, in contested hearings (such as remand or, even, sentencing – see section II.C.ii below), the remote defence lawyer is potentially an easier opponent. This is a problem if, under austerity, defence lawyers are financially pressured into (or rewarded for) appearing remotely in such hearings, via the opportunity to increase case volumes and associated fees.

ii. Sentencing

Many interviewees included 'sentencing' in their generally positive comments about other short hearings (above). However, others specifically considered these (unlike other non-trial hearings) inappropriate for CVP – at least where there was risk of custody. Many, such as Def-Sol-06, considered it practically easier to persuade judges of mitigation in-person:

> there's a lot to do with standing up and delivering your advocacy. It's a stage, it's a theatre. When you're sat there in a little room somewhere, either in your office or in your own house with your two-year-old banging on the door, it's difficult.

Like the above section, practical concerns in terms of ease of communication/ explanation (particularly for young, mentally ill, etc offenders) were also reflected in concerns regarding sentencing online:

> Def-Sol-08: So many defendants have mental health difficulties, learning disabilities. Speaking face-to-face to someone makes a difference to their understanding. Obviously, I will speak with the defendants by telephone at length, but you can just see the penny drop when you see them face-to-face.

Beyond purely practical or communication concerns, there was also a very strong moral or professional sense that defending in-person was simply more appropriate for sentencing. Many interviewees (both solicitors and barristers) spoke passionately about how the lawyer just ought to be there with their client when potentially facing prison, even if it did not make any difference to how persuasive they were to the judge:

> Def-Sol-03: It just looks awful if you're not there … I don't think anything's lost in terms of the submissions that I would make to a judge by way of video-link. I think it is just there are certain ways in which you can look after your client that fall short.

[27] Gibbs, 'Defendants on Video' (n 5).

> Def-Bar-01: if it's a sentencing hearing, it is quite emotive. They're sort of just left, abandoned. I wouldn't want to do that to my clients … obviously we're there to assist them with the law, but we also are humans trying to guide them through the process.

However, given the undoubted financial benefits of being able to fit in greater volume of cases online this does mean that (as in previous chapters) client care can be in conflict with financial sense. The compromises on client care discussed in earlier chapters in relation to TLC suggest there is a danger of some cutting back on this, or at least there being a sense of financial 'punishment' for attending nonetheless. Certainly, those with the *habitus* illustrated in those previous chapters are likely to perceive attending in-person for these hearings as one more thing that just cannot be done.

Some prosecutors, on the other hand, were happy enough to appear remotely themselves for sentencing (or at least, no less so than for bail, etc – recall that others considered anything contested as better off in-person). However, there were issues with this from the defence solicitor and barrister perspective (both for their client's own interests and the efficient administration of justice), as it could lead to inefficiencies and delay:

> Def-Sol-07: you can't speak to them properly … a lot of the CPS lawyers then have to ring another lawyer to get their decision okayed, so then you're ringing them, they're ringing somebody else, and they're ringing you back, it's taken 30 minutes and you've eventually got to the conclusion that you knew you were going to get to 30 minutes ago. You've wasted the court's time, everybody's annoyed, and you're leaving court at 6pm.

> Def-Bar-01: you might want to speak with the prosecutor privately beforehand and say, 'listen, I don't think count three is properly made out', or 'can we [negotiate a guilty plea] if we offer a [factual] basis of [plea]'… If they're on CVP, and you're there in person, you can't have that brief discussion beforehand, because you are then reliant on them picking up their phone during a hearing.

Hence, whilst remote sentencing may appear to some prosecutors as more 'efficient', that may only be the case in relation to them personally (and their, as we have seen in previous chapters, lengthy task-lists), rather than the system as a whole. In fact, plea arrangements (if they result in guilty pleas, as the above two quotes suggest) may operate to the prosecution's benefit too. The imperative for individual prosecutors to work through (or firefight) their task-list more quickly is not necessarily in the CPS's interests as a whole, if it means potential guilty pleas are lost.

iii. Trials

In contrast to the above, the suggestion of having trials online (fully or with at least some people appearing remotely) was largely received negatively. However, some did approve in limited circumstances. For example, in relation to very trivial offences:

> Pros+Def-Bar-01: traffic trials that are summary only … No prospect of prison, we're talking financial penalties only. Even if it's a case of at most they're getting points, and

> … the only way they're getting disqualified is if they tot up for instance …[28] I did six of those trials last week, with all of the defendants appearing remotely. That works fine.

Some even considered that cross-examination of witnesses could work well remotely:[29]

> Pros+Def-Bar-03: She then had to quarantine. She was beamed into court. I cross-examined her over a link for quite a few hours, and it was absolutely fine … maybe because it's question, answer; question, answer. It's slightly easier, more digestible perhaps, than the long speech over a link.

Others, whilst still in favour in some circumstances, were less sure about it for the majority of witnesses. Pros+Def-Bar-01 considered that only expert witnesses were suitable for this:

> There are very few witnesses who I think it would ever be appropriate to give evidence in a Crown Court trial over the video-link. I think medical experts, I wouldn't have an issue with them appearing over a video-link … their evidence isn't going to be controversial in the same way. Their conclusions might be criticised, but if they've complied with their duty to the court etc no-one's going to be calling them a liar.

Indeed, the above slightly positive views aside, the overwhelming majority of interviewees from both sides were completely against anyone appearing online for trials, on the basis that it was simply not as effective for advocacy or witness examination:[30]

> Def-Sol-05: I think one of the most important things is the barrister being able to look the jury in the eye when he's giving his speech, or the defendant being able to look the jury in the eye and tell them, 'I haven't done it'. I think that's so important. Over a computer, it's not the same.
>
> Pros-01: just to look at people when you're talking to them, to engage them, to actually get your point across. I think that's quite hard when you've got a bench of magistrates falling asleep because they're sick of looking at the TV screen.

Like the concerns about influence/coercion before court (in section II.B above) many were also particularly concerned about witnesses giving evidence from home. Whilst convenient (and potentially necessary in a dangerous pandemic), the scope for abuse or influence by others is high:

> Pros+Def-Bar-01: someone was giving evidence over CVP, and they were clearly just sat in their front room, [and you could] hear something in the background. Asked what

[28] This refers to the process whereby, if an individual receives 12 or more penalty points ('totting up') within three years, they face a 6–24 month ban unless they can persuade the court that doing so would cause 'exceptional' hardship. See Road Traffic Offenders Act 1988, s 35 and Sentencing Council, 'Explanatory Materials: Road Traffic Offences – Disqualification' (2022).

[29] This is of course not new in itself, as vulnerable witnesses have appeared by video for many years (see section II above), although not from home.

[30] Similarly, the Westminster Commission on Legal Aid, 'Inquiry into the Sustainability and Recovery of the Legal Aid Sector' (All-Party Parliamentary Group on Legal Aid, 2021) concluded [70] 'Where the honesty of a witness is in issue, it's harder to access [*sic*] credibility on a screen.'

> it was, the gentleman said, 'oh that's just my wife, she's watching TV, she's not listening, don't worry about her'!

Whilst this particular example is fairly harmless, it is not difficult to imagine spouses, family or others involved in the case putting pressure on witnesses giving evidence from their living room in a way that would not be possible in the more secure environment of a courtroom.[31]

Another problem in terms of witnesses appearing remotely (and in contrast to Pros+Def-Bar-03 above) was that some found it made cross-examination less effective:

> Pros+Def-Bar-02: it impacts the flow of our cross examination, because of the delay etc, on screen. The technology's good, but it's hard to pick up on the body language that you naturally take conversational cues from, that will help judge what you say next, or how you say it, or whether you say it, or whether you interject.

Others pointed out how lawyers appearing remotely in trials would make communication with their opponent and their client more difficult (and less efficient):

> Pros+Def-Bar-02: you can resolve issues more quickly; you can take instructions from your client very quickly [in-person], because they're just stood behind you in the dock.
>
> Def-Sol-06: if suddenly a legal argument comes up, because somebody says something they shouldn't have,[32] I would normally ask the judge or the magistrates if they can give me the opportunity to speak to the prosecutor. They leave, you spend five minutes either talking quite nicely or thrashing something out and having a bit of a row and then you try and work out what you're going to do. You just can't do that easily on a CVP.

Hence, whilst both prosecution and defence lawyers (generally speaking) had very positive views and experiences of new technology approaches brought about by COVID-19, trials tended to be the exception. Most regarded in-person attendance at trials to be highly preferable or, often, a total necessity.

D. Blessing in Disguise or Trojan Horse?

As the above demonstrates, with the notable exception of anything to do with trials, most lawyers (whether prosecution or defence) considered COVID-19 changes to working practices and courts as an unexpected positive from an otherwise horrific period. In contrast to the (largely negative) pre-pandemic literature discussed first, lawyers found online working and hearings made their working lives more convenient and helped defendants too. However, as some of the more critical respondents above suggest, this positive picture in relation to hearings

[31] For example: D Cherry, 'Court Exam Adjourned after Witness, Defendant Found Together in Livestream' (*Sturgis Journal*, 5 March 2021) https://eu.sturgisjournal.com/story/news/crime/2021/03/05/court-hearing-postponed-after-accused-found-same-house-witness/4587600001/.

[32] Eg, asking a witness an allegedly inappropriate question.

outside trials ought to be questioned too. Regardless of any benefits to defendant convenience, efficiency, saving court time, etc, there is also undeniably a significant financial advantage for lawyers to attend non-trial hearings via CVP. The complete removal of travelling time evidently means more cases can be fit into a given day (which, under the current payment system and associated imperative for volume working means more fixed fees):

> Def-Sol-09: [for magistrates' court remand] they don't have to travel anymore. They can all do it remotely, so it saves time, makes you much more efficient. From a Crown Court point of view, they could be logged into [Crown Court X], do one case, close that down, go and do one in [Crown Court Y] in the afternoon, and perhaps [Crown Court Z] just after that.
>
> Def-Bar-01: it helps financially for sure to be able to do more hearings in a day if you tended to stay at home.

Given the absolute financial imperative for volume working (for almost all criminal defence work apart from Crown Court trials) that we have observed in all previous chapters, the temptation is for this newly discovered 'free time' to be used to increase case volume, rather than giving individual cases greater attention. Likewise for prosecutors, whom again we have seen have huge volumes of work to 'firefight' through, at both magistrates' court and Crown Court level, this is a welcome opportunity to get through more of it. There are two key problems here. First, given the wealth of data discussed in previous chapters (from the current study and previous literature) on criminal defence and prosecution lawyers being (and, in qualitative studies, themselves telling researchers that they are) time-poor, it would be greatly unfortunate if the sudden free time provided by online hearings was largely used on taking on new cases rather than giving the current ones some sorely needed extra attention.[33] Second, the danger is that this understandable desire for more efficient and higher volume working can itself influence views on whether a given hearing being online or in-person is really in the best interests of the defendant, rather than purely their lawyer. As Pros-04 reflected in relation to both prosecution and defence:

> I think sometimes lawyers are thinking 'what's comfortable for us?' What's comfortable for the client (a bit like with GPs and patients) isn't always necessarily the same thing. And I think sometimes lawyers are thinking of their own interests first, rather than what's in the interests of the side they're representing, and overall of course in the interests of justice.

Indeed, other actors (with less or no financial stake), whilst sharing lawyers' concerns about online trials, were not nearly so positive about the other online hearings either. For example, Helm raised a number of concerns in the midst of

[33] Although such a response would not be unexpected, nor unique to lawyers. A long line of research on public service workers (beginning with M Lipsky, *Street Level Bureaucracy* (SAGE, 1980)) argues that more resources often lead to greater case volumes, rather than more time spent on each case.

pandemic measures, in relation to free decision-making, communication and guilty pleas.[34] Similarly, whilst a minority considered that 'when the system works, it works well',[35] a survey of 865 magistrates who sat in court between March 2020 and November 2021 (with follow-up focus groups), found views amongst the lay judiciary to be mainly negative.[36] Interestingly, some pointed out that (particularly for lawyers, from both sides) 'What started as a necessary expedient now appears to be employed as a convenience, to the detriment of the court process.'[37] Regardless of the type of hearing, respondents' views were that 'it is more helpful if professionals can be available in court to aid discussions'.[38] Communication (amongst all court parties) was considered to have been negatively impacted by online hearings[39] and difficulties with defendants' effective participation using remote links were further exacerbated for neurodiverse people or those with disabilities.[40]

Certainly, it appears that the opportunity to increase volume was embraced by some. The following quotations give a flavour of this:

> Def-Sol-03: I can just turn one off and turn the next one on, and go and see a different judge … It's been cracking. It's fantastic. And as far as managing limited resources, there's no way I would have been able to cover all three of those cases.
>
> Pros+Def-Bar-01: I'm able to do more work, which is good for me, because obviously I'm able to earn more fees, it's good for the system, because there's more people available to take the work that there is. And it's good for wellbeing.

Def-Sol-04 perhaps demonstrates most vividly what a day can be like with such an approach:

> Last night, I had three [not linked] duty clients arrested for rape. I dealt with the first client's interview last night, the second client's interview at 11am this morning [both online]. When I finished, I had to go to the Crown Court at [City], to take instructions from a client who was there with a barrister. On my way back down to the magistrates' court, I did the [3rd] interview by telephone from my car. When I got to the magistrates' court, I continued doing that interview by telephone but I had to stop that interview at 2pm to go in to see my client who was appearing for sentence in the magistrates' court. In the meantime, on CVP link, I was doing a pre-trial preparation hearing at [other City] magistrates' court. As soon as I finished that, I then got back onto the officer about the rape case. I then drove home. I got a phone call from a client who's in psychiatric hospital, dealt with that. Oh and I spoke to the psychiatrist this morning about his case which is in court tomorrow. And then five minutes ago, I got a phone call from the duty scheme for a case tomorrow of sexual assault with a voluntary interview. That is a standard day.

[34] R Helm, 'Pleading Guilty Online: Enhanced Vulnerability and Access to Justice' [2021] MLR Forum 001. www.modernlawreview.co.uk/helm-pleading/.

[35] MA, 'Magistrates' Courts and Covid-19' (n 18) 19.

[36] ibid 7. See also Clark, 'Evaluation of Remote Hearings during the COVID 19 Pandemic' (n 21).

[37] ibid 21.

[38] ibid 23.

[39] ibid 24.

[40] ibid 23.

> …
>
> This has been the advantage of COVID for us. Because there's been less pressure to physically see people or go to court, I do a lot of my conferences with the clients [online] … what COVID[/CVP] has allowed me to do is what I did today: appear physically in one court, whilst appearing by video-link to another court. And I'll do that tomorrow. If you are of the level of experience that I'm at, where I can look at a case and assess it in five minutes, it's positive. I can do a lot more work and in terms of cash, suddenly, I'm making money in a way that I wasn't before. In a way that I'd be scraping by under the old system, I'm now making great money.

I do not suggest that these lawyers in particular were lazy or unethical. Indeed, they also demonstrated a great deal of dedication to clients; Def-Sol-04 went on to say that their stress-levels were 'through the roof', that they 'don't sleep' and have calls with clients before 7am 'most mornings'. However, it is not fanciful to consider that some of the very positive views in relation to the administration of justice might be a little bit influenced by the happy coincidence that it is also financially better for most of these hearings to take place remotely. Qualitative research of this kind also always tends to suffer from self-selection bias: those who want to volunteer to speak to researchers also tend to be passionate about and care about their professional role. Even if all of these interviewees only did hearings online when it was truly in the interests of justice and/or their clients, the fact remains they could make more money and be better off if they did not take such a view and just maximised online hearings without regard to such things. The risk is that their colleagues may not all be so selfless. Every profession has bad apples. Much as we have seen elsewhere in previous chapters, diligence is financially punished and austerity makes such punishment all the more painful. As Sommerlad has pointed out, there are winners and losers in legal aid.[41] Equally, as we have noted in previous chapters, individuals with a well-adapted *habitus* to their *field* can follow their own *interests* there, almost sub-consciously, as the operation of *habitus* affects how they perceive their world.[42] The *habitus* conditioned to this *field* may affect the way 'the facts' are perceived even by perfectly well-intentioned people.[43] By operation of *interest/illusio*, those most inclined to view them in such a way as to find that 'happy coincidence' are more likely to stay in business, survive, or even thrive in an austerity field. In that sense, the responses here are an interesting application of the Bourdieusian constructs used throughout this book. The criminal law *field* has suffered from austerity for quite some time. Time enough for a corresponding

[41] H Sommerlad, '"I've Lost the Plot": An Everyday Story of the Political Legal Aid Lawyer' (2002) 28 *JLS* 335, 341, 360. In that study, the winners were 'legal aid factories' – ie firms which (according to hostile views in government and the media) perform high volume, but low quality, publicly funded work. Sommerlad viewed clients (because the work is allegedly poor), the taxpayer (because cases are run in ways which maximise profits rather than efficiency) and the committed 'political' firms (ie those who do legal aid work mainly for its political impact rather than to make money) as the losers.

[42] P Bourdieu, *Homo Academicus* (Peter Collier tr, Polity Press, 1988) 176.

[43] T Greenhalgh et al, 'Orthodoxy, *Illusio*, and Playing the Scientific Game: A Bourdieusian Analysis of Infection Control Science in the COVID-19 Pandemic' (2021) 6 *Wellcome Open Research* 126.

habitus to develop in those who survive and thrive in it. COVID-19 provided a sudden and unexpected change, but responses to those measures in accordance with that (such as using the opportunity to increase volume of work) would therefore not be unusual. On that basis, the fact that lawyers appear almost universally aware of the hazards from online trials, whilst generally much more positive in relation to other online hearings, makes a great deal of sense. It will be recalled that Crown Court trials tend to be worth the most and therefore were already highly profitable regardless of medium. A cynic would say it is no coincidence that this is also the area most lawyers (unlike, as noted above, some other court actors) were happy to keep in-person.

III. Sustainability

In previous chapters, we have already considered the toxic effects of burnout in the various contexts in which criminal lawyers work.[44] Lawyers consequently quitting the profession (for their wellbeing or in frustration) can itself be understood as an (indirect) consequence of austerity.[45] However, that is not to say that the more obvious/direct consequences of austerity as a reason for quitting (or closing) do not also apply. For some, the finances simply do not work (or only work if they practise unethically, which they are not prepared to do). We shall now examine the way in which this occurs and what this reveals about the logic of criminal legal practice for those who remain.

A. Criminal Legal Aid Solicitors

The Law Society has noted for some time the dwindling numbers and rising average age of duty solicitors.[46] This dearth of duty solicitors is particularly bad for rural areas, for example, parts of South Wales,[47] or (in England) the North Devon duty scheme, which has only been sustained by solicitors from further afield making three-hour round trips.[48] The SRA has similarly found that criminal solicitors

[44] Which very much reflects previous literature. See, eg, C Nicklas-Carter, 'Efficiency of the English Criminal Courts in a Time of Austerity. Exploring Courtroom Lawyers' Assessment of Government Policy (2010–2017)' (DCrim Thesis, Keele University, 2019) 138 (who found morale was 'awful') and V Kemp, 'Transforming Legal Aid: Access to Criminal Defence Services' (Legal Services Research Centre, 2010).

[45] See further my argument on the direct and indirect effect of cuts in J Thornton, 'Is Publicly Funded Criminal Defence Sustainable? Legal Aid Cuts, Morale, Recruitment and Retention in the English Criminal Law Professions' (2020) 40 *Legal Studies* 230.

[46] Law Society, 'Criminal Duty Solicitors: A Looming Crisis' (28 February 2023) www.lawsociety.org.uk/campaigns/criminal-justice/criminal-duty-solicitors.

[47] R Dehaghani and D Newman, 'The Crisis in Legally Aided Criminal Defence in Wales: Bringing Wales into Discussions of England and Wales' (2021) 41 *Legal Studies* 234, 246.

[48] M Fouzder, 'Solicitors Face Three-hour Round Trip to Stop Devon Duty Scheme Collapsing' (*Law Society Gazette*, 26 August 2022) www.lawgazette.co.uk/news/solicitors-face-three-hour-round-trip-to-stop-devon-duty-scheme-collapsing/5113499.article.

are generally older than those in other practice areas[49] and, more recently, the Westminster Commission on Legal Aid found the system was unsustainable.[50] Figures suggest the number of criminal defence firms has fallen by around 28 per cent even compared with relatively recently (2014/15).[51] *CLAR* found that 'while the rest of the [solicitors'] profession has been expanding, the criminal legal aid sector has contracted'.[52] Those longer-term trends have been worsened by the more acute consequences of COVID-19 (which aggravated a pre-existing criminal courts cases backlog). Given the emphasis of the payment scheme on the conclusion of the case, court delays severely impact firm cashflow.[53]

i. Firm Solvency

The above statistics affect individual practices, as might be expected. Firms make a judgement that it is not viable to continue criminal law work and shut down or do other things instead:

> Def-Sol-06: if you're running a firm, then you look at it and just think, 'why are we running a Criminal department, when we've got this [other] department? We're doing a divorce for somebody, and we're charging them this much, and then we're doing a huge trial for them, accused of drug supply or sexual offences and we're getting paid this much [less]'.

However, the problem may be even worse than statistics suggest: some considered that criminal firms could continue as a shell for many years, even if de facto insolvent:

> Def-Sol-01: where I practised in [recent years], I was head of the Criminal department. Every month it was struggling to pay the bills and to make a profit … it became rapidly clear in looking at the books that the firm had been practising as an insolvent practice for [several] years … needless to say, that practice folded.

This raises serious questions about whether the industry is sustainable in the current financial climate.

ii. Recruitment and Retention

Dramatic closures and slow-burning insolvencies aside, many firms appear to just plod slowly along the road towards that, with ever-dwindling staff numbers. Both recruitment and retention is problematic:

> Def-Sol-03: the number of people that we have in the department now is significantly reduced. Partly due to COVID, partly due to people simply moving on, and then not

[49] SRA, 'Criminal Advocacy Thematic Review' (2017) 76.
[50] Westminster Commission, 'Inquiry into Sustainability and Recovery' (n 30) 9.
[51] C Bellamy, *Independent Review of Criminal Legal Aid (CLAR)* (November 2021) 47.
[52] ibid 48.
[53] Westminster Commission, 'Inquiry into Sustainability and Recovery' (n 30) 44.

> being replaced … Cuts to Legal Aid have played their part enormously over the course of the last 10–15 years. X per cent here and there every few years or so, takes its toll … The last time we had any [new students join] was 2–3 years ago, who [both left] at the end.

As Def-Sol-03 shows, it is a combination of longer-term cuts and stagnation worsened by the more acute challenges from COVID-19, which means both that existing staff move on and are then difficult to replace. However, whilst many have noted recruitment difficulties, it is important to understand the nuances of this. For many years, available trainee solicitor positions have not kept pace with the number of Law graduates.[54] Hence, whilst legal study is not just training to be a lawyer,[55] any advertised trainee position can probably expect applications from Law graduates. The problems here are more nuanced. First, there is the financial liability of recruiting. With margins tight and prospects bleak, firms may not be able to pay new staff:

> Def-Sol-15: it has to stack up, so there's no point them being keen if there isn't a business model that can deliver the goods.

Second, as in many businesses/professions, until they get more experienced, trainees initially cannot contribute very much, or may even be a bit of a liability/cost:

> Def-Sol-21: I would love to pass my expertise on to somebody, but there is absolutely no prospect of being able to recruit a trainee. There's not enough work to go around and I couldn't offer that person a guaranteed position.

This reflects findings from recent reports. One respondent to the Westminster Commission considered it was 'virtually impossible to recruit' as it was an unaffordable business overhead that would not pay off until the trainee gained experience.[56] Hence, *CLAR* found, in 2018/19 'around 80% of firms doing some criminal legal aid work had no trainees at all'.[57]

Third, the *quality* of applicants goes down if criminal law is seen as the poor cousin of other practice areas:

> Def-Sol-05: [Law is] oversubscribed, so it's hard to get a training contract … So [criminal law] might be the only option you have … the quality of representation, I'll be frank with you, has probably decreased a little bit, because of the funding regime.

As Def-Sol-12 noted, *retention* of those few trainees who are recruited is then also a severe problem, making the financial gamble even worse:

> As soon as they've qualified, they go somewhere else! So you have invested in them, but you don't get any return, so trainee solicitors are very unattractive.

[54] See Law Society, *Trends in the Solicitors' Profession. Annual Statistics Report 2021* (2022).

[55] Unlike, say, Medicine or Nursing courses, many study Law with no intention of practising, in the same way that many who study History do not seek a career as a historian.

[56] Westminster Commission, 'Inquiry into Sustainability and Recovery' (n 30) 96.

[57] Bellamy, *CLAR* (n 51) 53.

As other partners noted, this could often be to other areas of law entirely, rather than just another firm. Def-Sol-10 explained their motivation for quitting early on in their criminal law career:

> I was barely making a minimum wage, which isn't really something that you think you'll be doing when you go to Law School. So you think, 'well what's the point'? You can obviously think of the legal career as a vocation, but at some point you have to think, <well I kind of want to be able to go to a café and get myself a cup of coffee without going into debt>.

Others find the nature of the work (in combination with its poor pay) to be extremely unattractive in practice and leave post-qualification:

> Def-Sol-02: They don't want to go out in the evenings. They don't want to be dealing with clients who are quite volatile and can also be quite threatening in certain cases. So you find that the individuals who wish to do that type of work are limited … So even if we've got trainees onboard, who are doing the work that we're doing, sometimes they don't want to qualify into crime.

Even those who do wish to work in *criminal* law post-qualification have other options. Many noted an increase in CPS recruitment:

> Def-Sol-09: Keeping them these last two years has been really challenging because of the CPS taking them. That's the big killer. If you're a trainee solicitor who suddenly becomes duty [solicitor] qualified, you might start as a duty solicitor at about £30,000. If you can go straight into the CPS as a Crown Prosecutor at £40,000, you've just had a £10,000 raise for doing the *same* magistrates' work.

This equally applied to more experienced lawyers, for example:

> Def-Sol-03: We've lost at least three [senior lawyers/partners] within the last year over to the CPS … I'm starting to see the cracks of this now that the dawn is breaking after the pandemic and people are starting to look around and think, 'is this where I want to stay, is this what I want to do?'

This reflects frustrations expressed to the Justice Select Committee, with respondents lamenting their firms becoming a CPS 'training ground' due to being unable to compete on salary.[58] However, such moves are not necessarily always about money, but also perceived quality of life, career development, or more indirect financial benefits:

> Pros-02: I wanted to move over, look at it from the other perspective, and work in a different environment to develop myself, my skills, what I could do … I was probably being paid more in private practice than in the CPS, but … you have the comfort-blanket of a pay scale and structured progression … Oh I said that I didn't leave for money, but I've realised how much pension I get now … which you just can't compete with in private practice … I've been told off at the CPS for doing too many hours. You would get that time back in lieu, which is just a foreign concept to a defence firm.

[58] HC Justice Select Committee, *The Future of Legal Aid* (HC70, 2021) 17.

Lastly, as with trainees/recently qualified, other senior practitioners left criminal law entirely, rather than join the CPS. Some diversified into other areas, and sometimes this was the first step towards leaving criminal law altogether:

> Def-Sol-19: I'm doing about 50-50 crime-childcare. The benefit in childcare being it probably pays better than any other legally aided work.
>
> Def-Sol-15: for many years I did nothing but legally aided criminal defence, but gradually moved into doing other things, particularly civil litigation, and to cut a long story short, their came a point last year where I couldn't stack up doing the proper job on legal aid with having a business that was going to be commercially viable. So, I personally went into other work.

As Def-Sol-15's reasons for leaving demonstrate, there is also that sense of frustration or (in Bourdieusian terms) *hysteresis* that comes from having a *habitus* out of sync with the austerity *field*. Def-Sol-15 reached a point where the disconnection between what they valued and understood to be good practice compared to what the *field* encouraged/required became too much to bear.

iii. Diversity

The above issues in recruitment and retention also have a particular impact on the diversity of the profession. After all, it stands to reason that those who are already disadvantaged will find it all the harder to survive on little money. As Def-Sol-01 notes:

> It's becoming a profession for the rich. I'm a working-class lad. I'm very proud of my achievements, but the job has almost taken a piece from me and the sacrifice you have to make to get here is hard and is it worth it?

Likewise, the extremely antisocial hours etc noted above have disproportionate impact on women in a society where they still shoulder much of the burden of childcare.[59] Indeed, *CLAR* found that, whilst the criminal law solicitors' profession had roughly equal numbers of men and women, 65 per cent of duty solicitors were men in 2019.[60]

Apart from the unfairness on individual practitioners, diversity is also important from the client perspective:

> Def-Bar-04: the more independent firms of solicitors, and particularly ethnic minority solicitors, that served small communities found that they couldn't be in business unless they joined up with other firms to be able to ride out the financial constraints. Their

[59] ONS, 'Women Shoulder the Responsibility of "Unpaid Work"' (Gov.UK, 10 November 2016) www.ons.gov.uk/employmentandlabourmarket/peopleinwork/earningsandworkinghours/articles/womenshouldertheresponsibilityofunpaidwork/2016-11-10.

[60] Bellamy, *CLAR* (n 51) [15.28], although accredited police representatives had a roughly 50–50 split, *CLAR* considered that this may have been down to the need to be frequently available at antisocial hours in order to be a duty solicitor [8.34].

> [ethnic minority] client base would be relatively small, so there were lots of firms that had just one partner or two partners per practice. Many of those small firms would take on cases and defend/represent their client base and sometimes they'd sustain the reduction in profit or losses because you believed in their case. It wasn't just a business. When it's a sole practitioner, they're face-to-face with the community where something's gone wrong: a lot of wrongful arrests to do with drugs, say. That partner would have to face the families and say 'yes, of course, I'll defend you'; whereas, if he was part of a firm of five or six partners, it's easier to say 'well, I'd love to, but the partners won't let me [financially].'

Similarly, one client respondent told Kemp in relation to ethnic diversity: 'I want someone who understands my ethnic background [Hinduism] and uses words I can understand'.[61] Others noted the benefits of being able to explain and advise clients in their native language and understand unique cultural issues.[62] More broadly, as Shute et al argue, confidence in the courts would be strengthened if more personnel from ethnic minorities were seen to be playing a part.[63] Kemp, reflecting Def-Bar-04's experience, noted how 'BME-managed firms tend to set up small niche practices' (to focus on the needs of their ethnic community) and are therefore more financially vulnerable.[64]

iv. Private Work

Many solicitors also increased the amount of private criminal law work they did (or tried to), which – taken to its natural conclusion – could result in doing no, or very little, legal aid work at all:

> Def Sol 05: I've survived from private work more than legal aid … a lot of people, I have to tell them, 'look, some cases I won't do on legal aid, but you're at your leisure and it's your choice. There are other people who I can refer you onto or you can find, but if you want me, this is what it's going to cost.'… I will sell the private side to say, 'well you're not going to get the best barrister' as well. 'If you need me and a barrister, there's a lot of people who will turn it away.' So that's how you convert …. luckily though, I've got the private work. That just sustains me, to be honest, and that is the future.

Whilst Def-Sol-05 was concerned with very serious crime, this equally applies to the less serious end of the process:

> Def-Sol-07: Quite a lot of the driving offences are privately funded. We do quite a lot of outside police station work, which is privately funded … and I've got a few magistrates' court trial cases which are privately funded as well.

[61] Kemp, 'Transforming Legal Aid' (n 44) 97.
[62] ibid 99–100.
[63] S Shute et al, *A Fair Hearing? Ethnic Minorities in the Criminal Courts* (Routledge, 2011) 131.
[64] Kemp, 'Transforming Legal Aid' (n 44) 109–10.

Most interviewees found there was significant competition for this private work though. Indeed, for Def-Sol-11, only the 'well-regarded' firms could count on this work:

> There's more private client work these days. (A) because legal aid is more difficult to obtain and (B) because, frankly, my firm is a very well-regarded firm and we will be briefed on cases where, for example, the client had legal aid, he didn't like the fact that he was seeing four or five different lawyers, so he came to me in particular.

The initial implications of this are troubling: only those with money can guarantee 'well-regarded' lawyers.

v. Hobbyists and Altruists

On the other hand, many good lawyers (who could count on private work if they wanted) nonetheless still do legal aid, out of a sense of altruism:

> Def-Sol-18: I don't go out chasing the private paying work. I do see myself as a legal aid lawyer. I'm very committed to it and I enjoy doing it and I think it's the right thing to do.

And/or out of interest:

> Def-Sol-05: if someone comes to me with a shoplifter, or a burglary case, or something on the lower crime level, then I probably won't do it. The only one I've done recently like that is for a friend's [relative], which was quite interesting as well. If it is quirky and a bit interesting, I think, <well actually I'll give that a go>.

Indeed, there are positives for camaraderie etc from a sense of altruism or mission. As Cooke notes, jointly experienced legal aid cuts can act as a motivator for shared values and rallying together in the face of adversity.[65] The danger is that interest and altruism can only take you so far. Even Def-Sol-01 (who considered their enthusiasm for the job as 'like a drug') reflected that:

> the addiction only goes so far … there comes a point where you can only do so much running around.

Whilst they make a laudable contribution, altruism and hobbyism is no panacea and, as we have seen, altruism is the kind of disposition likely to be driven out, since it does not match the *habitus* (illustrated in previous chapters) required to survive and thrive in an austerity *field*.

B. Publicly Funded Criminal Bar

In terms of numbers/economics, the Criminal Bar is also in a difficult position. Between 2015–2020, *CLAR* found 'significant' drops in the number of mid-career

[65] E Cooke, 'The Working Culture of Legal Aid Lawyers: Developing a "Shared Orientation Model"' (2022) 31 *Social & Legal Studies* 704, 717.

criminal barristers (8–22 years' experience) and KCs (the most experienced).[66] More recently still, Bar Council data suggests the number of barristers in full-time publicly funded criminal practice dropped by more than 10 per cent in 2020–21.[67] A 2021 Bar Council survey also found criminal barrister wellbeing was substantially worse than other practice areas, with over 50 per cent of criminal barristers reporting feeling down or in low spirits and only a minority finding the workload manageable.[68] Whilst the effects of working through the COVID-19 pandemic probably did not help, that cannot be blamed exclusively, as these results reflect similarly negative sentiments prior to that.[69]

i. Recruitment and Retention

Whilst some barristers noted difficulties in recruiting pupils, as with solicitors, this was generally not to the extent that Law graduates did not apply. Indeed, the pupillage market is even more oversubscribed than that of trainee solicitor positions.[70] Rather, similar to solicitors, the risk is that crime is seen by some as the softer option for those who cannot get pupillage in other areas:

> Def-Bar-03: like any industry, if you've got recruitment where you're attracting the brightest and the best and you're choosing between them, you can afford to not give jobs to people who are inadequate. Largely, legal-aid-based practices cannot compete with any private client, commercial, entities in terms of what they pay.

Apart from that, and much like we saw in relation to solicitors, the biggest issue is retention upon qualification and/or later.[71] Pros+Def-Bar-05 had experience in chambers recruitment:

> people come out of bar school feeling very enthusiastic about the criminal justice system, but they lose that pretty quickly afterwards. Those who don't go off to do civil often go in-house. We've had quite a lot of people who, for example, go to one of the regulatory prosecutors.

This reflected the perspective of three recently finished pupil barristers I spoke to, who had no intention of staying in pure criminal legal aid. Def-Bar-02 planned to use the experience as a springboard for a career as an international lawyer:

> I'm sticking with it because I ultimately want to get into international law and the only way I can do it is having gone through this.

[66] Bellamy, *CLAR* (n 51) 109.

[67] Bar Council, 'The Impact of the Covid-19 Pandemic on the Criminal Bar' (2022).

[68] Quality of Working Life Research Group, 'The Bar Council Barrister's Working Lives Survey Barrister Wellbeing Analysis' (2021).

[69] Bar Council, 'Barristers' Working Lives' (2017).

[70] Compared with the near 20,000 law graduates in 2021 (Law Society, *Trends in the Solicitors' Profession* (n 54)), 371 pupillages started in 2020/21, down from 404 in 2019/20: BSB, 'Pupillage Statistics' (April 2022) www.barstandardsboard.org.uk/news-publications/research-and-statistics/statistics-about-the-bar/pupillage.html.

[71] Reflecting Newman and Dehaghani, *Experiences of Criminal Justice* (n 23) 127.

Pros+Def-Bar-12 had already diversified (to almost 20 per cent in other areas) and intended to diversify further:

> Part of the reason I'm doing this and not just doing pure crime is that I do worry that the money isn't going to be enough and the work is too insecure.

Pros+Def-Bar-02, had spent substantial time working for the CPS (including as a fixed-term employee in a specialist department):

> Part of the decision to go to the [CPS] was undoubtedly to drum up another line of work.

Equally, as with solicitors, retention problems were not limited to the recently qualified, which reflects judicial concern about advocates avoiding criminal practice in favour of civil:[72]

> Pros+Def-Bar-08: of the people I went to Bar school with, at the Criminal Bar, I only know one other guy who's still in practice [out of 15].
>
> Pros+Def-Bar-09: I was called in [early 2000s] and there's almost nobody of my call still doing crime. Most people have got out into employment or family or something.

Much like solicitors, many also said CPS work was attractive and moved them away from defence, sometimes to a very significant extent: Pros+Def-Bar-13 had shifted to three quarters prosecution work (when it used to be three quarters defence) and Pros+Def-Bar-11 had (along with others from their chambers) accepted a short-term position at another state agency. These anecdotal reports reflect broader concerns from Lord Burnett CJ of a 'growing phenomenon in 2021 and into 2022' of ineffective Crown Court trials due to lack of available prosecution or defence counsel. Lord Burnett was (for a judge) surprisingly candid in blaming this on poor remuneration and resourcing by governments.[73]

ii. Diversity

Like solicitors, the above issues also have a distinct impact on the diversity of the profession. Those from poorer backgrounds have always struggled at the Bar to some extent. As Morison and Leith found, starting without other (eg parental) income is difficult due to the profession's structure.[74] Self-employed barristers have no guaranteed salary (after pupillage) and reputation needs to be built up over time. With the tighter margins of publicly funded criminal practice, these systemic challenges can quickly become prohibitive. Many interviewees found the effects of

[72] G Hunter et al, *Judicial Perceptions of the Quality of Criminal Advocacy* (2018) [4.1]. One judge provided a personal example of leaving the criminal barrister profession: by their becoming a judge!

[73] Burnett CJ, *The Lord Chief Justice's Report 2022* (Judicial Office, 2022) 18.

[74] J Morison and P Leith, *The Barristers' World and the Nature of Law* (Open University Press, 1992) 25.

this were discernible both in terms of those who even applied for pupillages and those who remained:

> Def-Bar-02: I've noticed that a few of the people who've done criminal pupillages tend to be from wealthier families.
>
> Pros-06: I have a couple of friends who are doing criminal law. The ones that I know that are sticking to purely criminal have a bit of cushioning already, in terms of finances.

Pros+Def-Bar-08, among others, considered that diversity at the Bar had 'peaked' and admitted that, without assistance, they could not have got going:

> My mum and dad kindly sent me £100 a week for about 8 months to help me get going, but some people don't have that .... and they really struggle.

This all accords with respondents to the Westminster Commission, who considered that 'the junior end of the profession was only open to those who could afford to work for nothing'.[75] Def-Bar-04 also pointed out that more senior practitioners moving away from criminal legal aid had consequences for those from ethnic minority or working class backgrounds:

> The role models have gone, especially for the ethnic minority youngster, or working class, to enter the profession of social legal services. When I was head of chambers, I arranged specifically for young people at about the age they were trying to decide on their O levels and A levels to come and spend a week in chambers. And the numbers of ethnic minority youngsters who subsequently decided they wanted to become lawyers and have become lawyers was remarkable.
>
> And it's not just a race thing either. There were working class youngsters who came along: white. I remember several who went home and told their parents there were barristers in chambers and some of them were black. They came and told me their parents couldn't believe it! So that changed the outlook of a lot of people.

Further, as with solicitors, in a society where women still shoulder much of the burden of childcare, the long hours and high-volume work required can also operate to the detriment of gender diversity. Def-Bar-01 considered her career sustainable as she did not intend to have children:

> I have no intention to have children. So that's not something that weighs on me. So at the moment, yeah, I'm fine.

It is difficult to imagine a male barrister making this sort of comment. Similarly, the Western Circuit Women's Forum found that two-thirds of those who left the Bar on the Western Circuit over a six-year period were women and that the vast majority of women left mid-career (conversely, almost all the men who left over the same period did so to became judges or to retire).[76] Data gathered for *CLAR* also suggests that the proportion of women in criminal practice drastically

[75] Westminster Commission, 'Inquiry into Sustainability and Recovery' (n 30) 101.
[76] Western Circuit Women's Forum, 'Back to the Bar' (2018).

declines after eight years of practice, with a 75:25 per cent split in favour of men by 23–27 years' experience.[77] The latest Bar Council report stated the criminal barrister gender pay gap as 35 per cent in favour of men.[78]

iii. Private Work

Just like solicitors, many barristers also increased the amount of private work they did (or tried to), which taken to its natural conclusion could result in doing no, or very little, legal aid work at all:

> Pros+Def-Bar-10: The general run-of-the-mill crime, at least defending, is not worth doing. So, if I do criminal cases at the Crown Court, it's privately paid only now.

Pros+Def-Bar-03 explained how this could mean legal aid was pushed aside:

> I get instructed on cases that pay better, and legal aid cases just get squeezed out. I don't have the time to take on any more, because I'm in demand to do other cases and I guess that is a problem … if someone's going to get paid £X to do the Legal Aid case on a Monday morning, but there's another case that they are instructed to do [for the same time], which is going to pay £XX, then you would be a fool wouldn't you?

Concerningly, they considered this was a frequent issue even in more serious cases, such as fraud or sexual offences.

Pros+Def-Bar-10 was candid about the difference being privately represented made:

> You get somebody who's had the opportunity to prepare your case, to read your case, to advise you properly, like we used to – when I started, you had to turn up actually knowing your case rather than reading it on the train on the way there. It gives you a massive advantage.

Troublingly, just as we saw with solicitors, some considered that is only the well-regarded who can get offered this sort of work:

> Def-Bar-03: Some people can [make a living off private work alone], you have to be successful, usually you have to have been at the job for a while

Leaving aside the question of whether market success always equals quality, it is obviously problematic if successful and experienced barristers are only available to rich defendants.

iv. Hobbyists and Altruists

As with solicitors, though, the effect of the above is mitigated somewhat by those experienced lawyers who nonetheless still do legal aid out of a sense of altruism.

[77] Bellamy, *CLAR* (n 51) Annex K, Table 32.

[78] Bar Council, 'Barrister Earnings by Sex and Practice Area – 2022 Update' (2022) 7. Albeit that this was slightly better than 38%, in the previous year.

For example, former head of chambers Def-Bar-04, reached the stage where they were doing some cases purely out of a sense of duty to their ethnic minority community, rather than it being financially viable:

> I felt clients welcomed having a barrister from out of town, because of being an ethnic minority, I've found it comforts clients: they felt they could talk more freely. And also who was not part of, as they saw it, 'the local establishment'. I have done it and I've known by doing it I'm going to be out of pocket. It's part of my commitment to social justice.

For others, and again, similar to some solicitors, it was also a case of interest, particularly for those who were independently wealthy already:

> Def-Bar-07: in some cases they have independent means and the job is more of a time filler than a necessity and so it doesn't matter – it's more important they do something they're interested in and the downsides are not as bad as they are for other people.
>
> Def-Bar-03: I only do crime for interest because I make my living on the public law, but I can tell you now that if my public law work dried up I would not be prepared to go and do crime full time legal aid … But … criminal legal aid work shouldn't be people's pastime, hobby or secondary things for people.

A more varied diet of work is not a bad thing in theory, however where only a little bit of a given area is covered and only infrequently, there is scope for problems. Empirical work from three in-depth studies examining the effects of lawyer specialisation suggests that 'specialists provide higher levels of quality than non-specialists and that in absolute terms, the quality of non-specialist advice is worryingly poor'.[79] Further, as Def-Bar-03 implies, if something is viewed as a pastime, it may receive less attention. Moreover, many (or perhaps most) criminal cases are not glamourous or intellectually/legally complex and therefore may pass the hobbyist by. Equally, as mentioned in relation to the problems of depending upon altruistic solicitors, altruism is the kind of disposition likely to be driven out, since it does not match the *habitus* (illustrated in previous chapters) required to survive and thrive in an austerity *field*.

C. Sustainability of Crown Prosecution

Given the reports above of significant movement from defence (both barrister and solicitor) to prosecution, one might hope that CPS practice at least was being sustained (albeit at the defence professions' expense). Unfortunately, there is little available data/research on this point. What we do know is that budget and associated personnel cuts (of 26 per cent/£185m) occurred from 2009–2016 and that, whilst there has been recruitment and investment since (£85m), this has not restored the profession to anywhere near 2009 levels (still £100m+ down) in

[79] R Moorhead 'Lawyer Specialization – Managing the Professional Paradox' (2010) 32 *Law & Policy* 226, 249.

absolute – let alone in real – terms.[80] Many (across both Specialist and Area teams) felt this recruitment was still inadequate:

> Pros-05: We could have five [specialist/complex] cases and only three people, which means we're then having to go to [City] or [City] or [City] to say, 'can you cover this case for us?' And likewise, we have instances where they come to us and say can we cover, so we all seem to be short of that sort of support.
>
> Pros-03: We are hiring more lawyers. We are hiring more paralegals. Not in the numbers we need, not in numbers that will make real differences to our caseloads. All they're doing is stopping them rising faster.
>
> Pros-01: The volume of work is at the point now where, with the staff that we have, people are struggling to get through everything.

Hence, whilst there is some recruitment (in the same way that there is *some* recruitment to criminal law firms and chambers), this does not necessarily mean it is adequate to address the workload problems discussed in earlier chapters.

Further, even with this recruitment, much like defence firms, there is no guarantee that those recruits will remain very long, chiefly due to the workload and pressures noted in earlier chapters at all experience levels:

> Pros-03: We will have people come over from defence. They will spend a bit of time [chuckle]. Once they realise the responsibility and pressure, and what is expected of them, but at the same time, how little time they're given to do it, they go back.
>
> Pros-04: One person who joined the same day as me, who after four months said, 'no, it's not for me' and has gone back to defending. Another one, who when I said I was joining CPS said, 'you must be mad', she stuck at it for nine months before she decided she couldn't do it. Went back to defending.
>
> Pros-06: I'll definitely be leaving! … If I stayed at the CPS, I think it would be a very long haul in the magistrates' team … You can't, it's not humanly possible to do 30 [case] lists like I've described to you for the rest of your life. It's just not. You will struggle. Your wellbeing struggles.

Self-employed barristers who had increased prosecution work were similarly in no doubt that it was unwise to rely on it:

> Pros+Def-Bar-01: You can certainly make a very respectable income doing prosecution [lists] in the magistrates', but there is no way that anyone could sustain it for any amount of time in a healthy way. And so I have to do family law to balance it out a little bit. Because, whilst that doesn't require any less work, or care and time, when you look at it comparatively, even the public funded family stuff pays significantly more than crime [*and therefore I need not do as much of it in a given week vs prosecution work*].

And yet, there was a sense from some that they themselves would never leave, similar to some of the defence practitioners noted above who were motivated by altruism and/or interest.

[80] CPS, *Annual Report and Accounts 2019–20* (House of Commons, 2020).

> Pros-03: It gets into your blood and you don't want to do anything else. I think the CPS relies on that. I think the government relies on that … I would imagine it's the same thing that lots of doctors and nurses think in the NHS.
>
> Pros-01: I think the people who do the job love their job and I think it attracts a certain kind of person. I don't think you would do the job if you didn't enjoy it. But I think the struggles more recently have just made it a little bit different than it's ever been before.

There is clearly a great deal of reliance on people with a very specific intellectual and/or principled interest in this area of work. However, whether such reliance is sustainable or wise, given findings in other chapters in relation to burnout with CPS work, is doubtful. Nonetheless, whilst the sense from many defence practitioners that the grass is greener might need to be revised, whether CPS recruitment and retention is quite as bad as the defence side remains debateable.

IV. New Technology, Old Problems and Sustainability

The necessarily fast move towards adopting new technology and approaches has much potential. However, parts of this have already been rowed-back on.[81] Online hearings and meetings have provided much efficiency and convenience for all concerned, whilst reluctance on the part of some appears Luddite. It is to be hoped that, in time and with calm reflection, some positives and lessons can come from the pandemic in the ways of working that it necessitated in criminal practice. That is not to say there are no hazards. There is the potential for views, for example on when it is best to appear remotely, being influenced, knowingly or not, by the financial benefits of such approaches at the expense of justice. There is a need to ask more than just whether a given measure is 'better' or 'worse' than the pre-pandemic status quo and to consider *who* it is better or worse *for* (court administrators, government, lawyers, the judiciary, defendants, witnesses, victims, etc – and appreciate that these may often point in different directions). As with other parts of this book, the financial stakes do not assist here. It is all too easy to see what we want to see in terms of 'the facts' or 'the interests of justice' if this means volume of work can be increased and consequent financial survival, when the alternative is risk of insolvency. This leads on to the later findings in this chapter. New *technological* resources help, but require the rest of the system to be adequately (*human*) resourced in order to unlock those efficiency and justice gains. The findings in the previous section suggest this is where the real stumbling block may be, as there are severe and genuine concerns as to the short-term stability of the criminal law professions, let alone the long-term prognosis. The increasingly dwindling numbers of duty solicitors and criminal barristers are indisputable and

[81] Lord Burnett CJ, 'Remote Attendance by Advocates in the Crown Court' (Court and Tribunals Judiciary, 14 February 2022) www.judiciary.uk/guidance-and-resources/message-from-the-lord-chief-justice-remote-attendance-by-advocates-in-the-crown-court/.

vindicate earlier criminal lawyer focus groups who viewed themselves as 'dinosaurs heading for extinction'.[82]

The financial conditions in the *field* are brutal and, as we have seen elsewhere, reward/require unethical practices. Many are unwilling to adopt such and therefore see no option but to leave. The danger is that we are left with the burnt-out, disillusioned and the (knowingly or not)[83] unethical. Hence, Johnstone's view that the 'clever technical lawyer' is a dying, albeit not (yet) extinct breed, in favour of one focused purely on speed has credence.[84] Nor, unfortunately, do the issues discussed above suggest that technology is a panacea. Technology may simply provide more opportunity to pack in ever-greater volumes of work. The changes to *habitus* we have seen throughout this book suggest that those who value justice etc will find themselves increasingly out of step with their *field*. Bourdieu called this feeling of being out of step *hysteresis*. Some such individuals may struggle on and suffer (particularly in the short term), whereas many others will leave, having found the career and profession they chose is no longer what it once was or what they thought it would be. Others still may, with alignment of their *habitus* to this *field* come to accept this (albeit sometimes with reluctance) as just the way it is and adapt their practices, utilising new technology as another way to prioritise volume, rather than quality of work.

[82] BVA BDRC, 'Civil and Criminal Solicitors' Views on LASPO. Report for the Law Society' (2018) 48.

[83] Greenhalgh et al, 'Orthodoxy, *Illusio*, and Playing the Scientific Game' (n 43).

[84] E Johnston, 'The Adversarial Defence Lawyer: Myths, Disclosure and Efficiency – A Contemporary Analysis of the Role in the Era of the Criminal Procedure Rules' (2020) 24 *International Journal of Evidence & Proof* 35, 54.

7

Understanding the Work of Legal Practitioners in Austerity

This book has sought to examine how external pressures, particularly austerity, influence criminal lawyers' work. We have now explored this issue across three key settings and considered what the future may hold for this area of practice, given that context. Two key conclusions follow. First, that legal practice, and the dilemmas thrown up by external pressures on it, cannot be understood in terms of a spectrum between free choice and irresistible compulsion. Obviously, few individuals inhabit each pole, but my argument is that even understanding this in an apparently more nuanced way (putting individuals somewhere on a spectrum between the two rather than at the extreme ends) can be misleading. Rather, a multi-dimensional analysis is required: one which appreciates the significance of both free choice and external pressures (along with, unlike a spectrum, their constant interaction and interdependence), which the Bourdieusian concepts discussed and refined in this book unlock the opportunity to consider. Second, that the chief way these manifest in the context of austerity criminal legal practice, is the (1) availability, (2) perception and (3) use of *time* by practitioners. Of course, time is limited for all of us as a matter of fact, but persistent austerity fuels a particularly strong sense of scarcity: of time as a rare *commodity* that must (as a matter of 'common sense' or 'the reality') be *spent* or *invested* prudently, on some things and not on others. This common sense places a premium on high-volume work and either (for defence) a few 'gold dust' cases or (for prosecutors) work that fulfils targets, ticks boxes and (most importantly) gets through a seemingly endless task-list. All of that feeds into the *habitus* of the thriving, or at least surviving, practitioner in this *field*. Bourdieu would say that those with such a *habitus* have obtained the ultimate form of (symbolic) *capital* in this *field* (like an elite athlete's intuitive 'feel for the game').[1] Those inclined to work against that high-volume mindset (with a different *habitus*), suffer from Bourdieu's *hysteresis*, manifested here as burnout and/or quitting.

[1] P Bourdieu, *The Logic of Practice* (R Nice tr, Polity Press, 1990) 66.

I. Understanding Practice

In Chapter 2, I considered a fundamental dispute in social science between objectivist and subjectivist approaches to understanding practice and how that had fed through even to some seminal studies on criminal lawyers. With such approaches, practice is understood as either a single (objective) reality for researchers to uncover, or as multiple (subjective) perspectives/realities (primarily those of practitioners). Research might try and avoid the poles (and purport to be *more* objectivist or *more* subjectivist, rather than absolutist), but the spectrum itself (whether expressly acknowledged or implicitly accepted) has proven tricky to escape, both for social scientists generally (as Bourdieu first set out to tackle) and in socio-legal studies.

I further noted a tendency in the severity of critique between these two approaches, partly driven by their differing analytical perspectives. Objectivist studies appear to demonstrate greater capacity to be critical, likelier to view 'the' reality as a practitioner failing in their deliberate and free choices, rather than responding to an imperfect system. In contrast, subjectivist approaches appear to demonstrate greater capacity to be sympathetic towards practitioners being studied, more inclined to accept practitioners' own rationalisations for behaviour (adopting such practitioners' 'taken for granted' assumptions about the world)[2] than a more objectivist approach is. Put another way: a spectrum between, taken to its extremes, an independent agent (who can therefore be judged for their unethical choices) or an automaton (who, as a helpless product of their environment, cannot fairly be criticised at all for unethical conduct – because it is not really done by choice). Again, whilst there is nuance in positioning in between the above absolutist poles of this spectrum, the spectrum itself can be tricky to escape.

However, as later chapters demonstrate, this is to miss a large proportion (perhaps the majority) of practitioners and to oversimplify much of human behaviour. In common with Bourdieu, I found it unrealistic to choose between or occupy a position on a binary spectrum. Instead, the two are different sides of the same coin – better understood together rather than at opposite ends. It is not freedom versus determinism, but a combined 'conditioned and conditional freedom'.[3] In arguing this, I am not saying that (at one end) overt (1) heroes, (2) villains and (3) those somewhere in-between (but, crucially, all on the same spectrum somewhere) do not exist. Some people freely make selfish decisions most of the time, others freely decide to do the right thing most of the time, even at great personal cost, and others freely make selfish decisions sometimes and altruistic ones at other times. Equally (at the other end), I am sure some people truly do lack agency sometimes and have no choice but to do bad (or indeed good) things. However, I contend that there is another aspect, outside of that spectrum, that such an

[2] ibid 25.
[3] ibid 55.

analysis misses – even though this could in fact be much larger than the first three: where agency and external influence (past and present) combine and interact to effect practice in a way that is greater than the sum of their parts; where individuals make conscious choices, but those choices (and the terms on which those choices are even conceptualised and made sense of) are influenced by something more sub-conscious. It is this aspect of practice which Bourdieu's concepts of *habitus* and *field* (and the more advanced ones which build upon them) help us to appreciate.

Most interestingly, this framework can account for the otherwise puzzling phenomenon of the practitioner who wants to do good, consciously tries to do good, thinks they are doing good, even makes great personal sacrifices in order to do good, but sometimes ends up doing the opposite and enhancing their own interests instead. In other words, those who are neither heroes nor villains, but consciously try to do the right thing without always managing it. Analyses which ignore or miss this will always be greatly limited, as it applies to most people. Most of us are neither heroes, villains, or powerless, but we are certainly guilty of sometimes being more inclined to see what we want to see. Interpreting 'the facts' so that the 'happy coincidence' can be found where everyone seemingly wins is intuitively appealing. Certainly, as Greenhalgh et al noted, many scientists who (with the best of intentions, but wrongly) dismissed aerosol transmission of COVID-19 did not (and, by their *habitus*, *could not*) realise for quite some time that they were wrong, and potentially even doing harm so as to uphold their powerful professional positions.[4]

Throughout the analysis of this book, I have used many of the concepts which Bourdieu developed (across a great many contexts) to help discern, illustrate and understand the operation of this fourth group here. By self-selection bias, many participants in this work might lean more towards the overt 'hero' archetype. They certainly seemed to care a great deal about justice, fairness and the rule of law, often (sadly) at their own expense. However, other examples also showed, via the operation of *habitus*, *field*, *illusio/interest*, *conatus* and *symbolic violence*, the possibility of acting in other ways (in one's own interests or, in the case of *symbolic violence*, even against their own interests, in favour of upholding the current logic of their austerity *field*), whether they realised this or not. Many spoke in terms of this simply being 'the economic reality of life',[5] or a 'happy coincidence'.[6] This demonstrates how an individual's *habitus* (their disposition and sub-conscious understanding of how the world works/what appears common sense to them), influenced by the (austerity) *field* can unwittingly lead them on to unethical choices. Such choices can appear unethical to an outsider, or in the abstract, but make perfect (common)

[4] T Greenhalgh et al, 'Orthodoxy, *Illusio*, and Playing the Scientific Game: A Bourdieusian Analysis of Infection Control Science in the COVID-19 Pandemic' (2021) 6 *Wellcome Open Research* 126.

[5] Def-Sol-13, Ch 4.

[6] Def-Sol-04, Ch 5.

sense to those with such a conditioned *habitus* to this *field*.[7] *Habitus* affects perception of the world and 'the facts'.[8] The well-meaning practitioner is either unaware they even have (or are making) a choice or, with their understanding of 'the facts' so distorted by their *habitus*, can self-justify unethical conduct as being good really.

Where does this leave our understanding of practitioners and the logic of their practice? First, this is not to provide an opportunity for cheap criticism. As argued above, only looking at the consciously selfish or heroic leads to an incomplete picture. Rather, we also need to acknowledge the existence of the many others who, 'without violence, art or argument'[9] will simply react and adapt to the conditions in their *field* (and end up perpetuating it) through a process which is extremely difficult for the individual to perceive. Indeed, so powerful is this process, that much of Bourdieu's work examined those for whom the operation of such concepts was self-harmful. By operation of *symbolic violence*, highly oppressive *fields* are lethally effective and long-lasting because the *habitus* of the oppressed means they see it as just the way it is (the only way it can be, 'common sense', etc) and therefore go along with it, even when this is at their own expense.[10]

Hence, second, rather than judgment or (for practitioners themselves) rumination, it is to instead encourage more frequent and productive self-reflection by practitioners. As I argued in Chapter 2, Bourdieu need not be read deterministically.[11] Rather, as illustrated in this book, the concepts allow a drawing back of the curtain to appreciate that what, at first glance, might appear self-evidently true or 'common sense' to individuals might not actually be so. Sometimes one's hand of cards really is weak, but sometimes it is not (eg in terms of plea advice, sometimes the defendant really is going to be convicted regardless, but sometimes they are not, and the understandable search for 'happy coincidence' might occlude realising that). Such reflection might reveal new opportunities, choices and strategies for a person to do good. At worst, you can be sure it really is a bad hand and the benefits of that should not be underestimated. In other contexts, Bourdieu noted how the 'internalised contradictions' of *habitus* can otherwise lead to severe mental anguish, even drug addiction and 'self-hatred'.[12] Appreciating when the deck really was stacked against you can provide a sense of 'intellectual pleasure'[13] or healing from understanding – and, anyway, maybe the next hand/case will be better. The difficulty is that, unlike card games, in practice this is fiendishly difficult to know. One must fight against one's own *habitus*, *field*

[7] P Bourdieu, *Homo Academicus* (Peter Collier tr, Polity Press, 1988) 176.

[8] Greenhalgh et al, 'Orthodoxy, *Illusio*, and Playing the Scientific Game' (n 4).

[9] Bourdieu, *The Logic of Practice* (n 1) 56.

[10] P Bourdieu and T Eagleton, 'In Conversation: Doxa and Common Life' (1992) 191 *New Left Review* 111, 115.

[11] Doing so would be rather at odds with Bourdieu's own life as a public intellectual. See M Grenfell, *Pierre Bourdieu: Agent Provocateur* (Bloomsbury, 2004).

[12] Bourdieu and Eagleton, 'Doxa and Common Life' (n 10) 121.

[13] ibid.

and (individual, group and system) *interests* to do so. It is not impossible though, and serious and frequent self-reflection could be fruitful.[14]

Third, for those researching legal practice, it is to appreciate the opportunities provided by analytical frameworks (particularly Bourdieu's) that move beyond the binaries of free choice versus determinism (or, indeed, positions between the two, which are still stuck on that same spectrum) and their associated tendencies to be critical or sympathetic. Instead, we should consider both how environments operate to influence, constrain, set the terms of and (sometimes) direct people's choices, and how those choices then operate to influence that same environment: two sides of the same coin. For policymakers, it is to strive to build the sorts of *fields* that prioritise and encourage ethical dispositions, rather than self-interest: in other words, as Bourdieu noted, to design *fields* which harness these natural human tendencies in a good way, by making it in one's self-interest to be ethical.[15] Unfortunately, as I have shown throughout this book, austerity tends to be unconducive to such fields.

II. Understanding Criminal Lawyers in Austerity

With the above in mind, there are two key points I would like to emphasise about the practice of criminal law in austerity in particular, which flow from this study. First, building on Morison and Leith in relation to barristers in the 1990s,[16] Newman and Dehaghani in relation to criminal legal aid lawyers in Wales more recently[17] and Porter in relation to prosecutors,[18] the importance of (constrained) time cannot be overstated. This book has demonstrated that the impact on the availability, perception and use of time for criminal lawyers is perhaps the most significant effect of austerity on this *field*.[19] Across the preceding chapters, I have found this to be the case at all stages (from the police station to appeals after trial), all levels of seniority, case severity and profession, for both prosecution and defence. Even when examining COVID-19 mitigations (Chapters 3 and 6), time emerged as the key theme, in the form of the welcomed – but ethically hazardous – ability to pack in greater case volumes thanks to time *gains* through increased

[14] See, more generally, S Armstrong et al (eds), *Reflexivity and Criminal Justice* (Palgrave Macmillan, 2017) 33.

[15] M Grenfell, 'Interest' in M Grenfell (ed), *Pierre Bourdieu: Key Concepts*, 2nd edn (Acumen, 2012) 165.

[16] J Morison and P Leith, *The Barristers World and the Nature of Law* (Open University Press, 1992) 19.

[17] D Newman and R Dehaghani, *Experiences of Criminal Justice: Perspectives from Wales on a System in Crisis*, Kindle edn (Bristol University Press, 2022) 111.

[18] A Porter, 'Prosecuting Domestic Abuse in England and Wales: Crown Prosecution Service 'Working Practice' and New Public Managerialism' (2019) 28 *Social & Legal Studies* 493, 505; A Porter, *Prosecuting Domestic Abuse in Neoliberal Times* (Springer, 2020) Ch 4.

[19] Reflecting a broader point by Bourdieu about the central importance of this for the logic practice. See Bourdieu, *The Logic of Practice* (n 1) Ch 6, 'The Work of Time'.

use of technology. Arguably, this desire for time may have clouded some lawyers' views on what was and was not appropriate for online/video work. Hence, as a *field* condition, austerity affects both the factual availability of time and, through the impact of that on individuals' *habitus*, both their perceptions of available time and how they decide to use the limited time that they do have. Again and again we saw weary, but clear, acceptance of the 'fact' that there was not enough time for everything regarded as 'good practice', or, as Pros-Bar-01 put it 'when everyone's pushed to their limits, everyone's overworked, underpaid, and being pushed to the very limits, errors *will* happen'. Instead, you have '*got to* pile it high, sell it cheap' (Def-Sol-09), 'as best you can, prioritise' (Pros-01), be 'ruthlessly efficient' (Def-Sol-03), or 'wing it' at Crown Court on the day of trial (Def-Bar-03). The specific areas where this bites in each context (such as prosecution disclosure and targets, defence plea advice and client care, etc) were detailed and analysed in the preceding chapters. Principally though, for defence, what limited time there is, has to be spent on those few lucrative 'gold dust' cases (mostly complex Crown Court trials), which financially sustain everything else, resulting in colossal stakes and problematic and unhelpful incentives in relation to, for example, plea advice. It is a similar story in relation to prosecution targets and statistics, although it is worth acknowledging that these may change direction more frequently (as Government and CPS policy revolves) than the more immutable financial mathematics which drive the defence focus, given their need to stay in business. Relatedly, this also means there are limits to what changing payment systems alone can achieve if conditions remain austere. As some interviewees stated quite candidly in previous chapters, the risk there is that one set of problematic incentives is simply replaced by another set. Something else might become 'gold dust' instead, but the fundamental issues would be the same. The stakes are always going to be high whenever people are struggling to make a living/profit or 'firefight' through the day.

Second, many interviewees noted how, in spite of all that, they stayed up late into the night to get things right, prepare properly, give every case the attention it deserved, etc. However, I greatly doubt that is sustainable in the longer term (never mind reasonable to expect of people). We saw how those who reported this also tended to be early in their career, or reflecting on a career they had since quit (or de facto quit), or clearly suffering from burnout and exhaustion. Indeed, the findings in Chapter 6, reflecting data elsewhere, suggest quit (or, at firm level, close down) many will (indeed many have).[20] That is not sustainable for individuals (nor is it fair to, effectively, punish diligence) and many others are of course not going to take such a self-sacrificial approach. Indeed, as noted above, whilst there are

[20] eg Law Society, 'Criminal Duty Solicitors: A Looming Crisis' (28 February 2023) www.lawsociety.org.uk/campaigns/criminal-justice/criminal-duty-solicitors; SRA, 'Criminal Advocacy Thematic Review' (2017) 76; Westminster Commission on Legal Aid, 'Inquiry into the Sustainability and Recovery of the Legal Aid Sector' (All-Party Parliamentary Group on Legal Aid, 2021) 9; C Bellamy, *Independent Review of Criminal Legal Aid* (2021) 47, 109; Bar Council, 'The Impact of the Covid-19 Pandemic on the Criminal Bar' (2022); Bar Council, 'Barristers' Working Lives' (2017).

probably some heroes in the mix (and probably some bad apples too), most people are likely to simply adopt dispositions (via their *habitus*) which are tailored to the *field*. They will then be more inclined to see what they want to see and therefore act in their own interests or that of the austerity *field* without necessarily realising it. It will affect the way they see and understand the world, such that they are more likely to perceive the facts as supporting those *interests* – just like Bourdieu found it does to anyone else across the variety of settings and times he studied during his career. Indeed, it seems to me that the average criminal lawyer has three realistic choices here (each represented across the interviewee sample). They can: (1) go above and beyond (and suffer for it); (2) quit (or drastically cut down) and do something else (potentially after having tried (1) until they and/or their family cannot do it anymore); or (3) they can, through their *habitus* being moulded into this austere *field*, come to that kind of wearied acceptance that being ruthlessly efficient, etc is just the way things are and get on with it as best they can. An austerity criminal justice *field* is more likely to bring about unethical behaviour by those within it because of its impact on their *habitus* and (consequently) dispositions, and which of those dispositions are rewarded or punished.

Being the topic of this book, the focus throughout has been austerity. I do of course accept that this is not the only reason people can behave badly. McConville et al, after all, found poor practices when finances were arguably better,[21] and conscious heroes and villains will always exist. However, given all the above, I am greatly sceptical of the potential for other changes to encourage ethical behaviour, unless and until the *field* can sustain and encourage it (which austerity appears to work against). As Bourdieu argued, the best way to ensure good practice is to make it in people's self-interest to be ethical.[22] Unless that happens, the disheartening tone of the findings from, in terms of prosecution, *The Case for The Prosecution* and, in terms of defence, *Standing Accused*, risk becoming timeless. As it stands, austerity appears to have resulted in a criminal legal practice field where, too often, it is self-sabotaging to be ethical and practitioners are set up to fail.

[21] M McConville et al, *The Case for the Prosecution: Police Suspects and the Construction of Criminality* (first published 1991, Routledge, 2017); M McConville et al, *Standing Accused: The Organisation and Practices of Criminal Defence Lawyers in Britain* (Oxford University Press, 1994).

[22] Grenfell, 'Interest' (n 15).

BIBLIOGRAPHY

Alge, D, 'The Effectiveness of Incentives to Reduce the Risk of Moral Hazard in the Defence Barrister's Role in Plea Bargaining' (2013) 16 *Legal Ethics* 162

Apted, M, *7Up* (Heinemann, 1999)

Armstrong, S, Blaustein, J and Henry, A (eds), *Reflexivity and Criminal Justice* (Palgrave Macmillan, 2017)

Ayer, AJ, *Language, Truth and Logic* (first published 1936, Courier Corporation, 2001)

Baker, S and Edwards, R (eds), 'How Many Qualitative Interviews is Enough? Expert Voices and Early Career Reflections on Sampling and Cases in Qualitative Research' (National Centre for Research Methods, 2012)

Bar Council, 'Barristers' Working Lives' (2017)

—— 'The Impact of the Covid-19 Pandemic on the Criminal Bar' (2022)

—— 'Barrister Earnings by Sex and Practice Area – 2022 Update' (2022)

Barry, J, 'A Barrister's Role in the Plea Decision: An Analysis of Drivers Affecting Advice in the Crown Court' (PhD Thesis, University of London, 2010)

Bauman, Z, *Modernity and the Holocaust* (Polity Press, 1992)

Bellamy, C, *Independent Review of Criminal Legal Aid (CLAR)* (November 2021)

Bernard, HR, *Social Research Methods: Qualitative and Quantitative Approaches* (SAGE, 2012)

Blackstock, J, Cape, E, Hodgson, J, Ogorodova, A and Spronken, T, *Inside Police Custody: An Empirical Account of Suspects' Rights in Four Jurisdictions* (Intersentia, 2014)

Blythe, M, *Austerity: The History of a Dangerous Idea* (Oxford University Press, 2013)

Bottoms, A and McClean, J, *Defendants in the Criminal Process* (Routledge, 1976)

Bourdieu, P, 'The Forms of Capital' in P Bourdieu and JG Richardson (eds), *Handbook of Theory and Research for the Sociology of Education* (Greenwood Press, 1986)

—— *Homo Academicus* (P Collier tr, Stanford University Press, 1988)

—— *The Logic of Practice* (R Nice tr, Polity Press, 1990)

—— *The State Nobility: Elite Schools in the Field of Power* (L Clough tr, Polity Press, 1996)

—— (ed), *The Weight of the World: Social Suffering in Contemporary Society* (P Parkhurst Ferguson tr, Polity Press, 1999)

—— *The Social Structures of the Economy* (C Turner tr, Polity Press, 2005)

—— *Distinction: A Social Critique of the Judgement of Taste* (R Nice tr, first published 1987, Routledge, 2010)

Bourdieu, P and Eagleton, T, 'In Conversation: Doxa and Common Life' (1992) 191 *New Left Review* 111

Bourdieu, P and Wacquant, L, *An Invitation to Reflexive Sociology* (Polity Press, 1992)

Bramall, R, Gilbert, J and Meadway, J, 'What Is Austerity?' (2016) 87 *New Formations* 119

Bridges, L, Hodgson, J, McConville, M and Pavlovic, A, 'Can Critical Research Influence Policy? A Response to Max Travers' (1997) 37 *British Journal of Criminology* 378

Burnett, CJ, *Lord Chief Justice's Report 2022* (Judicial Office, 2022)

BVA BDRC, 'Civil and Criminal Solicitors' Views on LASPO. Report for the Law Society' (2018)

Callaghan, D, 'Seeing through a Bourdieusian Lens: A Field-level Perspective of Anti-Bullying Interventions in a UK Police Force' (PhD Thesis, University of Liverpool, 2019)

Campbell, J, 'The Quality of (In)justice in London's Magistrates' Courts' (2020) 36 *Anthropology Today* 3

Cape, E, 'No Defence: The Erosion of PACE Rights' in J Robins (ed), *No Defence: Miscarriages of Justice, Lawyers and Poor Representation, London* (The Justice Gap, 2013)

Carlen, P, *Magistrates' Justice* (Martin Robertson, 1976)
Chan, J, *Doing Less Time: Penal Reform in Crisis* (1992)
Charmaz, K, *Constructing Grounded Theory* (SAGE, 2006)
Clark, J, 'Evaluation of Remote Hearings during the COVID-19 Pandemic: Research Report' (HMCTS, 2019)
Clarke, A and Welsh, L, 'United by Cuts: Exploring the Symmetry between How Lawyers and Expert Witnesses Experience Funding Cuts' (2022) 4 *Amicus Curiae* 455
—— '"F**k This Game … I'm Off": Financial and Emotional Factors in Declining Legal Representation in Miscarriage of Justice Cases' (2022) 49 *JLS* 518
Cooke, E, 'The Working Culture of Legal Aid Lawyers: Developing a "Shared Orientation Model"' (2022) 31 *Social & Legal Studies* 704
Cooper, V, 'No Fixed Abode: The Implications for Homeless People in the Criminal Justice System' (Howard League for Penal Reform, 2013)
CPS, *Handling Cases with Custody Time Limits: A Guide for Advocates Representing the Prosecution* (2014)
—— *Code for Crown Prosecutors* (2018)
—— *Annual Report and Accounts 2019–20* (House of Commons, 2020)
—— *Custody Time Limits National Standard for the Effective Management of Prosecution Cases Involving Custody Time Limits* (2020)
—— *Annual Report and Accounts 2020–21* (House of Commons, 2021)
—— *2025 Advocacy Strategy* (2021)
Dargue, P, 'An Analysis of Disclosure Failings in Murder Appeals against Conviction 2006–2018' [2020] Crim LR 707
Dehaghani, R and Newman, D, '"We're Vulnerable Too": An (Alternative) Analysis of Vulnerability within English Criminal Legal Aid and Police Custody' (2017) 7 *Oñati Socio-legal Series* 1199
—— 'The Crisis in Legally Aided Criminal Defence in Wales: Bringing Wales into Discussions of England and Wales' (2021) 41 *Legal Studies* 234
—— 'Criminal Legal Aid and Access to Justice: An Empirical Account of a Reduction in Resilience' (2022) 29 *International Journal of the Legal Profession* 33
Dezalay, Y and Garth, B, *Dealing in Virtue: International Commercial Arbitration and the Construction of a Transnational Legal Order* (University of Chicago Press, 1996)
Dezalay, Y and Madsen, M, 'The Force of Law and Lawyers: Pierre Bourdieu and the Reflexive Sociology of Law' (2012) 8 *Annual Review of Law Social Science* 433
Epstein, C, 'Faulty Framework: Consequences of the Difference Model for Women in the Law' (1990) 35 *New York Law School Review* 309
Equality and Human Rights Commission, *Inclusive Justice: A System Designed for All* (2020)
Fleck, J and Francis, R, *Vicarious Trauma in the Legal Profession* (Legal Action Group, 2021)
Fuller, S, 'Conatus' in M Grenfell (ed), *Pierre Bourdieu: Key Concepts*, 2nd edn (Acumen, 2012)
Gibbs, P, 'Defendants on Video – Conveyor Belt Justice or a Revolution in Access?' (Transform Justice, 2017)
Goriely, T, McCrone, P, Duff, P, Tata, C, Henry, A, Knapp, M, Lancaster, B, Sherr, A, 'The Public Defence Solicitor's Office in Edinburgh: An Independent Evaluation' (Scottish Central Research Unit, 2001)
Greenhalgh, T, Ozbilgin, M and Contandriopoulos, D, 'Orthodoxy, *Illusio*, and Playing the Scientific Game: A Bourdieusian Analysis of Infection Control Science in the COVID-19 Pandemic' (2021) 6 *Wellcome Open Research* 126
Grenfell, M, *Pierre Bourdieu: Agent Provocateur* (Bloomsbury, 2004)
—— (ed), *Pierre Bourdieu: Key Concepts*, 2nd edn (Routledge, 2012)
—— 'Interest' in M Grenfell (ed), *Pierre Bourdieu: Key Concepts*, 2nd edn (Routledge, 2012) 165
Harackiewicz, J and Elliot, A, 'The Joint Effects of Target and Purpose Goals on Intrinsic Motivation: A Mediational Analysis' (1998) 24 *Personality and Social Psychology Bulletin* 675
Harris, L, 'The Emotional Labour of Barristers: An Exploration of Emotional Labour by Status Professionals' (2002) 39 *Journal of Management Studies* 553
Helm, R, 'Conviction by Consent? Vulnerability, Autonomy and Conviction by Guilty Plea' (2019) 83(2) *Journal of Criminal Law* 161

—— 'Constrained Waiver of Trial Rights? Incentives to Plead Guilty and the Right to a Fair Trial' (2019) 46 *JLS* 423
—— 'Pleading Guilty Online: Enhanced Vulnerability and Access to Justice' [2021] *MLR Forum* 001
Helm, R, Dehaghani, R and Newman, D, 'Guilty Plea Decisions: Moving Beyond the Autonomy Myth' (2021) *MLR* 1
Hill, M, 'Disclosure – A Response from the CPS' [2019] Crim LR 611
HMCPS Inspectorate, *Making it Fair: The Disclosure of Unused Material in Volume Crown Court Cases* (Justice Inspectorates, 2017)
—— *Annual Report 2019–20* (House of Commons, 2020)
—— *2020 Charging Inspection* (Justice Inspectorates, 2020)
—— *Disclosure of Unused Materials in the Crown Court* (Justice Inspectorates, 2020)
—— *Disclosure of Unused Material in the Crown Court – A Follow-up* (Justice Inspectorates, 2020)
HM Government, *The Coalition: Our Programme for Government* (2010)
HM Inspectorates, *Neurodiversity in the Criminal Justice System* (2021)
Hodgson, J, *The Metamorphosis of Criminal Justice: A Comparative Account* (Oxford University Press, 2020)
Hunter, G, Jacobson, J and Kirby, A, *Judicial Perceptions of the Quality of Criminal Advocacy* (University of London, 2018)
Jacobson, J, Hunter, G and Kirby, A, *Briefing: Structured Mayhem: Personal Experiences of the Crown Court* (Criminal Justice Alliance, 2015)
—— *Inside Crown Court Personal Experiences and Questions of Legitimacy* (Policy Press, 2016)
Johnston, E, 'The Adversarial Defence Lawyer: Myths, Disclosure and Efficiency – A Contemporary Analysis of the Role in the Era of the Criminal Procedure Rules' (2020) 24 *International Journal of Evidence & Proof* 35
—— 'The Rise of Managerialism' in E Johnstone and T Smith (eds), *The Law of Disclosure: A Perennial Problem in Criminal Justice* (Taylor and Francis, 2020) 3
—— *The Role of the Defence Lawyer: Conceptions and Perceptions within a Changing System* (Lexington Books, 2021)
—— 'Pre-Charge (Lack of) Engagement: An Empty Gesture?' [2022] Crim LR 737
Jones, S, 'Under Pressure: Women Who Plead Guilty to Crimes They Have Not Committed' (2011) 11 *Criminology and Criminal Justice* 77
Judicial College, *Youth Court Bench Book* (2020)
Justice Select Committee (HC), *The Future of Legal Aid* (HC70, 2021)
—— *Fraud and the Justice System* (HC12, 2022)
Kemp, V, *Bridewell Legal Advice Study – BLAST: An Innovation in Police Station Legal Advice* (Legal Services Research Centre, 2012)
—— *Bridewell Legal Advice Study: Adopting a 'Whole Systems' Approach to Police Station Legal Advice* (Legal Services Research Centre, 2013)
—— '"No Time for a Solicitor": Implications for Delays on the Take-up of Legal Advice' [2013] Crim LR 184
—— *Effective Police Station Advice: Country Report 2: England and Wales* (University of Nottingham, 2018)
—— 'Digital Legal Rights: Exploring Detainees' Understanding of the Right to a Lawyer and Potential Barriers to Accessing Legal Advice' [2020] Crim LR 129
Kwarteng, K, *The Growth Plan* (CP743, 2022)
Law Society, *Trends in the Solicitors' Profession. Annual Statistics Report 2021* (2022)
Legal Aid Agency, *Standard Crime Contract 2022*
—— *Criminal Legal Aid Manual* (MoJ, 2022)
Ling, V and James, S, *Legal Aid Handbook 2022/23* (Legal Action Group, 2022)
Lipsky, M, *Street-Level Bureaucracy: Dilemmas of the Individual in Public Services*, 30th anniversary edn (Russell Sage, 2010)
Magistrates Association, 'Magistrates' Courts and Covid-19' (2022)

Maton, K, 'Habitus' in M Grenfell (ed), *Pierre Bourdieu: Key Concepts*, 2nd edn (Acumen, 2012)
McBarnet, D, *Conviction: Law, the State and the Construction of Justice* (Macmillan, 1981)
McConville, M and Hodgson, J, *Custodial Legal Advice and the Right to Silence* (HMSO, 1993)
McConville, M, Hodgson, J, Bridges, L and Pavlovic, A, *Standing Accused: The Organisation and Practices of Criminal Defence Lawyers in Britain* (Oxford University Press, 1994)
McConville, M, Sanders, A, and Leng, R, *The Case for the Prosecution: Police Suspects and the Construction of Criminality* (first published 1991, Routledge, 2017)
Ministry of Justice, *Transforming Legal Aid: Delivering a More Credible and Efficient System* (2013)
—— *Transforming Legal Aid: Government Response* (2014)
—— *Litigators Graduated Fees Scheme and Court Appointees Equality Statement* (2017)
—— *Government's Response to the Criminal Legal Aid Independent Review and Consultation on Policy Proposals* (HM Government, 2022)
Moorhead, R, 'Lawyer Specialization – Managing the Professional Paradox' (2010) 32 *Law & Policy* 226
Moorhead, R, Vaughan, S and Godinho, C, *In-house Lawyers' Ethics: Institutional Logics, Legal Risk and the Tournament of Influence* (Hart Publishing, 2018)
Morison, J and Leith, P, *The Barristers World and the Nature of Law* (Open University Press, 1992)
Mulcahy, L, Rowden, E and Teeder, W, 'Exploring the Case for Virtual Jury Trials during the COVID 19 Crisis. An Evaluation of a Pilot Study Conducted by JUSTICE' (Oxford Brookes University and University of Oxford, 2020)
Newman, D, *Legal Aid Lawyers and the Quest for Justice* (Hart Publishing, 2013)
—— 'Are Lawyers Alienated Workers?' (2016) *22 European Journal of Current Legal Issues* 3
Newman, D and Dehaghani, R, *Experiences of Criminal Justice*, Kindle edn (Bristol University Press, 2022)
Nicklas-Carter, C, 'Efficiency of the English Criminal Courts in a Time of Austerity. Exploring Courtroom Lawyers' Assessment of Government Policy (2010–2017)' (DCrim Thesis, Keele University, 2019)
Ocasio, W, Thornton, P and Lounsbury, M, 'Advances to the Institutional Logics Perspective' in R Greenwood, C Oliver, T Lawrence and R Meyer (eds), *Sage Handbook of Organizational Institutionalism* (SAGE, 2017)
Pattenden, R and Skinns, L, 'Choice, Privacy and Publicly Funded Legal Advice at Police Stations' (2010) 73 *MLR* 349
Peay, J and Player, E, 'Pleading Guilty: Why Vulnerability Matters' (2018) 81 *MLR* 929
Peräkylä, A, 'Reliability and Validity in Research Based on Naturally Occurring Social Interaction' in D Silverman (ed), *Qualitative Research: Theory, Method and Practice*, 2nd edn (SAGE, 2004) 297
Pivaty, A, *Criminal Defence at Police Stations* (Routledge, 2019)
Pleasence, P, Kemp, V and Balmer, N, 'The Justice Lottery? Police Station Advice 25 Years on from PACE' [2011] Crim LR 3
Porter, A, 'Prosecuting Domestic Abuse in England and Wales: Crown Prosecution Service 'Working Practice' and New Public Managerialism' (2019) 28 *Social & Legal Studies* 493
—— *Prosecuting Domestic Abuse in Neoliberal Times: Amplifying the Survivor's Voice* (Palgrave Macmillan, 2020)
Power, M, *The Audit Society: Rituals of Verification* (Oxford University Press, 1997)
Quality of Working Life Research Group, 'The Bar Council Barrister's Working Lives Survey Barrister Wellbeing Analysis' (2021)
Quirk, H, 'The Significance of Culture in Criminal Procedure Reform: Why the Revised Disclosure Scheme Cannot Work' (2006) 10 *Journal of Evidence & Proof* 42
Riddle, H and Kinch, C, *Magistrates Court Disclosure Review* (Judicial Office, 2014)
Robinson, G, Priede, C, Farrall, S and Shapland, J, 'Understanding "Quality" in Probation Practice: Frontline Perspectives in England & Wales' (2014) 14 *Criminology & Criminal Justice* 123
Sánchez García, R and Spencer, DC (eds), *Fighting Scholars: Habitus and Ethnographies of Martial Arts and Combat Sports* (Anthem Press, 2013)
Sandberg, J and Tsoukas, H, 'Grasping the Logic of Practice: Theorizing Through Practical Rationality' (2011) 36 *Academy of Management Review* 338

Sanders, A, Bridges, L and Mulvaney, A, *Advice and Assistance at Police Stations and the 24 Hour Duty Solicitor Scheme* (Lord Chancellor's Department, 1989)

Sartre, J, *Being and Nothingness* (Routledge, 1958)

—— *The Psychology of the Imagination* (Routledge, 1971)

Schneider, R and Zottoli, T, 'Disentangling the Effects of Plea Discount and Potential Trial Sentence on Decisions to Plead Guilty' (2019) 24 *Legal and Criminological Psychology* 288

Schubert, JD, 'Suffering/Symbolic Violence' in M Grenfell (ed), *Pierre Bourdieu: Key Concepts*, 2nd edn (Acumen, 2012)

Sentencing Council, 'Research to Support the Development of a Guideline for Reduction in Sentence for a Guilty Plea' (2017)

Shute, S, Hood, R and Seemungal, F, *A Fair Hearing? Ethnic Minorities in the Criminal Courts* (Routledge, 2011)

Silverman, D (ed), *Qualitative Research*, 5th edn (SAGE, 2020)

Skinns, L, 'The Right to Legal Advice in the Police Station: Past, Present and Future' [2011] Crim LR 19

Smith, D, 'Reform or Moral Outrage – The Choice is Yours' (1998) 38 *British Journal of Criminology* 616

Smith, T, 'The "Quiet Revolution" in Criminal Defence: How the Zealous Advocate Slipped into the Shadow' (2013) 20 *International Journal of the Legal Profession* 111

—— 'The "Near Miss" of Liam Allan: Critical Problems in Police Disclosure, Investigation Culture and the Resourcing of Criminal Justice' [2018] Crim LR 711

—— 'Changing Culture? Thinking Differently about Police and Prosecution Disclosure' in T Smith and E Johnstone (eds), *The Law of Disclosure: A Perennial Problem in Criminal Justice* (Routledge, 2020)

Smith, T and Johnstone, E (eds), *The Law of Disclosure: A Perennial Problem in Criminal Justice* (Routledge, 2020)

Solicitors Regulation Authority, 'Criminal Advocacy Thematic Review' (2017)

Sommerlad, H, 'The Implementation of Quality Initiatives and the New Public Management in the Legal Aid Sector in England and Wales: Bureaucratisation, Stratification and Surveillance' (1999) 6 *International Journal of the Legal Profession* 311

—— '"I've Lost the Plot": An Everyday Story of the Political Legal Aid Lawyer' (2002) 28 *JLS* 335

Soubise, L, 'Prosecuting in the Magistrates' Courts in a Time of Austerity' [2017] Crim LR 847

Stephen, F, Fazio, G and Tata, C, 'Incentives, Criminal Defence Lawyers and Plea Bargaining' (2008) 28 *International Review of Law and Economics* 212

Sukumar, D, Hodgson, J and Wade, K, 'How the Timing of Police Evidence Disclosure Impacts Custodial Legal Advice' (2016) *International Journal of Evidence and Proof* 200

—— 'Behind Closed Doors: Live Observations of Current Police Station Disclosure Practices and Lawyer-Client Consultations' [2016] Crim LR 900

Tague, P, 'Tactical Reasons for Recommending Trials Rather Than Guilty Pleas in the Crown Court [2006] Crim LR 23

—— 'Barristers' Selfish Incentives in Counselling Clients' [2008] Crim LR 3

Telford, M and Santatzoglou, S, '"It Was About Trust" – Practitioners as Policy Makers and the Improvement of Inter-professional Communication within the 1980s Youth Justice Process' (2012) 32 *Legal Studies* 58

Tenbrunsel, AE and Messick, DM, 'Ethical Fading: The Role of Self-Deception in Unethical Behaviour' (2004) 17 *Social Justice Research* 223

Terry, M, Johnson, S and Thompson, P, 'Virtual Court Pilot Outcome Evaluation' (Ministry of Justice, 2010)

Thompson, H, 'Austerity as Ideology: The Bait and Switch of the Banking Crisis' (2013) 11 *Comparative European Politics* 729

Thornton, J, 'The Way in Which Fee Reductions Influence Legal Aid Criminal Defence Lawyer Work: Insights from a Qualitative Study' (2019) 46 *JLS* 559

—— 'Is Publicly Funded Criminal Defence Sustainable? Legal Aid Cuts, Morale, Retention and Recruitment in the English Criminal Law Professions' (2020) 40 *Legal Studies* 230

Thornton, P and Ocasio, W, 'Institutional Logics' in R Greenwood and C Oliver (eds), *Sage Handbook of Organizational Institutionalism* (SAGE, 2008)

Thornton, P, Ocasio, W and Lounsbury, M, *The Institutional Logics Perspective: A New Approach to Culture, Structure and Process* (Oxford University Press, 2012)

Transform Justice, Fair Trials and National Appropriate Adult Network, 'Not Remotely Fair? Access to a Lawyer in the Police Station during the Covid-19 Pandemic' (Transform Justice, 2021)

Travers, M, *The Reality of Law: Work and Talk in a Firm of Criminal Lawyers* (Ashgate, 1997)

—— 'Preaching to the Converted? Improving the Persuasiveness of Criminal Justice Research' (1997) 37 *British Journal of Criminology* 359

Ward, J, *Transforming Summary Justice: Modernisation in the Lower Criminal Courts* (Routledge, 2017)

Weber, M, '"Objectivity" in Social Science and Social Policy' in E Shils and H Finch (eds and trans), *The Methodology of the Social Sciences* (Free Press, 1949) 80

Webley, L, 'Qualitative Approaches to Empirical Legal Research' in P Cane and H Kiritzer (eds), *The Oxford Handbook of Empirical Legal Studies* (Oxford University Press, 2010)

Webley, L, Tomlinson, J, Muzio, D, Sommerlad, H and Duff, L, 'Access to a Career in the Legal Profession in England and Wales: Race, Class, and the Role of Educational Background' in S Headworth, R Nelson, R Donovitzer and D Wilkins (eds), *Diversity in Practice: Race, Gender, and Class in Legal and Professional Careers* (Cambridge University Press, 2016)

Welsh, L, 'The Effect of Changes to Legal Aid on Lawyers' Professional Identity and Behaviour in Summary Criminal Cases: A Case Study' (2017) 44 *Journal of Law and Society* 559

—— *Access to Justice in Magistrates' Courts: A Study of Defendant Marginalisation*, Kindle edn (Hart Publishing, 2021)

Welsh, L, Skinns, L and Sanders, A, *Sanders & Young's Criminal Justice*, 5th edn (Oxford University Press, 2021)

Western Circuit Women's Forum, 'Back to the Bar' (2018)

Westminster Commission on Legal Aid, 'Inquiry into the Sustainability and Recovery of the Legal Aid Sector' (All-Party Parliamentary Group on Legal Aid, 2021)

Wigzell, A, Kirby, A and Jacobson, J, *The Youth Proceedings Advocacy Review: Final Report* (Institute for Criminal Policy Research, 2015)

Young, R, 'Exploring the Boundaries of the Criminal Courtroom Workgroup' (2013) 42 *Common Law World Review* 203

Ziff, P, *Semantic Analysis* (Cornell University Press, 1960)

INDEX

agency 8–9
altruists 148, 152–3
appeals 97–8
austerity
  and criminal court practice 4–7
    future of 127–56
  and Crown Court defence and prosecution practice 87–126
  and legal practitioner work 157–63
  and legally aided criminal defence at police stations 31–53
  and magistrates' court defence and prosecution practice 54–86
  meaning of 1–2

bail hearings 133–5
Bourdieu, Pierre, concepts 28 9 *see also* ***capital; conatus; doxa; fields; habitus; hysteresis; interest/illusio; symbolic capital; symbolic violence***
burnout 46–7, 82–4, 120–4

capital 20–1, 25, 29 *see also* **symbolic capital**
The Case for the Prosecution **(McConville et al)** 11–12, 14, 16
CLAR (Criminal Legal Aid Review) 2–4
cloud video platform (CVP) 132–8
conatus 25–7, 30, 77, 79, 114, 159
COVID-19 23–4
  courtroom mitigations 127–42
CPS *see* **Crown Prosecution Service**
Criminal Legal Aid Review (CLAR) 2–4
Crown Courts 87–9
  appeals 97–8
  burnt out 120–4
  court time 97–8
  criminal prosecution and defence, logic of 124–6
  Crown prosecution in 90
  demoralisation 120–4
  experience of staff 110–12
  financial challenges in practice 90–124
  gold dust 108–10
  legal aid in 89
  loss-making defence cases 108–10
  money and time 90–1
  plea advice 112–20
  preparation time 91–7
  prosecution disclosure, time for 98–102
  prosecution targets 104–8
  staff reductions 110–12
  'tender loving care' 102–3
  time and money 90–1
Crown prosecution
  in Crown Courts 90
  in magistrates' courts 56
  sustainability of 153–6
Crown Prosecution Service (CPS) 4, 11–12
  magistrates' courts 56, 60–1, 62, 65, 69–70
Crown Prosecution Service Inspectorate (HMCPSI) 98–102
CVP (cloud video platform) 132–8

defence lawyers 12–13, 14, 15
demoralisation 46–7, 82–4, 120–4
dichotomy, avoidance of 16–17, 28
diversity 146–7, 150–2
doxa 22–5, 27, 28

environmental pressures 9
experience of staff 47–8, 110–12

fees 2–4 *see also* **fixed fees**
field 20–5, 26–7, 28–30, 141, 159–63
  in Crown Court practice 114–15, 117–19
  in magistrates' court practice 61, 77
  in police station practice 37, 38, 41, 45–7, 52
financial challenges in practice
  in Crown Courts 90–124
  in magistrates' courts 56–83
  in police stations 35–51
fixed fees 15, 33–4, 36–7, 40, 55–6

gold dust 108–10
guilty plea incentives 112–15

habitus 18–30, 159–60, 163
- in Crown Court practice 98, 114, 119–20, 126
- in magistrate' court practice 60–3, 69, 73, 77, 85–6
- in police station practice 37, 38, 41–2, 45, 47, 51

hearings 132–8
HMCPSI (Crown Prosecution Service Inspectorate) 98–102
hobbyists 148, 152–3
hysteresis 20, 25, 47, 84, 124, 156, 157

illusio 22–5, 27, 29, 114, 117, 141
individual agency 8–9
***In-house Lawyers' Ethics: Institutional Logics, Legal Risk and the Tournament of Influence* (Moorhead et al)** 16–17
institutional logics 16–17
interest/illusio 22–5, 27, 29, 114, 117, 141
intermittent hearings 133–5
interviewees 5–6

***Legal Aid Lawyers and the Quest for Justice* (Newman)** 14, 15
legal aid system
- in magistrates' courts 55–6 *see also* magistrates' courts
- in police stations 31, 33–5 *see also* police stations

magistrates' courts
- burnt out 82–4
- court time 65–8
- criminal prosecution and defence, logic of 84–6
- Crown prosecution in 56
- Crown Prosecution Service (CPS) 56, 60–1, 62, 65, 69–70
- demoralisation 82–4
- experience of lawyers 79–81
- fees 55–6
- financial challenges in practice 12, 56–84
- legal aid system in 55–6
- money and time 57–8
- plea advice 75–9
- plea-hearing preparation 61–3
- preparation time 59–61
- prosecution disclosure time 63–5
- prosecution targets 69–73
- 'tender loving care' 68–75
- time and money 57–8
- trial preparation 61–3
- undesirable cases/clients 73–5

means testing 15, 55, 74

not guilty plea incentives 115–20

objectivist approach to understanding practice 9–17
online hearings 132–8

plea advice 75–9, 112–20
police stations
- challenges of setting 32–3
- legal aid system in 33–5
  - attendance in-person 49–51
  - burnt out 46–7
  - demoralisation 46–7
  - experience of staff 47–8
  - financial challenges 35–51
  - further investigations 42–4
  - investigations at the station 40–2
  - logic of 52–3
  - preparatory work 39–40
  - profitability 35–7
  - 'tender loving care' 44–5
  - time for 37–46
  - virtual attendance 49–51
- legally-aided criminal defence 31

practice in criminal law
- approaches to understanding 9–17, 158–61
- and austerity 161–3

preparatory work 39–40, 59–63, 91–7
private criminal law work 147–8, 152
prosecution disclosure time 63–5, 98–102
prosecution lawyers 11–12
prosecution targets 69–73, 104–8
publicly funded criminal bar 148–53

***The Reality of Law* (Travers)** 12–13, 15, 16
recruitment and retention of staff 143–6, 149–50

semi-structured interview studies 5–6
sense-making 17
sentencing hearings 135–8
solicitors 142–8
solvency of criminal defence firms 143

Standing Accused (McConville et al) 12, 14, 16
subjectivist approach to understanding practice 9–17
symbolic capital 24, 37, 38, 52, 77
symbolic violence 22, 25, 27, 29–30, 85–6, 159–60

technology enhancements 129–32, 155–6
'tender loving care' 44–5, 68–75, 102–3
transcripts 6

video-conferencing 129–32

youth justice 9

Printed in the USA
CPSIA information can be obtained
at www.ICGtesting.com
LVHW071258090524
779260LV00043B/450

9 781509 955312